Advice from a
GAMEKEEPER

John Cowan

MERLIN UNWIN BOOKS

First published in Great Britain by Merlin Unwin Books, 2009

Published by:
Merlin Unwin Books Ltd
Palmers House
7 Corve Street
Ludlow
Shropshire SY8 1DB
U.K.

www.merlinunwin.co.uk

The author asserts his moral right to be identified with this work.

Designed and set in Bembo by Merlin Unwin
Printed in Great Britain by TJ International, Padstow

ISBN 978-1-906122-11-9

CONTENTS

Introduction

The ivy clung to the building; jackdaws spilled from the chimney and out through a broken pane in the kitchen window, then all was quiet. No rosy-cheeked children explored the surrounding woods, their laughter echoing through the trees. The kennels lay bare with weeds and saplings growing from cracks in the paving and entwining the rusting railings. There, no loyal Labrador lay pining for the return of his master nor feisty terrier surveyed the scene for chance of mischief. The ferret boxes were rotten and collapsed, long empty of their charges that fed the keeper's family and earned him enough to make his life comfortable.

This was the world that I had returned to see, a most primitive way of life. The keeper depended for his livelihood on an ability to kill the predators that preyed on his game. Failure to do this would have lost him his job and, in turn, his house. This gave him an edge that only a primitive human being has: a life and death, black and white attitude that brooks no compromise and produces a single-minded, independent character.

The traps and snares that hung in his shed fascinated me, as did the collection of stoats, rats and feathered vermin that he caught and displayed to show to his boss that he was not slacking in his duties. I could not resist and I became a keeper myself – and have been for the last 35 years. I am not an expert; there are many keepers more qualified to write this book than me, indeed as the years pass I realise that I know very little and learn something new every day.

My visit to the haunts of my youth left me sad. The woods were bare and contained a fraction of the wildlife that they had in years gone by. Shooting had stopped years ago when the old Laird had died and his children, who were conservationists, thought that leaving nature to take its course would lead to a wildlife utopia. How wrong they were: gradually the predators took over as their food supply, the birds, rabbits etc did not thrive since no-one cared for them and the burgeoning population of predators started to reduce the survivors. The results were there for me to see and I resolved then and there to write this book and to argue the keeper's case, for he has been one of the most undervalued and over-criticised figures in history.

I would also like to record for posterity the stories that I learned from the old keepers who lived in a world where game was King, while my mind is still able to remember them. The keeper has been a significant part of rural life for centuries despite efforts by some to air-brush him from history. The various bodies which represent keepers strive to make their voices heard but are continually stonewalled by the media. Today's media is run by left-wing idealists who value the opinion of second-rate comedians above those of men and women who have contributed much to our country. We also live in a society which is as much class-ridden as any which went before, only now the elite are the people who have gone to University, especially Oxbridge, who believe that they are right and no-one who did not attend University is entitled to an opinion.

I will therefore put the keeper's point of view in this book and hopefully answer the questions: What is a gamekeeper? What does he do? And why does he do that? I would hope that this book will be of value to all people with an interest in the countryside and wildlife and not just potential and fully-fledged keepers. Many layman have difficulty understanding why an apparently sane, level-headed individual should give up the security and comfort of a 9–5 job with his own accommodation and take up the position of gamekeeper, with its associated insecurity of both employment and housing. I will try to explain this, probably with much difficulty, and perhaps I will even convince myself!

CHAPTER ONE

The First Step on the Ladder

For anyone considering a career as a gamekeeper – in my view one of the most rewarding you could possibly choose – your best initiation is to learn to 'beat'. It will offer you an insight into the working of a shoot and you will get a taste of the wonderful outdoor life that beckons. So, start be seeking out a keeper who is looking for beaters, offer your services and hope that he has a vacancy. Choose, if possible, a keeper who is both experienced and of good reputation. This will be easier said than done in some parts of the country where shoots have waiting lists to beat and pick-up. Keep trying, however, and eventually you will be successful. The keeper will provide you with a list of shooting dates. If not apparent, check the meeting time and place exactly, and be there early. Also ascertain whether a lunch is provided or whether the beaters provide their own.

Prior to your first day beating, it is advisable to undertake a fitness programme, especially if you intend to go grouse beating. Grouse beating can be the most arduous task, especially in August in hot weather. Twenty miles may be covered over rough terrain and if you are not used to such exercise it can be a humbling experience to be out-walked by pensioners and school girls.

It may be useful at this point to describe a typical day's grouse beating and the equipment necessary.

For the grouse beater, good, sturdy comfortable footwear which has been broken in during the fitness programme is your greatest asset. Light waterproofs, which can easily be stored in your game bag, may be necessary if the weather is uncertain, remembering that the weather in the uplands can be changeable as well as several degrees colder than on low ground. In short, you require light, versatile and comfortable clothing, bearing in mind you can always take clothes off if too warm, but you can't put them on if they have been left at home!

Take a lunch box with plenty to drink (it may be advisable to carry water with you if the day is warm) and try to use flasks that are very robust as the beaters' lunch is sometimes transported in the back of a Landrover to a lunch hut high in the hills. This will avoid the situation that occurred a number of years ago when a new shepherd was put in charge of the beaters' flasks and lunch boxes, and he wasted no time in negotiating the rough track to the bothy at the end of the fourth drive. The keepers and beaters arrived with a hunter's appetite and a blacksmith's thirst, lifted their flasks in anticipation and heard the unpleasant sound of broken glass. The shepherd luckily had returned home for his lunch and the headkeeper had to think fast to avert a mutiny.

So here we are: you are fit, eager and ready to go. You have arrived at the meeting place for the shoot. This may be at the headkeeper's house or on the moor itself. Get it right and make sure you know exactly the time and place.

As you are a newcomer, the headkeeper should introduce you on arrival to the other beaters. This may not happen: remember this man is under pressure and some people deal with this better than others; it is helpful if you understand this. The other beaters may, or may not, be friendly. Do not be offended if they are not forthcoming. Once they have discovered that you are prepared to work you will be accepted, and by the end of the day you will be on first-name terms with most of them. Indeed, if your performance is up to scratch you may be invited to beat on other shoots by keepers who are helping out on this one!

How to 'beat' a grouse moor
The time to move off arrives and, depending on how the shoot is run, you may have to go everywhere on foot or you may be transported by

8

vehicle. Whichever is the case you will arrive at a point where you will hear the phrase 'line out'. This means that beaters will drop off to left and right as they go forward.

The most experienced and reliable beaters will take the outside of the beat, and the keeper will be in the centre where he can control the line. You, as an inexperienced beater, will be next to him. Do as he says and watch the other beaters on either side so that you can keep in line. Where a ridge or similar occurs, walk along the top so that you can still see the beaters on both sides. This prevents a break in the line which can be disastrous to a successful drive.

You will be issued with a flag on arrival: use it when you hear the command 'flag up'. As you cover the ground, grouse will rise and, it is hoped, fly forward. They may go all the way to the guns which will result in a flurry of shots or they may land in front of the butts.

After you have covered some distance, which varies from drive to drive, the keeper will blow a whistle or a horn which signals to the guns that beaters are getting closer and no shots should be fired forward. The butts will be in view now and the grouse which alighted in the long heather in front of the butts will now be rising, giving good sport. On either side of the butts you will see men with flags. They are called flankers and are important to the success of the drive. A good flanker can make a drive; a poor one ruin it.

Picking up

The headkeeper blows his horn to signal the end of the drive. Now it is time to pick-up dead birds which the guns have shot. You will see dogs of all descriptions: labradors, golden and flat-coated retrievers, cocker and springer spaniels, all busily questing through the heather searching for the slain. Watch and enjoy but do not interfere unless asked to. Dog men can be possessive about giving their dogs retrieves and if you rumble about in the heather looking for birds yourself, you will ruin the scent for their paragons.

If a gun speaks to you, answer him politely and cheerfully but do not waste his time. If a decent number of birds have been shot, ask the headkeeper if he would like assistance to carry birds to the game cart. Do not become involved in a long discussion with the man on the game cart. He may be lonely and looking for a blether but remember to keep an eagle eye on the keeper, for soon he will be off to the next drive and you may be left behind, embarrassed.

There may be another two or three drives before lunch. If grouse are plentiful, the keeper's demeanour will change and he may become almost cheerful, the pressure will ease and everyone will relax. Take time to observe how he drives the birds, how the wind affects the drives and how the beaters and flankers are positioned to accommodate it. Also note how the butts are built and where they are positioned.

The Shoot lunch

Lunch comes and food has never tasted so good. Drink plenty of liquid but think twice about the free beer. The first drive after lunch will be hard enough without a pint or two sloshing around inside. Better to take it home and enjoy it over your evening meal. Shoot lunch banter is always entertaining; enjoy it and enter into the spirit of the day. The stories and characters encountered at a gathering of beaters and keepers are always fascinating, and at times hair-raising!

After lunch you will move off before the guns to line out. This will be done with plenty of time to spare and may be quite leisurely. The object of going out early is that the drive can be started whenever the guns are in position, which avoids a long delay before shooting starts. This means that there can be a delay for the beaters before the drive starts and it is tempting to lie down in the heather, especially if the weather is fine. Be careful you do not fall asleep. I remember when, as a young underkeeper, I started a drive in these circumstances leaving the headkeeper asleep in the heather. He eventually woke up at the sound of gun fire and ran to catch up at the last minute of the drive. Irate, the headkeeper was about to administer the mother of all rollickings when one of the guns congratulated him on the drive saying he had never seen it go so well. The head man, showing admirable presence of mind, thanked him and said he too never dreamed it would go so well.

The final drive

The last drive is here and you will be glad you undertook a fitness programme. Other beaters may be tiring: a sure sign is resting their hands above the knee as they walk. Be glad it is not you. A beater who cannot keep up will be treated quite ruthlessly. He will be left behind, the line will stretch to fill the gap he has left, and he will be told to catch up when he can. It is not pleasant to limp in, several minutes after the drive has ended; but do not fear, the other beaters will usually be sympathetic and sensitive to the laggard's plight.

The day is over, the keeper will thank you and if everything has gone well he will ask you back for the following shoots. You have taken a big step and walking the hill will never be so hard again. You have also been introduced to a wonderful new world which will interest you till the day you die.

You may not be lucky enough to have a grouse moor on your door-step so I will describe other types of beating which may be available to you.

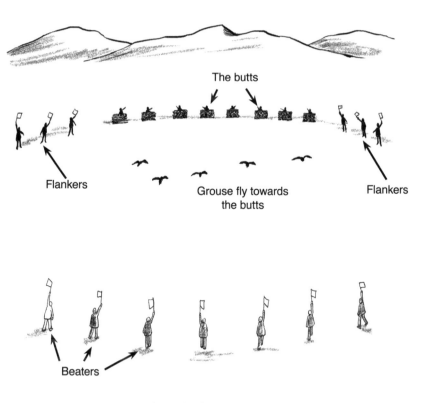

Grouse drive (scale compressed)

PARTRIDGE SHOOTING

The majority of partridges shot today are red-legged and reared. Improved techniques in rearing and releasing have meant that ground which was never conducive to partridge shooting now yield huge bags of very sporting birds.

Wild grey partridge shoots

However, it may be of more interest to the reader to describe a day at wild grey partridges, which many people believe to be the cream of the shootingman's sport.

The obvious difference between grouse and grey partridge shooting is the location. Grey partridge thrive best in an area of low rainfall, small fields, varied crops, good thick hedges and an absence of predators. Grouse exist only on heather moorland but the driving of both birds has some similarities in that the beaters carry flags, and flankers are employed for the same purpose in both grouse and partridge driving.

The partridge season begins on 1st September which means that partridge shoots span the time of year when the British countryside is at its most attractive, with the leaves on the trees changing colour and the stubble golden.

The aim of the partridge keeper is to drive the coveys into a crop or holding cover in front of a high hedge or row of trees, over which the birds are driven to the guns.

The drives tend to be short and sharp with as many as twelve in a day. Be careful when picking-up as many drives 'feed' other drives or are return drives (ie. the guns merely about-turn and the ground behind the guns in the previous drive is brought back to the original drive). This means that disturbing ground (and game) a long way behind is *verboten* unless permission is sought from the keeper.

October is the main month for wild grey partridge shooting and in the old days there were enough birds to run right into the pheasant shooting. There is every chance that you will be asked to beat at a pheasant shoot by a pheasant keeper who is helping out by picking-up or flanking at the partridge shoot.

12

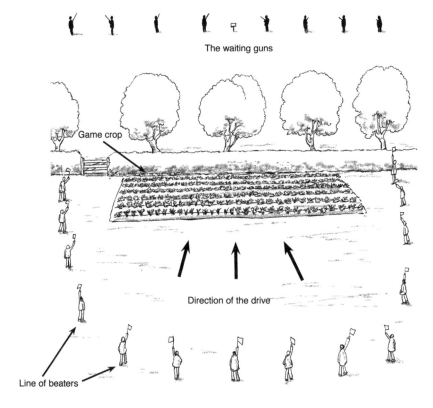

The waiting guns

Game crop

Direction of the drive

Line of beaters

The partridge drive closes in on the game crop sheltering the birds

Reared red-leg partridge shoots

Reared red-legs can be put into almost any habitat and be successful. They have revolutionised many average shoots and turned them into first class ones. The area which has benefited most from this innovation has been the marginal land next to grouse moors. This bracken-covered rushy ground has proved ideal for holding these birds and is excellent, where the ground is steep, for showing them. Beaters and flankers carry flags so there is a similarity to grouse and grey partridge shooting but because the birds are reared and because they flush akin to pheasants, there is a hybrid feel to the day. But make no mistake, when well-run and managed, this is one of the most spectacular and pleasant forms of driven shooting. Shoots can be held at any time between 1st September and 31st January. The ground can be steep, so preparation and equipment is as described for grouse shooting. The main difference between driving red-legs and grouse is that the latter tend to follow the contours of the hill while the former can be driven in virtually any direction, preferably with the wind and over steep gullies, or from one side of a valley to another, producing the high class sport which has made this form of shooting so popular.

Pheasant beating

The clothing necessary for pheasant beating is similar to that for grouse or partridge beating with the addition of heavier waterproofs, thorn-proof leggings and Wellington boots, due to the colder, wetter conditions and the type of terrain encountered.

Arrive at the meet in plenty of time and you will meet the other beaters. They will probably know the drives which will be shot that day and can tell you in advance which type of clothing and footwear will be necessary. Some beaters will arrive, then set off on their own: these are the trusted, experienced men the keeper relies on to blank ground in (this means to round up pheasants in unpromising areas and drive them in) before the drive proper starts. In this way, they may bring in many acres of hedges and rough ground then act as a 'stop' until the rest of the beaters arrive. 'Stop' is a term which applies to a beater whose role is to stand still at a particular place to stop birds from running out of a drive and so avoiding the guns. As the season progresses, most keepers use more and more 'stops' as the birds become wilder.

The keeper arrives; he may be harassed and nervous-looking as he has been trying to avert a mass breakout of birds towards the boundary, as well as feeding the drives which will not be shot that day. He may look at you with some trepidation; this is more likely if you have a spaniel on the end of a length of clothes line. Do not be alarmed: the worst case scenario is that you will be sent home. This is unlikely to happen however, unless the keeper is a complete psychopath, and you will most likely be asked to climb aboard a trailer towed by a farm vehicle. Some large commercial shoots have ex-army transporters and these move beaters in comfort from A to B. Every shoot is different and you may find that on foot is the preferred mode of transport, especially if the owner of the shoot is a 'prudent character'. Some keepers have been known to describe their bosses in this way, or words to that effect.

14

You have arrived at the first drive. This may be a game crop or a wood. The game crop is a crop of kale, maize or game-cover mixture which is situated to provide high, sporting birds. The crop is normally a convenient size and shape to facilitate the keeper's task, ie. to provide a steady flush of birds over the guns. If the crop has been well positioned, it is normally straight-forward to push the birds over the guns. The beaters line out in the same formation as for grouse or partridge shooting, the main difference being that they are far closer together; indeed on some shoots they are almost shoulder-to-shoulder. The wind may play some part especially if it is very strong and the keeper may slant one side of the line forward with the command, 'Right hand-side forward' or vice versa.

The pace of the line is far slower for pheasants than in other forms of shooting. This is because hasty or over-enthusiastic activity by the beaters may result in a massive flush, in which all, or the majority of the birds fly *en-masse* over the guns, giving the guns little chance to fire more than two or three shots. This is more likely to happen later in the season when birds are wilder and the cover has become flattened and withered due to the winter weather. The important rules to obey in this form of beating are to keep in line with the other beaters and to move at the same pace as the keeper who dictates the tempo of the day. That said, some shoots are run on a somewhat *laissez-faire* system with dogs running everywhere, beaters yelling and shouting at the flush of every bird and a general atmosphere of mayhem prevalent. This can work in woods with very thick undergrowth where the birds have only one option as to where they can fly, ie. over the guns. However, many employers look for a more professional approach.

As the drive progresses, birds will flush. When this happens, the line should stand still and be quiet while birds are in the air. This will help to prevent the mass flush mentioned previously and also give the guns a chance to reload. The keeper will sound a horn or blow a whistle to signal the end of the drive. This means that shooting stops immediately and the pickers-up can start to work. On many shoots the beaters do not become involved in picking-up, indeed they are hardly seen by the guns all day. Some employers prefer this but I personally feel that if the boss and his guests can speak to the beaters at some point in the day and show their appreciation for the work that the beaters do, it can boost morale, and promote that most important aspect of modern life, good public relations.

Beaters' dogs

On some shoots, however, the beaters who have dogs are welcome to help out after the drive. This is not always popular with the regular pickers-up who frankly are sometimes prima-donnas. The beater with a good dog should remember this and try not to 'rub it in' too much, if his dog 'wipes the eye' of the picker-up's dog. (The phrase 'wipes the eye' describes the situation where one dog fails to find a shot bird and the second dog tries for it and succeeds). Ill feeling can easily be generated but remember the keeper may value the picker-up more than you, and friction is something a shoot can do without as it depends on teamwork to be a success.

Wood drives

The next drive might be a wood. These are generally of mixed species, ie. softwoods and hardwoods with laurels or rhododendrons strategically placed at what are termed 'flushing points'. Flushing points are normally situated at the end of the wood where the birds are flushed over the guns. Well-designed coverts may have flushing points spaced throughout the wood thereby giving a steady flush throughout the drive. This, however, is usual only on well-established, carefully planned shoots where the land-owner demands perfection from his forester and his keeper.

The ideal wood will have many sheltered sunny spots as well as areas of spruce trees where birds can shelter in severe weather. Many woods have hedges and hardwood strips connected to the main cover. These will be blanked in and 'stopped' as described earlier. The main body of the beat will progress slowly with any dogs present at heel or on a lead. Indeed many shoots ban dogs from the beating line as there is a chance that a hunting dog will flush too many birds at once or flush them back over the beaters' heads away from the guns. Beaters on the low ground normally carry sticks rather than flags and these are used to tap the trees and poke the undergrowth to help evict the birds. As the beaters near the end of the wood, they may adopt a horseshoe formation or favour one side or the other by pushing men in front. The speed of the line will slow until almost at a standstill. Remember to stand still and be quiet at any sign of a flush of more than two birds.

At the end of the drive, the keeper blows his horn. The same rules apply as previously described. You will move on to the next drive, with normally 3–5 drives in the morning and 2–3 in the afternoon. Some shoots have 6–7 drives and do not stop for lunch, the idea being to go for a late afternoon meal.

There is nothing wrong with this system although some beaters miss having their lunch in the middle of the day. However, greedy guns may take advantage of the situation and try to fit in extra drives, especially towards the end of the season, and finish at 4pm or later.

Do's and Don'ts for beaters

Do turn up on time
Do wear smart and suitable clothing
Do take your own lunch
Do what you are told
Do keep in line
Do keep quiet
Do be pleasant and cheerful
Do help to carry game to the game cart and game larder
Do enjoy yourself
Don't drive at 70mph up to keeper's or Laird's house
Don't tell the keeper a better way to do his job
Don't criticise the shooting
Don't upset the pickers-up or other beaters
Don't phone the keeper at 10 o'clock the evening before the
    shoot to tell him you are going to his neighbour's shoot
    instead
Don't swear or curse in front of ladies
Don't chastise your dog
Don't let your spaniel off its rope without warning the
    keeper first that he has never been trained
Don't moan (keeper's prerogative)

The keeper's day

If the novice beater has proved his worth he will have been inundated with requests to beat and the season will have flown by. Towards the end of January he will be invited to shoot at the end-of-season 'Keeper's Days'. The purpose of these days is to thank the beaters and pickers-up for the work they have done during the season.

The usual format is for the assembled guests to be split into two teams who take it in turns to beat and shoot. The days are normally 'cocks only' so that they perform a service to the shoot as it is not good management to leave a surplus of cock pheasants who will fight amongst themselves and try to mate hens that are sitting on eggs. It would be useful for the would-be gamekeeper to treat these days as a privilege and a bonus, and not as a right. They are to be enjoyed but can easily be spoiled by lack of sportsmanship and selfishness.

Some keepers abuse these days by inviting guests who have not attended any of the season's shoots. The motives behind this are varied but the end result is usually the same: disgruntled and unhappy beaters. Some keepers even exceed this injustice by placing their guests at standing pegs all day while the beaters merely enjoy the privilege of beating with guns.

The proper system to be employed for the Keeper's Day is for each team to draw numbers, eg. 1–10 for the standing pegs, moving up two at each drive. A team leader should be appointed to enforce this fair method.

The keeper has a difficult role to play on these days. He must not be as strict as he would be on formal days as this could constrain the atmosphere of enjoyment. On the other hand some of the guns may not be experienced in this type of shooting and the keeper will have to observe each gun and nip in the bud any unsafe shooting or lack of etiquette.

Some keepers abnegate responsibility completely on these days and they become a free-for-all with guns jumping from moving Landrovers so that they can command the best pegs at each drive.

At this stage the reader may feel that he should give these days a miss. This would be a big mistake; he should take every opportunity to go shooting, as even a bad day is better then none and ninety nine percent of these days are enjoyable and will be remembered for years to come.

As well as his remuneration and his can of beer, the beater may bring something less welcome home from the shoot: ticks. These small inoffensive-looking creatures frequent moors and woodland, especially where there is groundcover such as bracken. They transfer from one host to another including sheep, hare, deer, fox and unfortunately, human beings. Any area of skin which is exposed may be infected but the most common area is the groin. The tick rather charmingly attaches itself to its victim by inserting a series of hook-like tentacles into the skin. Once attached, the tick grows to three or four times its original size as it sucks its host's blood. The most serious side-effect to humans is Lymes disease, a debilitating illness causing fatigue and other unpleasant symptoms.

There are many theories about the best way to remove ticks. After-shave and vaseline are meant to cause the tick to withdraw its tentacles, which is desirable as the parasite's body alone can otherwise be removed leaving the head in situ and the host liable to infection. It is best therefore to check for the presence of ticks especially in the peak month of September after grouse or partridge beating on the hill.

If the reader is about to embark on a relationship with a member of the fair sex it may be advisable to draw a veil over this, as such information may have a terminal effect on proceedings.

CHAPTER TWO

Unpaid Keepering Work

If the reader has persevered with this book thus far I may conclude one of two things: either he is interested in a career in gamekeeping, or, perhaps more unlikely, he is enjoying the text. To readers who are part of the latter group, I extend my sincere gratitude. To the former, I offer some advice and warning for you now have in the region of one percent of the knowledge required to make the grade. The next step on the tall ladder of becoming a gamekeeper is to offer your help to the aforementioned keeper in his day-to-day work. This assistance will vary from keeper to keeper, depending on labour supplied by his employers and the type of estate he works on. A single-handed keeper is probably the best bet to offer your services to, as they are invariably over-worked and under-funded. It is therefore up to the embryo keeper to assess the situation and offer to help where he thinks assistance would be most appreciated. This can take many forms: for instance, if there is a rabbit problem on the estate, a young trustworthy man could be a real boon to a keeper if he could be relied upon to clear an area of rabbits without damaging game interests.

Rabbiting

Even by accompanying the keeper on rabbiting on expeditions, the reader can be an asset by carrying equipment, clearing undergrowth such as brambles and gorse round burrows and waiting for a recalcitrant ferret to reappear while the keeper moves on to the next set of burrows.

I remember assisting the local rabbit catcher 'Auld Tam' by carrying spades, spare ferrets, nets and the poles for carrying the Bag. This usually involved Saturday and Sunday excursions dawn to dusk with the only payment in kind being the occasional shot with Tam's ancient four-ten at any rabbit which managed to evade the nets. Bags often exceeded one hundred for the weekend and the labour involved in hauling the paunched rabbits (my job as well) to the nearest road was quite arduous. 'Auld Tam' always dressed in rags and seemed to live in extreme poverty but, as I was to realise some years later, a hundred clean rabbits were worth approximately thirty pounds which was a good wage in those days. Little wonder that Tam was extremely disappointed when the naïve youth finally severed the rather unequal partnership. That said, the other side of the coin (and the reader will realise soon that there is always another side to a coin) was that I gained a superb grounding in the ways of rabbits and the means of controlling them. 'Auld Tam' was a self-employed professional, indeed I doubt that the Inland Revenue knew of his existence, and as such he depended on being efficient when he worked, having to produce results with the minimum time and effort, and the maximum return.

Tam was a perfectionist and a hard task-master who believed in the old maxim, 'If something is worth doing, it is worth doing well' and I learned this at an early stage of our partnership. Tam gave me twenty rabbit snares to set in a small meadow criss-crossed with well-padded rabbit runs. I set them carefully, or so I thought, as he had taught me, with five set right-handed (peg to the right), the next five set left-handed to facilitate collection and checking. (Some trappers used pigeon feathers to mark their trap-line, others different coloured cord which attached snare to peg, usually changing the sequence every 3–7 snares, meaning that if a snare was missing the area to be searched was greatly reduced and easily identified.) Tam inspected my handiwork, then methodically closed the majority of the snares, the remainder he pulled out of the ground completely. Turning to me he said, quite simply, 'Now set them in the middle of the run and between the claps.'

Predators were also encountered, especially when snaring, as the shrill scream of the rabbit in a snare draws to the immediate vicinity any creature which preys on rabbits. Foxes were rare in those days but I can remember an incident when we checked snares only to find several containing only the heads of the victims. Tam was beside himself with rage and did not rest until the culprit was accounted for.

Stoats, mink and otters can all be encountered during ferreting expeditions. The smell of the different mustelids when disturbed by an inquisitive ferret will never be forgotten and is a useful experience which will be helpful to the young keeper in future years. Interestingly many inhabitants of burrows apart from rabbits will be evicted by a ferret. Stoats, mink and fox have all been flushed by ferrets. The addition of a small bell attached to a ferret's collar is advised if there is a suspicion that some animal other than a rabbit is present. This will make the tenant more likely to bolt as well as giving the ferret (ideally a male) some protection.

One creature which Tam avoided at all costs was the rat. He was of the opinion that working ferrets on these creatures ruined ferrets, making them nervous and reluctant to enter as well as endangering them because of the infectious nature of the rat's bites.

All in all, rabbiting can be great sport and a good way to discover every nook and cranny of a particular piece of land.

Controlling foxes

Where the keeper employs the services of a pack of hounds to drive foxes to waiting guns, the reader should volunteer, as a large number of guns is required to completely surround a cover to ensure that no fox can find an escape route. The keeper at other times of the year may decide to hold impromptu drives for individual foxes. These drives require beaters and again the reader should offer his services enthusiastically. This should be appreciated by the keeper, as negotiating the type of cover that foxes inhabit, in late summer for instance, is not a pleasant task and cheerful and willing beaters are worth their weight in gold.

Cubbing time, when keepers check earths for signs of fox cubs, is an exciting time of year which every keeper looks forward to. The volunteer may be allowed to accompany the keeper and take his gun with him. Terriers will be used to enter earths and deal with cubs by bolting them or killing them. If the vixen is present, she may bolt and will be shot (do not miss, you may never be forgiven). If the vixen is not present, the keeper may ask his assistant to wait at the hole to deter her from approaching the earth and realising that the cubs are dead. Once she realises that they are dead she will disappear and may be difficult to account for, but while she thinks her cubs are still present she will return again and again. This is both the foxes' strength and weakness: they are wonderful parents. The dog fox will continue to rear the cubs if the vixen is killed and can be accounted for when he returns to the cubs as would the vixen. The keeper may arrange with you to leave the den at a prearranged time. In the period prior to this he will have approached into the wind to a position where he can see the den and the surrounding area. Quite often the vixen will investigate the earth soon after someone has left, and can be shot using a suitable rifle.

Helping with pheasant rearing

The rearing season offers great scope for the reader to offer his services as there are a number of arduous and onerous tasks which the keeper will be only too happy to delegate. If the keeper catches hens to supply a laying pen, the catcher-cages will need to be emptied twice a day or more. An extra pair of hands would be most welcome to enter the catcher-cages and fill the crates, then transport them to the vehicles. The hens will need to be handled to brail them (ie. tether the wing so that the bird is incapable of flight or inject them against the various diseases to which pheasants are vulnerable).

The laying pens will have to be prepared by furnishing them with fir branches, eggs need to be collected and the rearing field built. All these tasks are greatly facilitated by an extra pair of hands. When the rearing season is in full flow, the keeper will welcome any assistance he can get; even feeding his dogs at weekends will be a relief as he has absolutely no spare time at this most hectic period.

The two most stressful periods in the rearing season are bitting and releasing. Bitting – to stop feather pecking – entails driving the three-week-old poults into a confined area (usually a hot and dusty job). Someone (guess who) has to enter this space, make himself as comfortable as possible, catch the poults, then hand them to the keeper who inserts the 'bit' (a roughly u-shaped piece of hard plastic) between the mandibles of the bird, using a particular device. This is one of the most unpleasant tasks to be encountered as it is invariably claustrophobic, oppressive and dirty. However, it is one of the most important jobs which, if not done at the right time, can ruin the entire season.

Three weeks later, when the birds are six weeks old, releasing will start. This involves catching the poults, placing them in crates and transporting them to the release pens. Again many hands make light work if they know what they are doing.

The day the keeper releases his birds to the wood is the day when the shoot has the highest number of birds. From this day on, they become fewer every day and it is the keeper's job to keep these losses to a minimum. To do this he must feed and water them, protect them from predators, poachers, stray dogs, disturbance from walkers, farming activity and forestry operations. The poults must also be chased by dogs back to the centre of the shoot when they stray. This is called 'dogging-in' and when birds really start to stray the reader will be most welcome to assist in this operation, especially if he has a steady dog which does not 'peg' birds. 'Pegging' birds means that the dog, instead of flushing the birds into the air, catches them. Although many dog handlers believe that their charges are so soft-mouthed that they can catch birds which the handler subsequently releases unharmed, my experience is that many if not all these birds die within a short time. If you have an inveterate 'pegger', a solution may be to fit a muzzle which does not restrict the dog's breathing. Whatever you decide, remember the birds are sacrosanct and if your dog cannot be trusted, leave him at home.

Few people outside the keepering fraternity realise how much feed and water pheasant poults consume and it is no exaggeration to say that from July to the end of October the keeper will be fully occupied seven days a week fulfilling these tasks. Obviously if the reader could help by filling drinkers and hoppers at the weekend, he would be a godsend to the keeper.

Unless the keeper is very efficient or works in an intensively-keepered area, there is every likelihood that he will have problems from a fox or foxes at some stage after release. When this happens the keeper can usually deal with the predators before too much damage is done. However, occasionally a cunning fox appears which is lamp-shy, snare-wise and just very difficult to account for. When this happens, an extra pair of eyes and ears can be very useful to observe the movements of 'Charlie', especially if the estate has high seats strategically placed near the release pens.

If poachers are a problem, an occasional night spent watching would be a useful service. Be sure to take a mobile phone so that you can contact the keeper or the police if something occurs which you cannot deal with yourself. Use your discretion, however, as it would defeat the purpose if you called the keeper out only to find it was the local farmer checking his cattle. Time seems to drag when night-watching and you will find yourself hoping that poachers appear, just to break the monotony. Remember the good night's sleep the keeper has gained will have done him the world of good as he has more than enough to do during daylight hours without staying in the woods every night.

This brings us full circle to the shooting season and if the keeper is a gentleman he will have told his employer of your assistance. This will put you in good stead for the future if you decide to pursue a career in keepering, as a reference from an owner of a reputable shooting estate carries a lot of weight. The reader should remember one thing however: he has been put in a position of trust and if he betrays that trust, few keepers will forgive him as they are invariably the hardest of men and you are unlikely to be able to repair the relationship.

Other help you can offer

Low ground keepering may not be to the reader's taste and he may feel drawn to the glamorous world of the grousekeeper. There is less scope to assist a high ground keeper, not I hasten to say, because they do not do so much, but rather the tasks they fulfil tend to be of a solitary nature. There are exceptions however. Fox control at cubbing time follows similar lines as on the low ground and only the terrain differs.

Heather burning is labour-intensive and extra help is always welcome. The aim of the keeper, when heather burning, is to burn old heather in strips roughly 35–40 yards wide to allow new young heather to regenerate. Young heather is desirable as it provides the best feeding and the 35–40 yards strip provides the ideal conditions for young grouse as it has been found that they seldom feed more than 15–20 yards from escape cover.

The season for heather burning runs from 1st October to 15th April but the majority of heather will be burnt in March. On arrival at the moor you will be taken to the area to be burnt. You will then be placed in a team of three and, as you are inexperienced, at least one other member of the team will be an old hand. You will be given a beater to extinguish the flames. These flame-beaters take a number of forms: the oldest type is made from birch twigs attached to a birch pole. Newer versions use strips of conveyer belting attached to a pole, or there are deluxe models made from aluminium shafts and mesh. Whichever type you are given, the object of the exercise is to use the beater to confine the fire to the 35–40 yard strip. Every fire has a hot side and a hotter side. While the less hot side can be controlled by one man, the hotter side is held by two men taking it in turns to get close to the fire. The intense heat requires protective clothing, ie. leggings, gloves and some form of face protection. Check that these are provided by the estate, and if not, take your own. When a fire gets out of control you will be glad you did.

Heather burning is a satisfying experience. The weather conditions (obviously fine weather is necessary for burning) and the scenery at this time of year make for an enjoyable time.

The spraying of bracken using asulox or other chemicals is beneficial to a moor, because if left unchecked, bracken encroaches, choking the heather and increasing every year. Application is usually by a knapsack-sprayer which, as the name implies, is strapped to the user's back, an arduous task which obviously a grousekeeper would be only too happy to delegate to someone else.

A more constructive form of assistance can be offered when the grousekeeper repairs or builds new butts. The reader can offer great service moving stones and turves or even wooden pallets depending on what type of butt is preferred on the moor. Some keepers are artists when it comes to butt building and the novice will learn a vast amount in a short time from such a man.

At any time of the year the grousekeeper is grateful for an extra pair of eyes to survey his moor, and the would-be gamekeeper who takes up a good vantage point at dawn or dusk with a powerful pair of binoculars, observing the presence or otherwise of predators and trespassers, provides a priceless service which should be appreciated by the keeper.

This takes us through to the shooting season, as I've described in the previous chapter.

Taking stock: is this the career for you?

I would suggest that the reader assists a keeper for two seasons before deciding for certain whether or not to pursue a career in gamekeeping. It may not take this long to decide that this way of life is not for him. If this is the case, no harm will have been done. It is better to find out at this stage rather than embark on a career then terminate it in its infancy.

If the reader has become even more enthusiastic about becoming a gamekeeper after the two years then there is every chance that he may make the grade. Keenness to the point of obsession is a prerequisite for the successful keeper and if this is not present, you are doomed to failure.

There is one more factor that the reader may not have considered and that is the plunge he will take in social status when he wears the green suit. I believe that this has been exacerbated in modern times by the media portrayal of the gamekeeper as a simple servile bumpkin employed by a rich land-owner. The fact that he lives in a tied house in a society where everyone aspires to home-ownership puts him, in the public perception, even lower in the social scale.

The high profile character-assassination of gamekeepers by environmental groups; and with bird and animal protection societies painting the gamekeeper as nothing more than a rural criminal, demeans the profession even further. The result of this climate of opinion is that the reader (and his family) will encounter prejudice when he assumes the position of gamekeeper, that he will not have experienced previously – unless he already belongs to a persecuted minority group!

One disturbing aspect of this prejudice is the persecution of gamekeeper's children by teachers holding animal rights views.

I do not apologise for revealing these unpleasant facts as I believe they should be aired and my reader is forewarned. That is my duty in producing this book: to endow my reader with all possible knowledge regarding this subject. You must realise therefore that to be successful you must possess a strong character and a thick skin.

Fall-back career option

In a perfect world I would suggest that, prior to his first appointment, the keeper should have acquired a trade or skill that he can fall back on should his keeping career terminate prematurely. As well as this he should, if possible, try to gain a foot on the property ladder in some way such as the so-called buy-to-rent system whereby the purchaser of a house does not reside in it but lets the property to a third party, the rent received going towards paying the whole, or part of, the mortgage.

The reason for me suggesting this is that, once you embark on your keepering career, your wage will reflect the fact that you receive rent-free accommodation. The down-side of this is that the amount of mortgage offered to you will obviously be reduced because of your reduced salary. You may, however, be fortunate to be employed on a estate where a free cottage will be offered to you on retirement, but as this is probably forty years in the future, it is impossible to count on this with any degree of certainly unless a contract is drawn up (and I have never heard of this happening). This problem has been made more acute by the high rents attained by country cottages nowadays. It is not uncommon for the keeper's house on an estate being put up for rent after a keeper retires and the new keeper being offered a lowly terraced cottage in its place. It is little wonder, under these circumstances, that free available housing for retiring estate workers is scarce and liable to get scarcer.

Skill requirements

There are some skills and equipment that the aspiring keeper should acquire before assuming his first position. They are as follows:

- The ability to drive a Landrover or other 4wd vehicle over rough terrain. Coupled with this, the experience of towing and reversing a trailer. This should be acquired when assisting the aforementioned keeper.

- The experience of driving a quad bike, again towing and reversing a trailer.

- The use of a chainsaw. Preferably the young keeper should acquire relevant certificates. These require the acquisition of a power-saw and the full safety equipment, ie. helmet with visor, gloves, safety boots and Kevlar leggings. Maintenance and felling techniques must be learned before passing the test. This experience is not perhaps mandatory but is an extremely useful addition to your CV.

- Gundogs and terriers. A gundog would normally be considered a necessity for a gamekeeper, as would a terrier on a grouse moor. Too many dogs (more than three) may be a disadvantage, as your employer may become suspicious if you spend too much time training and trialling dogs.

- Welding equipment and the ability to use it are a great asset to a keeper as he can repair trailers, hoppers and other metal-work on the spot rather than have to wait for others or incur the cost of employing an outside firm.

- Experience of tractors and trailers, as well as JCBs is, again, a real boon and a plus point on your CV.

- Knowledge of natural history, the ability to identify the various predators, their habits and movements, as well as the different birds of prey is another prerequisite.

- Experience in handling various types of firearms is essential to a gamekeeper. I would suggest that the reader becomes proficient enough to shoot 20 out of 25 clay pigeons on a sporting bird layout. Practice will make perfect. Rifle shooting, both .22 and centre-fire, is where competence is again a necessity. I would suggest the ability to shoot a 1 inch group at 50 yards for rim-fire and a 2-inch group at 150 yards for the centre-fire. Practice will achieve this standard and probably exceed it. Safety is paramount and it is a waste of time to achieve a high standard of marksmanship, yet be an unsafe and untrustworthy shooting companion.

- A certain level of physical fitness is required to be a gamekeeper. I would suggest the following level to be attained. Ten chin-ups, twenty press-ups and fifty trunk-curls. You should also be capable of carrying 50 kilos for a 100 yards on level ground and 25 kilos for one mile over rough country.

- The modern keeper should have an out-going, cheerful and optimistic disposition. The ability to get on with fellow workers in the game management staff, as well as other workers and tenant farmers, is essential. This is a marked contrast to yesteryear when the keeper was not expected to mix with other inhabitants on an estate, indeed he maintained a rather aloof manner which probably made him even more unpopular. The last thing an employer needs is a keeper who causes friction and cannot co-operate with other members of staff or tenant farmers.

- The would-be keeper should make himself familiar with the operation of traps and snares until he is comfortable handling them. Your friendly keeper will be invaluable in showing you how they work and the best sites for them. The important ones are fox snares, fenn traps and Larsen traps. There are others which will be dealt with in subsequent chapters, but these will be enough for a basic introduction and again a useful addition to your CV.

• One last point to consider is your clothes and appearance, if you are called for an interview. A long-haired unshaven individual wearing a t-shirt, jeans and dirty trainers would be most unlikely to be successful in gaining employment. A tidy appearance, conservative dress and polished brogues would be the best approach. Remember your prospective employer will expect you to have put in some effort to impress, and a lack of a sign of this effort will mark you down, in his eyes, as lazy and lacking enthusiasm.

So there you have it. You are young, fit, presentable, with suitable skills, experience and knowledge to apply for a job as an underkeeper, beatkeeper or even single-handed keeper. This may seem a bold statement but occasionally an individual comes along who is so talented that he requires only the most basic training before he can go single-handed. You may be one of these lucky men but remember you will require an understanding boss when things go wrong which can happen to any keeper. In your case the cause of the problem may be identified as your lack of experience, not bad luck. It may be better to receive a good grounding on a first class prestigious estate for several years and then take your pick of the excellent jobs on offer, rather than being impatient and settling for second best, stuck in a dead-end job with no potential for furthering your career. Remember also that your potential employer may have an ulterior motive for employing an inexperienced man, as he may think that such a person will be cheaper, naive and more malleable: in short; a soft touch.

The most important factor when considering whether you should accept a position is the fact that your first position will affect all your subsequent employment. This is because keepers depend on references from previous employers to gain new positions and therefore they must leave every job on good terms, after having done the job to the best of their ability without alienating the entire population of the surrounding countryside. You will now realise that if you accept a very difficult position on a second class estate with many problems, it may be difficult for you to build a good reputation and because you have no previous employers to provide references as to your keepering ability, you may find yourself in a rut from which is hard to extracate yourself. In the trade, keepers who have started from the very bottom on poor estates and worked themselves to the top are regarded with much respect on the grounds that 'they came up the hard way'.

Another consideration for the aspiring keeper is the fact that he may not meet his prospective employer, but instead will be interviewed by an agent, or in Scotland, a factor. This can be a satisfactory arrangement, but it may also mean that the employer is not very enthusiastic and does not attach much importance to employing a keeper. The infernal triangle of employer, factor, and keeper can be problematic, explosive, and even disastrous, needing skilful diplomatic skills from all sides.

The following scenario sums up this special relationship, if one can imagine the cowboy as your previous employer, the Indian chief as your new boss/landowner, the medicine man as the factor, and the horse as the keeper.

The cowboy sets out on a journey across the desert mounted on his favourite horse. Halfway across, the horse collapses, exhausted, and apparently dies. The cowboy salvages the saddle, reins etc and continues on foot. After a few hours an Indian chief spies the prostrate horse, coaxes it back on its feet and rides it back to his camp in triumph, racing the poor animal before his friends until it finally does expire this time. The chief then takes his family to feast in his tepee, handing the body of the horse to his medicine man, who strips the flesh, hanging it up in the sun to make jerky, stretches the skin to cover his tepee, boils the internal organs in a pot to make broth and then finally grinds the bones to make medicine. There are many keepers who know how that horse felt!

Jobs advertised

I have digressed, so let us return to the task of finding a position as a gamekeeper. The *Shooting Times* is a weekly magazine which usually has a Situations Vacant column, especially in the first six months of the year. Buy it every week and keep the copies: you will memorise the jobs advertised, so look out for jobs which are advertised on a regular basis This is not a good sign as it could point to an unreasonable employer, broken promises, poor accommodation or other problems. In any event, if you are in any doubt, check on the grapevine and if there is any suspicion of underkeepers being over-exploited, leave well alone.

A good source of information is the National Gamekeepers Association, which keeps a register of keepers looking for employment and employers with situations vacant. It is advisable to join this organisation as it is the main voice speaking for gamekeepers in the British Isles.

Local newspapers can be a source, especially in areas where shooting estates are numerous. Those living outside these areas must ask acquaintances to inform them when local positions become vacant. In general, keep an ear to the ground, use initiative and common sense to make sure that you are aware of any vacancy when it occurs or even before, as the early bird often catches the worm. By this I mean that an approach to an employer as soon as a position becomes vacant can sometimes be successful, as it avoids the expense of advertising, the sorting of applications, the interviews and the letters of apology to unsuccessful applicants. The employer may also be swayed by the early starting date that you could offer, and the fear, because you are a first-class candidate, you may find another position in the time he takes to advertise. In short, he may feel that a bird in the hand is worth two in the bush.

Keepers are notorious gossips. One of their favourite topics is jobs about to come up and they are undoubtedly one of the best sources of information, not only as to when a vacancy is likely to occur but also about the nature of the job and calibre of the employer. Be aware, however, when talking to a keeper about a vacancy, be sure that his son or friend is not interested in the job as he may be cunning enough to discourage you from applying especially if he feels that you are a superior candidate. This happened to the me once and since then it has always been my policy to never take one man's opinion on any subject to be gospel.

Your application

We will assume that you have selected a vacancy which you would be happy to fill. Your first task is to write to the address given in the advertisement, furnishing them with your c.v. I would suggest you attach a hand written letter stating your reasons for applying for this particular position, emphasizing the skills and experience which you possess and which are particularly relevant to the job in question e. g. a position for a grousekeeper would not require rearing experience, but would require pest controlling experience, ownership of terriers and an excellent level of physical fitness. The exact layout of the c.v. I cannot comment on, as every employer will be 'turned on' by something different, indeed some applicants for certain jobs are sent a rather impersonal application form with a list of questions, many of which can be answered yes/no. My personal opinion would be to be particularly wary of this type of estate as it suggests to me that a minimum of effort is being expended to find the right candidate and the successful one would not be a valued member of staff.

Once you have sent off your application you should receive an acknowledgement (within a week). The next contact may take several forms: the least desirable obviously is the straightforward 'thank you for your application but you have not been successful in this instance'. Deep disappointment will be felt but do not be discouraged, there will be many more opportunities. The other option may be a letter or phone call asking you to attend for interview at a certain place and date.

Impress at interview

Now that you have an interview, make sure that you have everything in place to impress your prospective employer: get a haircut, polish your sensible brogues, check that the clothes you are to wear are clean and pressed and remember to wash and polish your car. You will be nervous in the period running up to the interview but this normally disappears as the interview progresses, so do not worry excessively and make the most of your opportunity.

An agent or factor will have some role to play in your interview. He may conduct the whole affair himself, introducing you to the headkeeper or employer who may have the final say by offering their seal of approval to his choice or you may face a triumvirate of factor, headkeeper and employer. They will ask you questions to see if your application was accurate as to your knowledge and experience. Answer truthfully and do not be afraid to say that you do not know the answer to any particular query. This is far preferable to an applicant who bluffs and waffles his way through an interview portraying himself as untruthful and opportunistic.

One of your inquisitors may try to unsettle you and attempt to determine whether or not you have a 'short fuse'. On no account, despite the worst provocation, should you rise to the bait as a keeper with a quick temper is not desirable. (This may be news to some guest guns and beaters on certain shoots up and down the country).

The terms and conditions which you are prepared to accept are entirely up to you. It would be prudent to make enquiries and try to find out the going rate for an underkeeper/beatkeeper and what perks are to be expected. This varies from area to area, for instance a beatkeeper in England will be paid more than a single-handed keeper in Scotland. Also the quality of accommodation must be taken into account. Remember that a house which you feel is perfectly habitable may be viewed by your wife as a hovel not fit to keep the dogs in. It would therefore be advisable to allow her to inspect the offered abode before accepting the position (believe me this has happened on more than one occasion). If the accommodation offered is obviously sub-standard, even to your eyes, extricate yourself from the interview as quickly as possible. On no account accept a position with the promise that things will be put right after you move in, as my experience is that, in many instances, this just does not happen, or if it does, the improvements are carried out over a protracted period. Be polite, make suitable excuses, but whatever you do, do not accept poor accommodation!

I would offer the same advice as regards the vehicle offered. An aging van, rusting Subaru pick-up or vintage Landrover are sure signs that money is scarce or the employer is lacking enthusiasm for shooting, but feels he must not let the side down by not having a shoot, while not providing sufficient funds to run one properly. Such a job is a nightmare for a keeper as he tries to make bricks without straw. This is not to say that it cannot be done: resourceful and talented keepers produce unbelievable results year after year proverbially making silk purses from sows ears. But it is far easier to make a name for yourself on a good estate with adequate resources than to take the 'rocky road to Dublin' because you were desperate for a 'start'.

If the reader takes my advice he may decline many offers of employment. Do not be discouraged, the right job will come along. The credit side is that he will become experienced in interviews and will be able to compare different jobs and therefore the going rates of pay, perks and accommodation.

The Estate personnel

He will meet many different characters among these agents or factors. These men are charged with the complete running of an estate and as such can wield considerable power and influence. They also carry an enormous burden, as decisions which they make can literally cost or earn an estate hundreds of thousands of pounds. They are also called upon to act as intermediaries between the estate and tenant farmers when disputes occur, a thankless task if ever there was one! The important thing to remember is that they are only human (I have been assured of this!) and if they view you with an air of trepidation and suspicion it is only because they do not want to be blamed for employing an individual who turns out to be a complete disaster because he is a thief, psychopath or just completely idle.

The landed gentry can be quite disconcerting if you are not acquainted with their various foibles. The first anomaly you may notice is an eccentric or disastrous dress sense. Battered shoes, tired old corduroy trousers, moth-eaten pullovers all seem to have a special place in the landed gentry's idea of acceptable clothing. Indeed on arriving at the interview you may find the headkeeper attired in his tweed suit, the factor or agent in his classic polished brogues, checked shirt, mustard chinos and immaculate tie, leaving the applicant to wonder which is which. The answer to this is of course that the land-owner does not feel the need to impress, while you, the agent and the headkeeper undoubtedly have to.

The older generation of land-owner can have difficulty relating to their own employees which can be off-putting at first, but once they get to know you, they will become less aloof and many can be great company with a wicked sense of humour. It is as well to remember that the majority of this generation were plucked from their family at a very early age and packed off to boarding school where they were expected to endure all sorts of unspeakable ordeals with a stoic resolve and never ever show any emotion. While at one time this was an essential part of the production line that produced a race of empire builders, it did little to form a rounded individual at ease with the modern world. However, never underestimate a public school education, or indeed the upper-classes themselves: they have regrouped and refocused as they always have done and now produce young men and women who are at ease with anyone from a Duke to a Dustman and are completely comfortable in present day society. The common denominator to both the older and younger generation of land-owner is that they are gentlemen, their word is their bond and they are invariably easy to work for, providing you try your best. They have a unique talent which allows them to disarm any individual and make them feel that they are important to them. This is a great gift but the reader should realise that this is a vehicle for them to get their own way and he should never feel that he is special as this may lead to a rude awakening.

The following story will illustrate this point as well as reminding the young keeper that you can never ever say with certainty that you have 'cracked it'.

In February 1987 I purchased the weekly edition of *Shooting Times*. As usual I opened the magazine at the wrong end and surveyed the situations vacant column. One advertisement stood out, for me, from all the rest: it called for applicants for a vacancy that had arisen on a Lancashire grouse moor due to the imminent retirement of the headkeeper. This interested me because the incumbent, Angus Macdonald, was something of a living legend who had served with my uncle in the Army Commandos in the last war and my childhood antics had been accompanied by my uncle praising or berating me with such phrases as 'Angus Macdonald could not have done it better' or 'I don't know what big Angus would have said about that'. Angus became almost a mythical figure in my eyes and it was almost a surprise when years later I met keepers who had known him and I realised that he did indeed exist and that real life exceeded legend.

Angus Macdonald was born and grew up on one of the western isles of Scotland. At 14½ years of age he left home to work as a pony and kennel boy on a highland estate. Such were Angus's natural attributes and skills that he became responsible for his own beat at the age of 17, gaining an enviable reputation as a deer stalker, vermin killer, rifle and shotgun shot as well as a prodigious grousekeeper. Add to this a formidable 6ft 4 inch frame, exceptional strength and fitness and it is not difficult to see why he was one of the most promising keepers of his generation.

War cast a dark cloud over the land and Angus' highland estate was one of those few in the highlands to be used as a training camp for the newly formed Commandos. Angus assisted, unofficially teaching recruits field craft, living off the land, shooting and trapping. It was obvious that he was a natural Commando and when his call-up papers arrived it was not long before he returned home for training to be Commando via a short stint for basic training in the 'Argyles'. Angus survived the war, many of his comrades did not, and like my uncle he was reluctant to recall the experiences he went through. Suffice to say that they were all very brave men.

After the war Angus was head-hunted by one of the largest land owners in the highlands and was charged with restoring his grouse moors to their former glory. In this Angus was spectacularly successful and became a firm favourite of the Laird who took Angus fishing, stalking and shooting on his other estates up and down the country. Unfortunately Angus allowed his new-found status to affect his judgement, as he realised that the Laird would back him whatever he did. This resulted in Angus making a huge mistake which he lived to regret.

A new young assistant factor named Snodgrass arrived on Angus' estate and Angus wasted no time in making sure that the young man knew his place. This culminated in Angus humiliating Snodgrass in front of other staff at an end of season grouse shoot where the factor shot very badly. There were two repercussions from this incident: firstly the factor was put off shooting for life, and secondly he never forgave Angus for belittling him.

A number of years passed with Angus reigning like a King in the laird's absence until the day that changed his life forever. His employer called him to a meeting one day, informing him that he had acquired a grouse-moor in England (some say he won it in a bet) and he wanted Angus to go there to work his magic and restore it to full production. Angus was reluctant to go as he was very happy where he was and wanted for nothing. However, his boss was persuasive, conceding that he need only stay long enough to sort the neglected estate out, then return to his present position.

And so it was that Angus moved to Lancashire, becoming as famous there as he was in the highlands, the keepers affectionately nick-naming him Trevor after his namesake the ITV news broadcaster. Angus resurrected the moor and was starting to looking forward to returning home when tragedy struck: the Laird died from a massive heart attack. This meant that his estates were put into the hands of trustees and purse strings were tightened to the point of strangulation.

A further hammer blow was suffered when a new factor was sent down from Scotland to make the Lancashire moor pay its way. The factor was Snodgrass and he wasted no time in showing Angus who was in charge now. Half the moor was planted in trees and the remainder let to tenant farmers for grazing cattle. A syndicate of undertakers from Birmingham took the grouse shooting and added to the feeling of gloom and melancholy that prevailed over the estate.

Angus was now trapped. There was no way back to Scotland and the estate deteriorated as his enthusiasm waned. Sadly he started to gain solace from the bottle and became a shadow of his former self, and his peers who had at one time respected and even feared him now viewed him with disdain and called him 'Tragic Trevor'.

This was the background to my travelling down to Lancashire to be interviewed for his erstwhile post. The southern uplands and the Lake District were magnificent with their snow capped peaks, making my journey a pleasurable experience. Eventually I reached my destination, driving slowly into a courtyard of natural stone-built offices which formed the hub of the estate.

I entered the door to the main estate office where a secretary escorted me to the factor Snodgrass. He was a thin, wiry man with thick lensed glasses. Shaking my hand firmly he motioned for me to sit down and ordered tea and toast from the secretary while he pored over my application asking me questions as he delved deeper into my past experiences. All the time he wrote notes in a book, only looking over his glasses to ascertain my response to his questions. Tea and toast arrived and I began to relax, noting the wonderful view from the window and the pleasant atmosphere. I could picture myself working here.

'The keeper who is retiring is Angus Macdonald,' the factor stated. 'Yes I know of Angus, he is a living legend,' I replied. The factor stopped writing suddenly, looking at me intently over his spectacles. 'Do you know Angus personally?' he asked. 'No, but my uncle served with him during the war.' My words had barely left my mouth when the factor slowly closed his book and stood up offering his hand 'I think we covered all the ground we have to today and you realise that we have had a massive response to our advertisement; we will be in touch.' I felt the atmosphere change and shook his hand looking him in the eye as I did so, hoping to detect a clue as to whether or not I was wasting my time. He looked me in the eye fleetingly then dropped his gaze, a thin smile on his face. I knew then that it was all over, bar the 'Dear John letter'.

I left the factor, disappointed, but was determined to visit Angus Macdonald so that at least some good would come from my long journey south. Driving up to his house, which was a large single storey building in the natural stone of the district, I was impressed by the location and its wide vista covering almost the entire estate with the industrial heartland of Lancashire beyond.

The door knocker took the form of a stag's head which was a fitting centre piece to the massive oak door forming an impressive focal point to the Macdonald residence. I chapped twice, a solid satisfying sound that fitted the massive structure perfectly. After a short delay the door slowly creaked open and an elegant lady stood framed in the doorway. This was Angus' wife Moira, who spoke to me, her voice blessed with that most beautiful lilt of the western isles. A great beauty in her day, now her smile masked a sadness in her eyes. 'Come through, Angus will be pleased to see you.' I followed her down a corridor to a large kitchen with low oak beams and flag-stoned floor. A fire glowed at one end of the room, an old grey-muzzled labrador lay lapping up the heat as only a labrador can, his only reaction to my presence was a quizzical raising of the eyebrows and there on a bench beside, slumped the husk of Angus Macdonald. He lay with his right hand precariously clutching a half-filled glass of the water of life which almost but not quite spilled some of its contents. His long left arm lay languid clasping the neck of a bottle of Islay mist, leathery skin draped loosely over his skull, cheek bones trying to erupt beneath his eyes while his nose dominated his face like the beak of an eagle.

As I entered the kitchen, his piercing blue eyes fixed on me as a peregrine views a grouse. 'I believe you know my uncle,' I nervously offered. Almost immediately Angus metamorphosed into a man 25 years younger. Standing up, he put the whisky aside and shook my hand with a grip like a sea-eagle. 'It's good to speak to a Scotsman again,' he said. I had neither the nerve nor the heart to tell Angus that, in his eyes at least, I was actually a Sassenach, and we spent the rest of the afternoon discussing topics that only keepers find interesting: fox hunting trips to the middle of nowhere, cunning vixens with uncanny intelligence, stalking trips, 'rifles' who couldn't shoot, didn't tip and wouldn't walk, employers and their estates, grouse-moors and their drives, their great days and their disappointments, other keepers and their shortcomings, dogs and retrieves that would never be surpassed, but always Angus returned to the highlands and as he looked out of the window in the late afternoon I realised that he longed to see the sun lying low over the Atlantic from the western isles rather than set behind the smoke stacks of Salford.

Finally it was time to go and as I stood on the porch outside his house I asked Angus what were, in his opinion, the greatest obstacles to game preservation and the worst vermin to be dealt with on an estate.

He thought for a second, then leant forward to emphasise the point:
'FOXES, FORESTERS, FARMERS, AND F***** FACTORS –
not necessarily in that order!'

CHAPTER THREE

The Fox

You are now a gamekeeper, so from this point on, the reader must adopt a realistic and pragmatic attitude to what has been previously, in effect, a leisure activity. Any advice given in this book from here on will apply to a single-handed keeper or a beatkeeper with a high degree of responsibility.

My reason for this is that an underkeeper is usually under direct instruction of a headkeeper and should follow these instructions to the letter, even if he feels that his boss is wrong in some aspect of his management. I would also caution against mentioning to your head that you have a book at home which suggests doing things differently from his methods. Your sincere attempts at enlightenment may not be received with the same good will as they were offered. The reason for this is that many head men are highly insecure individuals who worry endlessly that their job may be put in jeopardy by a new underkeeper who is younger, fitter and more intelligent. If you then add a young man who questions his knowledge and experience the relationship between head man and his underkeeper may be tainted by suspicion and jealously which eventually will lead to disaster.

February fox control

The commencement of your employment will hopefully be in the month of February. I say this because a keeper new to his beat must waste no time in reducing the population of birds and animals which are detrimental to the preservation of a healthy population of game birds.

There is only a limited time to make inroads into their numbers, even from the beginning of February, before they start to breed, occupy territories and rear their young and it is always better to nip such activities in the bud, than to mop up the results of neglect over a protracted period of time.

The number one priority on any shooting estate is to reduce fox numbers to a minimum. It matters not whether the estate is grouse moor, partridge manor or intensively managed pheasant shoot: good results cannot be obtained unless there is a scarcity of our ginger friend. Prior to your appointment, evenings lamping, days working terriers and the attendance at fox hunts were pleasant pursuits. This has now changed. The success of your career, the security of your family home and your own peace of mind will from this time onward depend largely on your ability to control the red outlaw.

Foxes mate in January and February as a rule, although there are recorded instances of cubs born in December, so obviously it is possible for a vixen to come into season before or after the usual period. When the breeding season is in full flow the fox is at his most vulnerable, taking risks he or she would not normally take. He or she may be seen abroad in daylight in the middle of the day, oblivious to human presence, and it is advisable for the keeper to never venture forth without his preferred fox rifle as there is nothing more galling then to watch Charlie 100 yards away when the rifle is at home locked in the gun cabinet.

Foxes at this time of the year are also at their most vocal: the vixen screaming is the most unforgettable sound the keeper will ever experience. The scream or squall as it sometimes is called is difficult to describe but if the reader imagines something between the shriek of a women in distress and the wail of a stricken hare he may gain some inkling as to the sound to listen for. He need not fret, however, as any night out in the countryside at this time of year, especially in 'foxy' country, will give him ample opportunity to hear this, one of nature's most exciting sounds. As the squall is heard most frequently during January and February, it is assumed it plays some part in attracting dog foxes to a vixen in season.

Certainly if the keeper on his beat at night hears a number of vixens calling, he can be sure that there are dog foxes to match and if something is not done in the next seven and a half weeks there will be many fox cubs born on the estate in late March and early April. Another sound which may be heard is that emitted by the vixen immediately prior to and during mating; this again is difficult to describe but if the reader imagines a jay doing battle with a wood pecker he will have some idea.

Lamping

To avoid a plague of foxes on your beat, the first step is to start 'lamping' on a regular basis. Lamping is the pursuit of foxes at night using a high powered torch lit from a four-wheel drive or a battery pack. These lights are gauged as to their power by the term candle power, a very powerful one being 1 million candle power or more. The purpose of lamping is to shoot the animals in the beam of the light using a high powered centre-fire rifle. If the foxes have not been lamped regularly by someone taking pot shots at long range, with the inevitable misses, it may be possible to reduce their numbers by merely traversing the ground on foot or in a four-wheel drive vehicle, and shooting them when they pause to assess the situation.

Foxes are naturally inquisitive and when something they are not familiar with encroaches onto their territory they will often sit and observe, which should be a fatal mistake for them if you are a competent shot. A filter which covers the lamp and softens the glare can be successful, as it seems to be less alarming to foxes than a bright white light. These filters can be red, blue or amber and I will leave the reader to decide by trial and error which is the best (I have been successful with all three). A good quality telescopic sight is a necessity when lamping as it gives you extra range where you can identify for certain the target. Every year sheep and other farm animals are shot by mistake by 'marksmen' who took a chance at long range. My own view is that a shot at 150 yards while lamping is a long shot (I can hear shouts of derision already) and even then you need an excellent scope rifle combination to be confident every time.

It might seem odd that someone could mistake a sheep for a fox, but it is easy to mistake one set of eyes for another when they are reflecting the light from a powerful torch. An experienced lamper can say with 95% certainty which animal owns the eyes he illuminates at night, but I have seen many experienced men swear that a deer was a fox and a black-faced ewe alone in a field has caused a number of mistakes. The bottom line is that the lamper must be able to see and identify his quarry before squeezing that trigger.

This course of action will yield some foxes if they are reasonably plentiful and have not been lamped by incompetents. However, there can be few areas of Britain where foxes are not lamped and have not been educated: this will manifest itself in Reynard given one flash of his eyes, then departing into the next parish, when the lamp is shone on him.

It is important when lamping not to shine the light centrally on the fox but to try and catch him in the periphery of the beam. This may help to tempt a lamp shy fox to linger for just a second which may be enough. Some foxes display an impressive awareness of their predicament when lamped on ground from which it is difficult for them to escape. They run to the nearest patch of cover eg. rushes or a ditch and refuse to look at the light despite all efforts by the lamper to attract their attention. If this happens and you have two assistants, it is possible to keep the light trained on the spot where the fox disappeared while the duo armed with hand lamp and shotgun approach from a down-wind position to flush and dispatch the cunning animal.

An alternative strategy adopted by some keepers is to use a lurcher, normally a greyhound bull terrier cross, which, when released from the Landrover or pick-up, has been trained to follow the beam of the light and kill the fox when it is flushed. Many of these dogs are worth their weight in gold to a keeper who has a healthy population of foxes on his beat.

Fox snares

The lamping sessions that you have undertaken may or may not have yielded a number of foxes but at least they should have helped you to assess the number of foxes on the land and the areas which are their favourite haunts. Go to these areas and check for runs through hedges and under Rylock fences. Rylock fencing is the standard, squared, high tensile stock fencing. These may have fox hair caught where the animals push their way though a gap or there may be the strong pungent odour of the fox indicating that he passes that way regularly. If there are runs present, and they are obviously well used, then the setting of snares will reap dividends. Fox snares are made from 2mm thick steel rope which can be hard or soft. The soft type is excellent for snaring runs below fencing as it is more flexible and can be made to fit the gaps exactly. They can be purchased ready-made from a gamekeeper supplier; or a roll of wire can be purchased from the same source and the snares can be produced yourself with a considerable saving, especially if a large number are required.

Snares which are purchased ready-made usually consist of the snare itself attached to a length of wire by a swivel which reduces the likelihood of the snare wire fraying when a fox is caught. The swivel is unnecessary when the snare is set on a fence and all that is required is a length of wire with a small loop made at one end by tying the wire as you would when making a slipknot in a length of rope. The end of the wire attached to the small loop should be lashed using garden tying wire and the other end of the wire is passed through this loop forming a snare.

When setting the snares, gauge how much wire you have to spare when the snare is set in the gap, then attach the end of the snare by tying it in a slipknot to the strongest part of the fence. Extra security can be obtained by lashing the short end of the wire to the rest of the snare using garden tying wire. Some trappers gouge a small trench to hide the bottom of the snare which also allows rabbits and pheasants to pass through without disturbing the snare.

Similar results can be gained by forming tying wire into a 'U' shape and using it to pin the snare to the ground at the bottom of the loop. The snare should be held in position either using a piece of fencing wire lashed to the snare outside the loop or the snare can be attached to the fence using garden tying wire again outside the loop.

All snares should be fitted with a 'stop'. This is a piece of wire twisted round the snare 3–4 inches from the end of the snare which restricts the snare so that it cannot shut tight, so catching a bird or any animal by the foot.

When snares are first purchased the wire will be bright and shiny and keepers use various methods to camouflage them. Many keepers boil the snares to remove the smell of grease from the wire. This will result in the snares going brown with rust after a period of time. Unfortunately this shortens the life of the snare considerably and makes them stiff and unmanageable. Other keepers bury the snares or soak them in a solution containing oak bark or similar after the boiling process. My own view is that this is unnecessary and expensive (boiling included) and I have for many years dipped snares in forest green Cuprinol or similar, then hung them up to dry.

Obviously the longer the snares are stored before use the better, but I have still had good results after the snares have only been hung for a fortnight. Great care must be taken when setting these snares as every precaution must be taken to ensure that only foxes are caught. The first non-target species the trapper should check for is the badger. On a reasonably sized estate, say of 3,000 acres, if there are no known badger sets it should be safe to commence fence snaring with the proviso that snares are checked at first light every day. If by mistake brock is caught it is usually a straightforward task to release him from the snare using wire cutters especially designed for the purpose (obtained from gamekeepers suppliers).

The young keeper should also be careful to ensure that no farm stock can reach a snare by setting them inside the wood away from the field side of the fence or hedge. If there is a good run which cannot be protected from farm stock eg. lambs, then the solution is to block the gap using scrap Rylock or blackthorn branches, so forcing the fox to the snares.

Snaring on open runs requires much more skill than snaring on fences, the skill taking some men years to learn while others remain ignorant forever. The advent of lamping has meant that many young keepers have not had to learn how to snare. The advantages of lamping are that it can be exciting and a sport. It is also less controversial and does not occupy a man every day for 2–3 hours, as snaring does. If lamping was more effective than snaring, then snaring could be discontinued altogether, but this unfortunately is not the case and in most areas the only really effective weapon against the fox is the piece of wire.

Snares used on open runs are made from hard wire forming a 6–8 inch loop which is attached to another length of hard wire 18 inches long by a swivel. A 'stop', which is a short piece of wire twisted round the snare to prevent it closing completely, should be fitted so that the snare will only hold its victim without strangling it. It is a legal requirement that any snare is free running, ie. when the fox ceases to struggle, the snare should slacken preventing the animal being choked to death. A 'teeler' is used to position the snare on the run. A teeler can take many forms: many trappers use lengths of hazel or ash saplings 9–12 inches long by ¼–½ inch in diameter. These are pointed at one end while the other is split so that the wire can be pushed into the cleft and gripped. It may be necessary to use tying wire twisted round the top of the teeler to ensure the snare is held rigidly in position. Other teelers can be made from lengths of plain fencing wire which should be lashed to the snare by garden tying wire. This type of teeler is useful where the hanging type of snare is preferred as it is easier to disguise the wire and adjust the position of the snare.

The snare can be attached to a peg or a drag. Drags are preferable as the fox will pull the snare away from the run leaving it undamaged so that a new snare can be set in the same place, time after time. The same sites can be successful year after year, so once the favoured runs are known, good results can be gained using the minimum of snares. The drags must be heavy enough to ensure that a fox or other animal can only move themselves a short distance. Extra security can be gained by leaving six inch nails protruding or by stapling scrap Rylock to the drags which are often two old fencing stobs or posts. Always check that they are sound and not rotten. A length of fencing wire wound round, then stapled to the stobs will be essential to attach the snare to the drag, leaving sufficient scope to hide the drag in adjacent cover.

Pegs must be made substantial enough that they are impossible to break or pull out of the ground. This is another argument for snaring with drags, as on hard rocky ground or very soft ground it may be

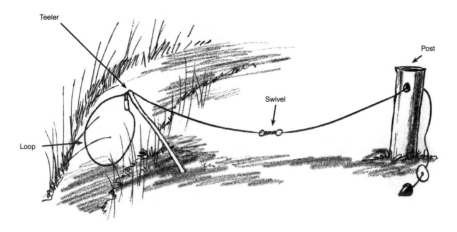

A simple fox snare set on a run with the amgled teeler (a simple stick with a notch) holding the loop in the right position.

impractical to use pegs. Added security can be ensured by drilling holes 3 inches apart at right angles to each other near the point of the peg. Push ordinary fencing wire through the holes and staple them to the peg using small staples, then feed end of snare through one of the holes before winding round the peg and securing. The ends of the wire should only reach halfway up the peg and be slightly flared so that when the peg is driven into the ground the fencing wire acts like an anchor.

Snares should be set in trios at slightly varying heights on the same run. The heights should vary from 5–7 inches or even higher in rough cover. The reason for setting in trios is that a fox carries his head at various heights as he walks along and may knock a snare out of the way or partially close it. Because he may return along the same route, another chance to catch him will be gone. Trios treble your chances. Natural gaps should be utilised wherever possible to set snares. However, it can be effective to form artificial gaps using branches or scrap Rylock. Where a run is not well defined, it may be worth walking the same route a number of times using a garden hook or similar to clear a run in an area which you feel would be used by Charlie.

Siting your snares

When deciding the best sites for setting snares, the first consideration should be to find the favoured woods and hillsides that foxes use to rest during daylight hours. These almost invariably will contain an eastern aspect as Charlie loves to sun himself first thing in the morning after a long night's hunting. This is especially true after rain, and a survey of such an area at first light with a good pair of field glasses and a centre-fire rifle will often yield a dividend. Weather conditions will determine the area the fox decides to lie up in: a cold east wind will send him to the other end of the wood, heavy rain will take him to heavy cover or underground and hot weather makes him search for shade and water.

A sunny hillside covered in broom and gorse is a favoured lie for Reynard and it is up to the keeper to find which are the favourite sites. If he has been lamping not long after nightfall and sees a fox, then obviously the animal has been lying up nearby and this is potential target area. The keeper may have large tracts of forestry or unkeepered land on his boundary and almost certainly these will supply him with a steady supply of foxes, especially from late August onwards when big cubs start to forage into new territories. An interesting phenomenon is that the

Snare attached to a substantial 'drag' made from pieces of scrap timber lashed together with fencing wire.

male cubs start to wander first and can travel long distances from where they were bred.

Once you have found where Charlie is lying up or entering the estate, look for barriers which will channel him to a narrow point where a concentration of snares are likely to be successful. These barriers may be a river which is traversed by a bridge, an electric fence, or an area of brambles which he will choose to skirt rather than force his way through. Reynard will always take the easy route using footpaths made by sheep, cattle, rabbits hares and even man. The keeper will, with experience, learn to recognise the likely sites as second nature. Ponds and lakes are excellent areas which attract foxes, especially if you feed the water to attract ducks and geese. Make a path round a pond and set snares as described and they are almost certain to be successful. Experiment with different sites and methods as it is only by trying different techniques that the trapper can become truly proficient.

If these natural sites are scarce on your beat, an alternative method is to use 'middens'. This involves placing dead rabbits, deer offal, reject pheasants or other tit-bits at strategic places over the estate to draw foxes to where you want them. The best sites are rushy ground which can be traversed with narrow paths, like the spokes of a wheel with the bait at the centre. Always remember that a wary fox likes to circle a potential meal before approaching it fully, so provide him with a convenient path to do so, well furnished with snares of course. Four or five paths should be sufficient, with 3–6 snares set on each.

If livestock is present, the area should be fenced off. The easiest way to fence it off is to use five strands of plain high tensile wire with two strands of barb on top 5 inches apart. Another method of snaring where your beat has pheasant release pens is to shut the doors and pop-holes on the pens so that they are secure, hang rabbit skins, pheasant wings or similar from the branches of trees inside the edge of the pens, then set snares round the pen, possibly utilising the snares left from the previous season's release.

Pens containing hens or ducks are deadly for attracting foxes to a specific area. These can be permanent, but strong weld mesh with one inch squares must be used to floor the runs. This keeps the birds in clean conditions as droppings fall through the mesh. The runs should be 3–4 feet off the ground and be portable with adequate shelter and constant food and water. Ducks require water containers to wash themselves if they are to thrive. The calling of the ducks or hens is irresistible to Reynard and as he must come to investigate. You then have an excellent chance to account for him with a few well-placed snares, a lamping expedition or an early morning check with a rifle

Night vision equipment

Some employers dislike snaring and ban their use. This makes things difficult for the keeper as he needs as many methods as possible to counteract the red menace. However, the views of the man who pays the wages must be respected and obeyed. In these circumstances I think it is reasonable for the keeper to ask his employer to countenance the purchase of night vision equipment. Night vision equipment allows the user to observe and shoot at night, using infra-red illumination and image intensifiers. Infra-red is invisible to the naked eye so the advantages are obvious as a fox can be seen and shot without the operator betraying his presence. The catch is the cost. A very basic monocular, which can be clipped onto a scope, will cost over £1,300 and a much more sophisticated system with goggles and a permanently fixed night vision scope could cost from £5,000. The plus side is that lamp-shy foxes can be accounted for and 'calling' foxes using animal distress calls are more likely to succeed. A high seat in a likely spot such as a pheasant release pen, near a hen-house, a lambing field or cubbing den can be used with good results.

Calling foxes

Calling foxes is a sport in its own right and can be successful at dusk, during darkness and first light. A good vantage point should be chosen giving a clear all-round view downwind from the area where you think the fox will be present. Have your rifle cocked and ready, but with the safety catch on, then try your call. Call for thirty seconds then allow a few minutes to elapse before trying again. After twenty to thirty minutes move to another area.

If lamping, use the light sparingly until you see the fox's eyes, then try to keep him in the edge of the beam. If he stops within a hundred yards, shoot him as he may decide to circle to wind you (to get downwind of you) and if that happens he will be gone. Calls can be purchased and take many forms: some are simple plastic tubes with a reed which, when blown, imitates the shriek of a rabbit or hare in distress; others are meant to mimic a vixen in season.

More sophisticated designs use modern compact disc recordings which can even be remote controlled. This can be advantageous in large open spaces, as a fox circling the call may get downwind of the operator, but if a decoy hare, rabbit or even a dummy fox is used it can be deadly. The simplest but surprisingly effective call is the human hand when sucked between thumb and forefinger on the palm side, the plus points being that it costs nothing and you almost never forget your hands when you go out!

Practice calling beforehand, a good idea being to go to a playing field near a housing estate. If your calls draw domestic cats, then there is every chance you can fool a fox also. (Note: do not shoot any cats that respond to your call, indeed make sure that you are not armed in any way as in the present climate the boys in blue may be so perplexed and intrigued by your activities that they could incarcerate you for weeks!)

An important point to remember for the young keeper at this stage, especially if he is employed on a Scottish estate, is to ponder long and hard before asking his boss to finance the purchase of night vision equipment. If his employer is of a certain vintage, ie. whelped pre-World War II, it may be better to consider other job opportunities, rather than broach this subject and be found guilty of causing the poor chap to suffer an apoplectic fit.

Humane methods

Fox cages have been developed in the last few years to answer the call for a humane, safe method of catching problem foxes in urban areas, and some keepers have tried them in rural situations with varying levels of success. I have no knowledge of any keeper who runs a network of cages with any degree of effectiveness, but to counter this the ready-made cages bought from gamekeeper suppliers are sold steadily and as they are relatively expensive, somebody must be getting results somewhere. As with all trapping, the siting of cages and the bait used are all-important. In Scandinavia large cages made from heavy slab wood boards forming a tunnel with a weld mesh end are placed near forest roads and baited with rabbits, hens and offal. These are successful but that may be because the winters are harder in these countries and prey species may be scarcer. I feel therefore that the way to proceed with cages would be to construct homemade versions and place them permanently at hen-houses or similar, possibly placing them under a raised house and run or pre-baiting them in early winter before setting them when the weather turns really hard in February/March and when prey is at its scarcest.

An old-fashioned cage of sorts was used in some parts of the country to catch foxes, badgers and otters. These cages were placed at single entrance rock holes from which it was impossible to dig out. Once such a site was found to be used on a regular basis, a lair made from heavy flat stones was built at an angle from the entrance but without barring entry to the original hole. Sand was then placed and rolled flat at the entrance to allow the trapper to ascertain when an animal had entered. When this happened a flat stone was moved to block the original entrance but allowing access to the new trap which was sprung by the victim scratching at a small opening which dislodged a stick attached to another flat stone which slid down behind the fox, trapping it in the artificial lair. This method was effective in areas with large deep rock holes where the use of terriers was dangerous but it is possible that a resourceful keeper could adapt this system so that it could be more widely used.

Fox-hound gun packs

The use of fox-hound gun-packs has become common practice since the passing of legislation banning traditional fox hunting with hounds. Most packs can now be used legally only when driving foxes to standing guns.

Prior to the ban there were a number of packs which hunted exclusively to waiting guns with many keepers taking advantage of an extremely effective service to reduce their fox population. Now the keeper is spoilt for choice as every pack in the British Isles is a potential gun-pack. This situation has caused a few wry smiles from the older generation of keepers who would have been sacked if found guilty of the heinous crime of vulpicide: indeed, many a keeper had to provide a fox to hunt when the local pack came to draw his coverts, or else there was a huge inquest. You may ask how a keeper could guarantee a fox to be hunted and guarantee game for his boss at the same time. The answer was: often with great difficulty, as foxes were fewer in the old days and it was always possible that a neighbouring keeper or farmer might quietly dispose of the animal which you had carefully preserved for a number of months.

Artificial fox earths

There was, however, a fool-proof method which involved building a number of artificial fox earths. These are constructed using concrete pipes or flat stones. Usually there are three entrances leading to a bedding area which must be dry and can be furnished with straw or bracken to make it more attractive. Around each artificial earth, a 6ft high fence is constructed similar to a pheasant release pen with running water and a number of gates to allow access. The keepers on the estate would keep an eye on all known natural earths until cubs were seen to be present whereupon they would be disturbed, causing the vixen to move them, hopefully to one of the artificial earths. When this happens the keeper would wait until the cubs were fully weaned, then shoot the dog and vixen, closing the gates of the pen to contain the cubs. From this time on the keeper became the fox-cubs' surrogate parent, supplying them with food until they were advanced enough to be released to fend for themselves, although even then they would still be fed, the keeper being careful not to approach them so that they retained their fear of human beings. The advantage of this system was that the adult foxes who would have killed large numbers of game to feed their cubs were killed early in the season and the cubs were not released until the reared pheasants were going up to roost and therefore relatively safe.

The main requirement for a fox-hunt is a large number of guns, fifty or sixty sometimes turning up, causing a logistical nightmare for the keeper. Quantity may not mean quality with guns who only shoot once a year turning out. Safety, as always, is paramount, but with such a large number of guns it may become self-regulatory. A good idea is to spread experienced, reliable men throughout the line to supervise conduct. The worst example of dangerous gun handling I witnessed was at a fox hunt. The assembled guns waited rather nervously in a farmyard for the owner of the farm that was to be hunted to appear, which he eventually did, carrying an old hammer gun. I noted with some apprehension that it was loaded and fully cocked. The other guns, not surprisingly, parted like the Red Sea at his approach then fell in behind in a remarkably straight single file. After we had walked fifty yards, the old hammer gun, which its owner carried in one hand aiming straight forward, discharged first one barrel, the second then going off in sympathy. The farmer cursed, reloaded and cocked both barrels only for the same thing to happen again after another fifty yards. 'Christ she's keen tae get stairted the day,' he stated, swinging round to face the following guns who skipped sideways to avoid looking down the muzzles of the defective weapon.

The keeper who organised the hunt would not have tolerated such conduct from anyone else, but the farm belonging to this man contained one of the best fox-holding coverts in the district and the keeper considered the risk involved worth taking to kill a vixen in late February. The problem was solved partially when the keeper acquired a cheap but safe hammerless shotgun from a local gunsmith and presented it to the farmer. However, his gun handling was incurable and fox hunts at his farm always uncomfortable occasions.

If hounds are being used it is essential to completely surround areas to be hunted.

Sewelling can be used to reduce the area that has to be covered. The most cost-effective is the type invented by Alan Cousins using hazard tape, baler twine and purpose-built reels. This, when augmented by the day-glow high visibility safety vests hung at intervals can turn foxes towards standing guns and can mean the difference between success and failure.

This is both to comply with anti-hunting legislation and also to ensure that any foxes flushed by the hounds are accounted for. The gun of choice for many keepers nowadays is the semi-automatic on firearms certificate up to eight shot capacity. This obviously gives the marksman great margin for error should he miss with his first or even second shot. The lack of recoil means that multiple shots can be fired very quickly once the user becomes proficient with this weapon. Shot size can be controversial, some maintaining that smaller shot, say 3–5 throws a better pattern and is therefore more likely to be effective, others stating that BB is the best size as each pellet has more shocking power. I would suggest that the reader tests various cartridges on a sheet of cardboard or similar at various ranges to determine the best load and shot size for his particular weapon.

A fall of snow is welcomed by all keepers, once the shooting season has ended, as a quiet reconnoitre of the known fox dens will show if they are being used. Snow by itself can often send foxes underground and while it is not good practice to interfere with fox earths before the breeding season, if an animal has betrayed his presence by leaving his footprints leading into the hole, it can save much work later in the year if the keeper can bolt Charlie using a terrier and despatch him with a shotgun. All exits must be covered, so enlist help if necessary. Again the eight shot auto provides insurance if you miss the first shot and some keepers take out extra security by utilising a fox-catching lurcher. Grousekeepers in well-keepered areas tend to spend more time checking earths from November onwards as there is less likelihood of a fox moving to an unkeepered area to breed if it is disturbed at a cubbing den. In areas where you are surrounded by large tracts of unkeepered country it is advisable to leave known breeding earths totally undisturbed until the beginning of April. This is doubly important if the surrounding area contains large tracts of forestry.

The old methods of fox control

In the past, the task of controlling foxes was a simpler task as poison was widely used and legal. Most keepers carried a small bottle of strychnine as they patrolled their beat, which on low ground seldom exceeded one thousand acres. They used it to dose any dead animal or bird which they found or shot. In springtime eggs were treated similarly, mopping up any predator that survived eating carrion during the winter months. When one considers that on unkeepered ground farmers operated the same policy, you can understand why vermin was scarce in the old days and why game was plentiful.

Another hazard for foxes in the old days was the gin-trap, generally used for rabbit trapping. This trap was widely used by rabbit trappers and keepers to reduce rabbit numbers and to provide an income from the sale of the victims. The traps were set at the mouth of the burrows, buried just below the level of the earth and covered with finely sieved soil. Then a specially-made tool like a 1ft long length of broom shank which tapered to a point at one end was used to roll the soil flat and compact it. Obviously any animal which showed an interest in rabbits, ie. cats, foxes, stoats, otters, hedgehogs, stray dogs, and polecats were at risk from these traps and when you realise that a trapper might run 8–10 dozen traps at a time then it is little wonder that pests were scarce.

Late March

It is now the end of March and any vixens on your beat will either have had cubs or are confined near or in the cubbing den at the later stages of pregnancy. This period, which includes the time suckling her cubs, lasts for 3–4 weeks. During this time, the vixen is totally dependant on her mate to supply her with food, although there may be a cache or caches of prey nearby which has been caught previously. It is possible for a dog fox to supply two vixens who may be mother and daughter, the daughter being subservient to her mother. This situation explains the phenomenon which has been described by keepers as 'split litters'. The understanding was that the vixen moved some of the cubs to a separate earth to ensure the survival of at least some of the cubs, but I am sure that what has actually happened is that the subservient vixen's litter has been discovered close to the mother's litter and because of the close proximity, bearing in mind that a breeding vixen is extremely territorial, the conclusion has been formed at that they were all from the same litter and from one vixen. Another twist to this scenario is that the subservient vixen does not produce cubs but assists with the rearing of what are actually her little brothers and sisters. If the dog fox is killed during this critical period it can trigger a reaction which will not have been anticipated by the keeper or sheep farmer. The vixen will suckle her cubs without any food for a number of days then all hell will be let loose. Driven by hunger she will head for the nearest and easiest source of food, and if that is a field of newly born lambs, then slaughter may ensue.

First-hand experience

I experienced such a situation twenty years ago. I had been checking fox-holes on a moorland area of the estate I was responsible for when I met the shepherd Eric about to go to the hill. Asking him if there was any sign of foxes, he laughingly replied, 'No but there won't be many left after Jock has put his eggs out.' I enquired further and found out that Eric had observed a dog fox lying dead over the march (boundary land) beside a poisoned egg which the neighbouring farmer had placed for crows and other vermin. I bade Eric farewell and wished him luck with the lambing, which was in full swing, but at the back of my mind I wondered if there would be trouble. I had checked all the known fox earths in that area and had found nothing, and as it was 'foxy' country with forestry and wild areas there was almost a certainty that the dog fox had a mate with cubs somewhere in that wilderness. Moreover prey species were scarce, there being few rabbits or game birds, meaning that a hungry vixen would be severely tempted by the lambs which abounded in the fields around the shepherd's house.

In the upland areas of Scotland and England shepherds are reluctant to divulge the whereabouts of vixens with cubs. This stems from the fable spread by hunt supporters which blames fox predation on lambs to be the result of the vixen taking revenge for her cubs being killed. This is embroidered even more by the theory that a fox will not kill lambs on his or her own patch, ie. the farm that they are rearing their cubs on. I have always found this scenario quite amusing, that every farm could have a family of foxes passing each other every night to raid each other's territories. To be fair the latter theory does have some credibility as both dog and vixen at breeding time will defend their territory vigorously against other foxes, but I am convinced that the former was proposed by the hunt to placate the farmer when foxes had predated lambs in hunting country and to deter any punitive action being taken against the hunt's quarry which might have spoiled the season's sport. Also, many shepherds are ardent hunt supporters and refuse to accept that a fox can do any harm.

A week or ten days passed when my phone rang; it was Eric to say that he was losing lambs to a fox and it was serious, with two or three being killed every night. The dead animals were being left in the field, sometimes the head severed, but always the rib-cage ripped open and the heart and lungs removed. I immediately realised that this was the work of the vixen whose mate had been poisoned. She must have been too weak to carry the lambs to the den, so preferred to gorge herself on the lambs lights then regurgitate them to her cubs when she returned to them. This obviously meant that she needed to kill two or three lambs daily to provide sufficient food for her litter, a disastrous situation for the shepherd. I told Eric that I would sit that night at the lambing field and at least deter the animal if I could not kill her.

There was little wind, but what there was came from the east, meaning that the vixen would leave her den and travel into the wind straight to the lambing fields. This was assuming that I had guessed right as to the location of her den, ie. the forested area to the north of the farm. I decided therefore to take up a position two hundred yards to the south of the main lambing field hoping that my scent would not be carried to the incoming fox. It was a beautiful April evening with excellent visibility allowing me to spot the vixen as she trotted purposefully through the heather using sheep paths and burn-sides that traversed the hill opposite. She was not wary, perhaps because of hunger or because she had not been disturbed previously and was now making a bee-line for one particular field which housed older lambs than I thought she would be capable of killing. I now had a problem as the field that the vixen was heading for was 350 yards away and the light was starting to fade. I waited for her to disappear into some low lying ground, then started to move closer while at the same time observing the area she would appear into. I had reduced the distance to 250 yards when I saw her again. I froze, watching her with fascination as she approached the lambing field. Leaping on top of the dry stone wall which surrounded the field, she paused for a quick look round, then entered the field.

My heart was beating fast at this point, the vixen quartered the field, sizing up her quarry, causing the ewes to stand up, stamping their feet and calling their lambs close to them. One lamb was slow to answer his mother, the vixen sensed this, and with a speed rivalling a cheetah singled out the unfortunate animal, coursed it for a short distance then killed it by gripping it behind the head, breaking its neck. I realised that I had a short time, while the fox was occupied, to get close enough for a shot, so moving as quickly as I could without making a noise, I headed for a heathery outcrop which overlooked the field. Crawling into position I was lucky enough to see the vixen ripping open the rib-cage and devouring the contents and, a second later the treble two repaid the compliment and she died quickly, shot through the heart.

Although I did not realise it at the time, few people have witnessed foxes killing lambs, indeed some authorities question whether foxes do kill lambs, claiming that they only take lambs that are already dead or are so sickly that they were going to die anyway. The lamb I saw the vixen kill was quite large and very healthy but despite this, the fox killed it effortlessly, so easily in fact that I have wondered ever after why more lambs are not taken by foxes. It may be that in normal circumstances a fox is quite content gathering still-born lambs and afterbirth, especially if there is a good supply of voles, game birds, ground nesting birds and rabbits. The other scenario where I have heard of large-scale lamb killing has been an old fox, often with an injury or disability, being driven by hunger to attack sheep flocks.

April: checking fox dens

Most keepers check fox dens for the first time in April, the exact date depending on the altitude of the estate, as it is generally believed that low-ground foxes breed earlier than high-ground ones. Tradition also plays a part, with each district having a different starting date.

Depending on the number of holes to be checked and the amount of time the keeper has available, the dens will then be checked approximately every fortnight after this for incoming vixens and cubs, up to the end of June. Two people are better than one when checking dens. Each should carry a shotgun loaded with suitable shot and if possible a centre-fire rifle. The reason for this is that a quiet approach into the wind may find the vixen sunning herself outside the earth and she can then be shot saving time and trouble later. A terrier is essential nowadays to enter the holes and alert its owner to the presence of a fox.

In previous years when gas (cymag or phostoxin) was legal to use at fox earths, many keepers observed the dens from a distance and when it was observed that cubs were present, waited for the dog to appear then shot him and gassed the earth with the vixen *in situ*. This method could be effective, a twist being that the keeper kept a marking dog which could be of any breed so long as it is too large to enter an earth. This dog usually had a dislike of foxes and would show its handler by growling, digging or even by its birse (hackles) rising, that a fox was present. The hole was then gassed, saving time and energy that would have been expended especially if a dig was necessary. The other plus point was that a terrier did not have to be kept and the marking dog was generally a multi-purpose dog and so earned his meat. I first learned of this method from a keeper who, despite being a Cumbrian, when asked by me the best type of terrier for a keeper to use replied, 'English springer spaniel with a tin of cymag.'

If you have approached the earth and decided that neither dog nor vixen is above ground offering a shot, then it is time to enter the terrier. But first make sure that you have positioned yourself and your companion so that the fox cannot bolt unseen, bearing in mind there can be exits up to fifty yards from the main entrance. Many keepers use a lurcher as a back-up to cover areas which cannot be covered by the gunmen, or if, horror of horrors, a fox is missed. On approaching the den the reaction of the terrier will have told you whether or not the vixen is likely to be present, as most terriers know before they enter a hole if it is occupied or not. So when you release him, if the terrier charges enthusiastically to ground, be ready, because if the vixen is to bolt, she may bolt early. This, however, only happens in a minority of cases, possibly because the vixen wishes to stay to protect her cubs or perhaps more likely, the confines of the small earths and cubbing den itself mean that the vixen would be hard pushed to pass the terrier to get to an exit.

So, if a vixen is present, all hell will break loose with the terrier giving tongue. This is preferable to the hard type of terrier which chooses to engage the fox in a mortal fight, because the vixen often positions herself round a corner in the den where she can ambush the terrier as he tries to negotiate the bend. This type of terrier, far from being deterred by this, becomes if anything more determined and a bloody battle can ensue which only ends with the death of the vixen, or the terrier being dug out. This is not a satisfactory scenario as much time can be wasted, the den damaged so that it is not used again and the terrier so injured that he is not fit for active service for a week or more (which is why some keepers keep a small pack of terriers). The keeper should make sure that only one terrier is entered at a time as the first entered will be prevented from retreating and taking evasive action should his companion press him from the rear, intent on engaging the fox, resulting in the first terrier sustaining severe injuries. If your terrier has given tongue for 3–4 minutes with no results, it is now time to call him out by whistling down the main entrance. If you are lucky enough to possess a terrier which is tractable, he should come out after a short time. Tie him up out of harm's way and take up a position where you can take aim down the entrance the terrier used to exit the earth. Have the gun to your shoulder, safety catch off. Within a few minutes or even less, the vixen will come out to investigate where the terrier went. Shoot her in the head then reward your terrier by allowing him to rag the dead fox. Once the terrier has satisfied his lust to fight and believes he has scored a victory, remove the vixen and send him into the earth to despatch the cubs or retrieve them from the earth where they can be despatched humanely.

If things have not gone to plan and a dig has to be undertaken, an electronic detector attached to the dog by means of a collar is a real asset. This allows the keeper to pinpoint the exact location of the fox underground and can save much wasted effort when digging at the wrong place. After the vixen and cubs have been killed, every effort must be made to repair the den using flat stones and returning it, as much as possible, to its original condition.

Staking out the den at cubbing time

Once a den has been successful, no other dens should be visited that day as the keeper will want to wait for the dog fox to come back to visit the earth. This can happen at any time of the day or night so it would be prudent for someone to stay at the den with a rifle in case the dog fox comes to visit not long after the keeper leaves. I would recommend a position two hundred yards downwind of the expected approach route with a commanding view of the surrounding area. If the dog fox returns and discovers the vixen and cubs dead he will never return, so it is imperative that the first time he returns he is shot. Most keepers stay all night at the den to bag the dog fox or in the circumstances where the cubs are killed when the vixen is not present, the vixen herself. Two people are preferable, with night vision, which unfortunately few keepers possess, a real advantage. Failing this, a battery pack powered spot-lamp with a filter should account for him or her. If this is not successful, first light will see the surviving parent or parents circling the den looking for some sign of their cubs.

Some keepers use a different tactic and leave a coat hanging on a spade at the den to keep the parents away, then attend that evening or next morning if the former visit is not successful. There is some debate as to the right approach at cubbing time, with some fox controllers extolling the virtues of killing the parents first, then killing the cubs at their leisure. The theory of this is that when the cubs are alive the dog and vixen will always return to them, making them predictable and so susceptible to a waiting marksman. The other view is that the cubs should be killed when you have the chance as the vixen, despite your best efforts, may move them unseen and you may not get another chance. My own view is that on big open hillsides with little cover, such as grouse moors, where foxes are relatively scarce, it would be advisable to kill the parents first. However, where there is a good population of foxes and many alternative areas of unkeepered ground such as forestry, take your chance when it comes, use the scarecrow and sit out night and morning or all night if you can afford the time.

In the old days when keepers would have viewed the modern centre-fire rifle with telescopic sights as a magic wand and night vision as heaven-sent, cubbing time was a different affair, with most keepers setting gin-traps at regular cubbing dens, so catching breeding vixens before they even had their cubs. This meant that the surviving vixens sought out large rabbit burrows to cub in.

When the keeper discovered that one of these burrows was being used by foxes as a breeding site, he would set the traps in the following way. A single trap was set facing into the hole or holes in order to catch a cub or cubs, the entrance was then blocked by building stones into a wall with the trap set inside the hole. The area outside each hole was then trapped using 2–3 traps close to the wall of stones.

Some keepers used to cut circles of rabbit netting and fitted them into the holes as an alternative to using stones. The advantage of this method was that the wire circles were easily carried in a game bag and also the trapped cub, being visible through the net, was more likely to lure the dog or vixen into the traps. The aim of this technique was to bring a cub to investigate the wall or wire and be caught in the trap causing it to squeal; this would immediately bring the vixen and often the dog to answer the cub's distress call, and they would in turn be trapped themselves. Some vixens tried to dig in from the top of the hole to avoid the traps and many trappers placed traps above the burrows as well, to counteract this. A refinement to this system which some keepers felt was an improvement was to take the trapped cub and place it in a cylindrical cage formed from the rabbit netting. The cage was then placed in the burrow and traps set as before. These techniques were deadly and did much to keep foxes at the reduced level they enjoyed prior to the banning of the gin trap in the 1960s. The effectiveness of this method was entirely dependant on the fact that foxes are extremely good parents and will do everything possible to save and protect their offspring, as the following stories will illustrate.

A keeper from Wigtownshire had set traps as described above, and had no luck until evening when he discovered a cub held by the forefoot. The traps used to catch the cubs were generally old weak traps so that they did little harm to the cub, indeed some keepers filed the teeth or padded them to reduce damage to their victim. It was too late to use the cub as bait, so the keeper put the unfortunate animal into a sack and took it home, locking it in his garden shed. He then fed his dogs, had his evening meal, then left home to visit a relative who was unwell. On his return, his wife told him that a terrier had been outside yapping, driving the dogs mad. His puzzlement, however, turned to disbelief the next morning when he discovered that the vixen had chewed a hole in his shed, rescued her cub and made good her escape.

Another fascinating incident which shows the fox's determination to protect and save its cubs occurred in Kirkcudbrightshire. The keeper was using the wire netting cage technique, when he had to leave the estate to take up another position. He left the traps for the local shepherd to check, who saw a dog and vixen standing a yard away from the traps two mornings in succession, so he decided to move them further away from the cage. The next morning the traps were still set but the cage was gone, the adults having pulled it from the hole, moved it a hundred yards, then ripped it open to release the cub. Incidents like these are the reason why few keepers lack respect for foxes.

The reason for checking dens as described in early April is that there is a likelihood that the vixen will be present with the cubs and therefore be accounted for with little difficulty. As the cubs grow, however, they can become more difficult to find as the vixen will move them to inaccessible sites to avoid detection. These moves may be made as a result of disturbance such as a shepherd changing his route one morning and passing closer to an occupied earth than usual or it just may be that the remains of their prey, ie. lambs, pheasants, grouse, curlew, lapwing, rabbits and hares strewn round the den has attracted flies and the vixen decides that it is time to move on. If these moves are voluntary, they generally take place when the cubs can move on their own, without having to be carried by their mother or father as would be the case if disturbed and the cubs too small to walk.

A moonlit night is generally chosen with the dog and vixen yapping to each other and the cubs throughout the journey to their new den, which is normally a more roomy abode than the cubbing den and with more entrances. These den sites have usually a number of features in common: they are secluded, they have a sunny sheltered aspect, they have cover such as bracken, broom or gorse nearby for the cubs to play in while staying out of sight. The final requirement is a good steady source of clean drinking water as the cubs will grow through the driest time of the year. In real drought conditions it is often a good idea to check areas on the shoot that are blessed with a good water supply, as any foxes in the area are bound to visit them.

Late spring/high summer

As at other times of the year, early morning and evening sojourns can yield dividends and detect cubs that have slipped through the net of checking all known fox earths fortnightly. If the weather is fine there will be a point when the cubs spend more and more time above ground where they will reveal their presence by the tell-tale areas of flattened ground cover, be it grass, bracken or standing crop such as wheat or barley. These flattened areas will contain signs of prey such as wings and hind legs of rabbits and hares as well as the characteristic tapered fox droppings. It is possible to tell from these droppings the age of the cubs and how long ago they were produced. Jet black shiny droppings are a sure sign that cubs are present while dry almost white ones indicate that they have moved on. If you think that cubs are present it is a good idea to raise a small team of guns to cut off likely escape routes, then take terriers and/or spaniels to hunt the area dealing with any going to ground using the terriers, the waiting guns taking care of the cubs lying loose and choosing to break for cover.

Where cover is extensive eg. forestry blocks and large hillsides covered with gorse, broom and bracken, many keepers utilise the services of a gun-pack of fox-hounds, the aim being to hunt all areas of the shoot for foxes prior to the release of pheasants in July/August. This is extremely effective in mopping up any animals that evaded the control as described earlier, the only problem being getting enough guns and persuading the local farmers that the hounds will not do their stock any harm.

Protecting poults from foxes

If the keeper has followed the advice as I have laid it out, he should have a trouble-free pheasant and partridge release as far as fox predation is concerned. However, foxes can reappear at any time, as if they have descended by parachute and they must be dealt with as quickly as possible, before they cause so much damage that the season can turn out to be a disappointment or even a disaster. I will describe in detail in subsequent chapters the defence strategies to minimise random fox damage and protect your birds. These include electric fences and soundly constructed release pens which will stop a fox entering a pen, which is the worst case scenario, resulting in mass kills of hundreds of poults. The young keeper, believe me, does not want to enter his release pen one morning to feed his birds and be presented with the carnage which is the result of Reynard entering the pen when the birds are 6–9 weeks old and at their most vulnerable.

Snares set round the pen and on any track leading to the pen are the first line of defence. These are effective for the first 2–4 weeks after release, but once the birds start to fly over the fence and then try to get back in to the pen, they tend to knock the snares so rendering them ineffective. The keeper should have been lamping in the period before release, but because the cover and corn is still standing it may be difficult to cover the ground adequately. The plus side is that cubs are usually quite easy to call and seem to be so curious that they will investigate the most unlikely sound and seem almost oblivious to the light. High seats overlooking release pens can be very useful in ambushing foxes as they try to catch birds which are flying down from roost, often in a field adjacent to the release pen woods. If night-vision equipment is available and the seat comfortable, an all-night vigil may yield dividends with the advantage that you will not disturb the fox approaching the seat.

There are new products on the market, which have been developed in America, to mask the human scent. These take the form of a deodorant or a special suit, perhaps to be sure, the young keeper should use both. If these work, and I have no reason to believe that they will not, they will provide another useful tool in the fox-hunter's armoury, and should be used, as the keeper needs every assistance in his never-ending battle with the fox.

The layman reading this chapter may be thinking that the demise of the fox as a common predator in the British Isles is only a short time away: sadly, this is not the case and in most areas foxes have never been more numerous, keepers finding that as quickly as they clear an area of the red menace then it is re-populated from unkeepered areas and forestry blocks.

Urban foxes

Another source of frustration is the so-called urban fox. These are accepted and even encouraged by town and city dwellers until they become a nuisance by killing domestic pets such as rabbits and cats and rearing litters under garden sheds or even in the basements of houses themselves. The stench of foxes and the decaying prey that they leave strewn around their earth when rearing cubs quickly changes attitudes and a pest controller is contacted to rid the householder of the offending animal or animals – the proviso being that the animals are unharmed and relocated to an idyllic home in the country where they will live happily ever after!

This is apparently a lucrative occupation and therefore, while I have no doubt that some unscrupulous operators dispose of their catch round the next corner, most captive urban foxes will end up released in open country and there is anecdotal evidence of large numbers of disorientated foxes, often with mange, in a small area unable to cope with life in the true wild. The release of these foxes is at best environmental vandalism and at worst downright cruelty. The only good point from the keeper's perspective is that these animals are so naïve that they are easily dealt with.

To end this chapter I would like to ask all keepers, especially the younger generation, to realise that the fox is a worthy adversary and as such deserves our respect. He also deserves to be killed quickly and cleanly, without unnecessary suffering, despite his crimes, always remembering that if there were no foxes there would be little need for gamekeepers and the countryside would be a poorer place.

CHAPTER FOUR

Birds of Prey

In days which now seem long gone, life was much simpler for the gamekeeper: he strode the fields, woods and hills of his empire and all, save his employer, paid heed to his word. Unfortunately, in the early twenty first century, this is no longer the case. Where the keeper of yesteryear could be single-minded to the point of ruthlessness in his desire to protect his game and his employment, the modern man must always look over his shoulder and make decisions as to the wisdom of his actions.

One of the areas which most highlights this dilemma is the entire question of birds of prey. In the past it was a straightforward question: does it threaten my game? If the answer was in the affirmative, then it was killed, often by the most convenient method available. I can see members of the bird-watching fraternity who might be reading this book swooning in horror crying, 'I thought as much!' The important thing, however, is not what keepers used to do, but what they do now.

A political football

The RSPB, because of their large membership (over one million members) have considerable clout where politicians and the media are concerned. They have become much more than a bird protection society: they own large tracts of land, they often hold the balance of power where planning decisions are taken in the countryside, they have contacts and lobbying power which reaches to the very top of government, they have activists who are employed by the media, acting almost like cold war Russian 'sleepers' and, perhaps most worryingly to gamekeepers, a network of sympathisers who appear to be unpaid surveillance agents on grouse moors.

The reader may feel, after reading my views, that I hate the RSPB, but in fact I do not – they are only doing their job. The size of their organisation demands that they raise income on a large and continuous scale, many jobs are at stake and basically it is a good cause. However, politicians, the media and the great British public should realise that these charities rely on a threat being delivered by a big bad bogey man, otherwise little old ladies will not be divested of their life savings to help negate that threat. Obviously the greater the threat and the more demonic the bogey man, the greater the reaction and thus the greater the funds realised.

This is all well and good, but when the same methods are used to press for custodial sentences and at the same time calling for the burden of proof to be removed, it is time to call 'foul'. I know a number of RSPB members and employees who wince when the standard message is churned out time after time following some incident concerning a bird of prey. A disturbing development to this aspect of media coverage was evident in the recent alleged shooting of a pair of hen harriers. The three witnesses, who appeared to be nature wardens of some sort, asserted that gamekeepers were responsible. 'They would be the only people with anything to gain by such actions.' No bodies or feathers were found at the scene and, despite police enquiries, no charges were brought. Despite this, the damage was done and the bird of prey lobby had publicity that they could only have dreamt of. The witnesses may have made a genuine mistake, a fact that was not investigated by any member of the media, but the end result was another black mark against the keepering fraternity.

It is suspected by some that there is a political element in all this: the landed gentry have always been hated by a certain section of the community, the ownership of land by one individual being anathema to these people. The gamekeeper, who is described by this element as a lackey or foot-soldier, is obviously a soft target, a fact exacerbated by some employers dropping any responsibility for their keeper's actions like the proverbial hot potato at the first sign of trouble. Gamekeepers, who are the last of nature's individualists, have formed reluctantly and perhaps belatedly into organisations to protect their interests. This is the classic David and Goliath situation and hopefully the British public will see it as such and give gamekeepers a fair hearing at last.

I make no excuses for spending the early part of this chapter on politics, for birds of prey have become a political football and it would be wrong of me not to point out, in a book of this nature, the background and repercussions of any action a gamekeeper might take. The law is the law and if a keeper is caught and convicted for breaking it, he cannot blame anyone but himself. The future, in my opinion, lies in management of the situation. The keeper must identify the problems associated with birds of prey and find solutions to these problems, if game shooting is to continue as it is presently practised. I will therefore, with this aim in mind, describe in the remainder of this chapter the natural history of the various birds of prey and the threat to game that they pose. I will offer opinions subject to my own experience, or failing that, the experience of men that I know and trust, with no whitewash or holds barred.

The barn owl

My list is alphabetical but some readers may be surprised that the barn owl is included at all. The species is completely innocent of any predation against game and is one of the most charismatic of birds. For this reason I have included the grey ghost, as the gamekeeper can provide nest boxes to encourage pairs to set up territories on his beat. This will quickly increase the population as it has been found that the limiting factor to barn owl expansion is a shortage of suitable nest sites. These boxes can be placed in trees where there is a shortage of suitable buildings, the gamekeeper gaining satisfaction and propaganda value from seeing this most graceful of birds sailing in the 'gloaming'.

The buzzard

The buzzard is the most common bird of prey in the British Isles. I was almost thirty years of age before I saw a buzzard; now I see one almost every day. Some underestimate this bird, describing him as a scavenger who lives exclusively on carrion and earthworms. In reality he is an efficient hunter of live game such as rabbits and game birds. Although he is more adept at catching the young of these species, he can kill adult birds, especially the smaller females.

Some authorities claim that the buzzard can only deal with pheasants up to sixteen weeks of age but I have witnessed successful buzzard attacks on adult pheasants, especially when snow is on the ground. It may be that he prefers carrion (although I doubt it) but when this is scarce he is capable of taking live quarry, be in no doubt. His *modus operandi* is to perch in a position which gives him a clear view of a likely area, for example a rabbit warren at breeding time. When a young rabbit appears, the buzzard swoops silently and kills its victim by crushing its abdomen. The prey will be eaten on the spot or carried to the nest if young are being reared. Birds are not normally taken in flight but I have observed attempts by buzzards to catch pheasants which presumably flew to avoid an attack which began whilst they were on the ground.

Buzzards love to soar, circling for hours, their wings outstretched, congregating before they pair off for breeding. The nest, which is large, is normally in a substantial tree, larch, spruce or hardwood, often based on an old carrion crow's nest. There are usually three eggs laid and once the hen starts to incubate, the pair become quite secretive, although the cock bird will observe, sentry-like from a prominent position which allows him to see the approach of unwelcome visitors. Should someone approach the nest, the cock bird will raise the alarm by calling to his mate, alerting her so that she can escape before they come too close. If the hen is killed or dies, the cock bird will incubate the eggs himself and may even bring a spare female to assist. The first eggs may be laid in March, with incubation starting in April, taking more than a month to hatching. The young are fully fledged a further seven weeks later, although they are still dependant on their parents for another two months.

Research has shown that losses to buzzards are greatest where release pens are in the vicinity of successful buzzard nests. It is therefore obvious, given that the young birds are fledged at the same time as poults are released to the release pen, that care should be taken to avoid releasing poults in a wood where buzzards nest. If this is impossible, it is advisable to use smaller pens with a plastic top net. This is a good method of release, the only drawback being that the poults cannot roost as freely as they would in an open-topped pen. To counteract this, good shrub-like ground cover should be readily accessible to the birds when they eventually have to be released from the pens. This should be done by trickling a few birds out every day until all are released, with the feeding area and water regime replicated outside the pens.

If foxes are a problem, a good system of electric fencing should be installed. This can be expensive, but then so can a large number of headless poults! If open topped pens must be used, escape cover, if it is not already present, must be provided in the way of fir brashings, while at the same time the keeper should plant shrubs such as rhododendrons for the future. A good method of protecting your poults is to use old Rylock fencing, cut into 6–8ft lengths, placing them in the corners of pens to form tunnels of protection, while allowing the poults to pass through unhindered.

Deterring birds of prey

Deterrents may help to prevent attacks and are advisable, especially in the early stages of release. These take many forms, the simplest being empty plastic feed bags hung on the sides of the pen or from tree branches. An added refinement are the game feed bags which have been printed with a large eye on the back. For some reason the sight of the eye seems to deter birds of prey. The best method of using these bags is to cut a length of high tensile fencing wire, then form it into a circle, lashing the two ends together with garden tying wire. The circle is then squeezed into the bag, producing a kite-like construction which, when hung by a wire or string from a tree, moves and rotates making it more prominent.

Another deterrent is to hang compact discs (CDs) by a wire or string. These rotate and on sunny days flash intermittently and can be quite effective. (Despite rumours to the contrary, I have found that Des O'Connor in concert has no greater deterrent value than any other!)

Where a feed ride is used, it can be useful to stretch thin baler twine across, making it difficult for a bird of prey to swoop along the ride attacking the feeding birds. This is important as poults which are continually harassed at their feed become stressed, do not feed well and become more susceptible to disease.

Where hopper feeding is practised, it is recommended that the hoppers are placed under corrugated iron shelters. These should be six foot high to allow easy access for replenishing them and shielded by applying brashings to the sides, providing shelter from the weather as well as protection from birds of prey. These precautions should help to reduce the damage done by all birds of prey, not just buzzards. However, a goshawk can still land in the pen, then attack the poults at ground level.

Eagle owl

The eagle owl is very rare in Britain with his main foothold in the pennine area of England. He is a supreme hunter and at nearly thirty inches tall is the largest of the European owls. He is capable of killing a fully grown hare, so it is obvious that there is no game species, possibly even young deer, outside his capabilities. Perhaps the most interesting habit, from a gamekeeper's point of view, is the bird's propensity for killing other birds of prey, buzzards appearing to be a favourite, while hen harrier remains were found at a nest in Lancashire.

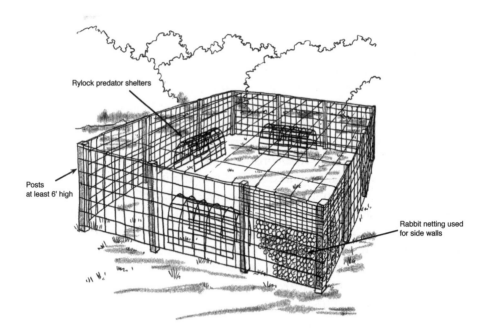

The enclosure must be at least 6 feet high, with rabbit netting used for the side walls and Rylock for the shelters.

This has caused much controversy in naturalist circles, with some claiming that the eagle owl has never been a native of the British Isles, while others claim equally vehemently that it was, before being driven to extinction. The dilemma for bird watchers is that they feel that they must protect everything, but what do they do when an interloper like the eagle owl appears on the scene which could conceivably undo much of the good work they have undertaken in the last few years? I will not claim that gamekeepers have viewed this RSPB dilemma with any degree of sympathy but it does show how the actions of a few irresponsible people can have far-reaching consequences, for the original breeding stock of eagle owls was thought to have been released by falconers or the owners of captive birds.

The eagle owl hunts at dawn and dusk, roosting close to the trunk of a tree or, if available, inside a hollow tree which is also the preferred nesting site. The disused nest of other birds of prey are sometimes utilised, and eagle owls have been known to kill buzzards and use their nests. The arrival of an eagle owl on to a keeper's beat would be a nightmare, with nothing safe for 365 days of the year.

Golden eagle

The golden eagle has recovered from very low numbers at the beginning of the twentieth century and has doubled his numbers in the last thirty years. This would seem like good news but some authorities are never happy, suggesting that this magnificent bird is restricted in its range by persecution. This is the classic glass full or half empty scenario, my own view being that, given modern legislation which makes it illegal to leave fallen domestic stock on the hills and the vast areas which have been afforested this century, we should rejoice and give credit to the land management which has allowed this bird to increase its numbers. One has only to look to Ireland, a country with many mountain ranges which would be suitable habitat for eagles but which has none. Indeed, rather bizarrely, Scottish eagle chicks were given to the Republic of Ireland for release in Donegal to boost their tourist industry. These chicks were taken, under licence, from eyries in Scotland which contained more than one chick, the lay man perhaps being perplexed by this action when set against the furore caused by a nest being robbed of its eggs or an adult being killed.

Recently an adult breeding eagle was found poisoned in the Scottish borders. This news received huge publicity, with a large sum of money being offered for information leading to the conviction of the culprit. This senseless act caused much damage to the image of the keepering fraternity and the tone of the subsequent media coverage, orchestrated by a member of Lothian and Borders police, did nothing to improve the situation. The hectoring and bullying made the chance of a conviction less likely and caused keepers to close ranks and defend the indefensible, so that co-operation and progress were set back years. One wonders if this is a deliberate tactic, to demonise and discredit, so that the keeper's voice is never heard and debate gives way to propaganda.

The golden eagle is one of the earliest nesting birds of prey, with nest building starting in February in some cases. The nest is usually situated on a cliff ledge with a commanding view of the surrounding area but nest sites in trees are also used. The nest itself is large and built using branches lined with heather, sheep's wool or other finer materials. Two eggs are normally laid in March or early April but usually only one chick is reared. The eggs take 43 days to hatch and the chicks are fledged over two months later but are dependent on their parents for a further three months. This poor reproduction rate is one reason for the slow expansion of this bird but this is somewhat balanced by the fact that the golden eagle is long lived, with some individuals reputedly living to fifty years old.

The goshawk

The goshawk is the supreme predator, capable of killing birds and animals up to the size of hares. He is an opportunist who will take any prey available, including other birds of prey. He will do more damage to birds in a release pen than any other bird of prey, being faster, more agile and more persistent than a buzzard and larger than a sparrowhawk. He prefers to hunt in open woodland, either swooping from flight or waiting on a perch, then attacking his victim when it appears. He is bad news to barn owls and red squirrels so it can be assumed that, if his numbers continue to increase exponentially, there will be a conflict between those who wish to see more goshawks and those who wish to preserve red squirrels, barn owls and probably black grouse.

The precautions the keeper can take to minimise losses due to goshawks are similar to those used to deter buzzards, with the proviso that the goshawk is more bold and determined, so deterrents may have to be more elaborate and moved more often.

The goshawk is similar to a sparrowhawk in plumage but is larger, giving the impression of a streamlined, leggy buzzard. In flight he does not flap his wings intermittently like a sparrowhawk and is more direct and purposeful than a buzzard. The nest is usually in a tall tree such as a larch in a large mature wood and positioned on a branch next to the trunk. Four eggs are laid in May with incubation taking 35 days, and a further 35 days seeing the chicks fledged. The cock bird becomes very territorial during incubation and will challenge any threat, including human, which ventures too close to the nest.

Buzzard-reared goshawks

Numbers are increasing rapidly, due to the high percentage of chicks reared, the large increase in forestry providing suitable habitat and the large food supply in the way of reared game which is now available throughout the year to this versatile hunter. As well as these advantages, the goshawk is also helped along the way by individuals who substitute buzzard eggs for captive-bred goshawk eggs at suitable sites up and down the country, the buzzards rearing the young goshawks and teaching them to hunt as they would their own offspring. It would be interesting to know if the habits of these substitute goshawks are different from naturally-reared birds because the goshawk is more of a hunter of live game than a buzzard, who relies more heavily on carrion to survive.

This nature-or-nurture question has probably been answered by the people who carried out this experiment, as they would be unable to play with nature without examining the effect that they had caused and I fully expect in the years to come some self-satisfied bird enthusiast to publish a paper describing the procedures they undertook and the results.

The goshawk has given the gamekeeper one valuable tool which has now become commonplace in his armoury against the corvid family: the Larsen trap. This trap was developed by a Swedish gamekeeper to catch goshawks, which were perceived in Sweden to be a sufficient threat to game that it was legal to control them. The trap, which I will describe in greater detail in subsequent chapters, used a pigeon or game bird as bait in one compartment next to a catching compartment, which is activated by a perch/trigger. The Game Conservancy saw the goshawk trap and adapted it to catch crows and magpies, using a member of the same corvid species as bait because territorial defence was the spur, not the pursuit of a prey species.

It is, of course, illegal to use the Larsen trap for its original purpose of catching goshawks: indeed it is illegal to take or kill any bird of prey by whatever means available.

The hen harrier

The hen harrier is the most controversial bird of prey in the British Isles. The reasons for this are complex. It is the only bird of prey to have been scientifically researched as to its effects on a specific prey, ie. the red grouse. The result of this research is: *Birds of prey and red grouse, the report of the joint raptor study* but is more commonly described as the *Langholm Report*.

Before describing the results of the report it is important to examine the background to the report. The owner of the Langholm moor was an intelligent, broad- and fair-minded man who was, as one of the largest land-owners in Britain, a target for those political conservationists who despise private land ownership and especially fieldsports, with grouse moors being a particular grievance. The land-owner, being a gentleman, met with these people and listened to their arguments over many years, their main case being that a predator had no effect on prey populations because the predators moved on or bred less successfully when the prey became scarce. The land-owner was impressed by their arguments, as they had some scientific research to back them up from other countries. He, however, was loyal to his own employees who were equally convinced that predators would seriously reduce the shootable surplus, without which a grouse moor becomes unviable.

The argument simmered for years, until in the early 1990s, it came to a head. An ex-employee went public, describing how he had killed large numbers of birds of prey. This was obviously an embarrassment to the land-owner who decided the time had come to get to the bottom of the matter. To this end the *Joint Raptor Study* was set up, with the objective of examining the impact of raptor predation on red grouse numbers. The study was based at Langholm but also included 'in part', five other study moors elsewhere in Scotland. The study ran for five years from 1992-1996 with the moor being keepered as before in terms of legally culled predators. Shooting was to have continued but as events ran their course little or none took place.

Speculation was rife during the study, with some rumours suggesting that the results would show that raptors had no effect on grouse populations. As the study reached its conclusion, however, it was apparent that stocks of grouse on Langholm moor had crashed, with desperate attempts to divert the predatory hen harriers by feeding them with dead hen chicks, failing to save the grouse.

The study showed that hen harrier numbers rose from four to 28 in the five years, although this was disputed by some locals who were positive that the figure was 34 birds. Raptors removed on average 30% of the potential breeding stock of grouse in each year of the study. In the summers of 1995 and 1996 harrier predation removed an average of 37% of the grouse chicks hatched. In each year raptors killed on average 30% of the grouse between October and March.

The end result of this was that grouse numbers did not recover as they should have done in 1996, when it would have been expected that shooting should have taken place. This was predicted using shoot records going back for more than a hundred years, showing that grouse numbers had peaked and troughed in a similar cycle over this period, with 1996 being the first time that the peak did not occur. Moreover neighbouring moors which did not carry high raptor numbers, peaked with high densities of grouse in 1996.

Conservation groups who had, up to this point, been confident in their own righteousness immediately began a campaign of damage limitation, blaming the poor performance of the moors on bad management and loss of habitat. Bodies one would have expected to be sympathetic to shooting interests were reluctant to use the results as vindication for a policy of predator control. The problem, of course, is that no matter how much damage a bird of prey causes, it is illegal to damage or kill it in any way. This means that many gamekeepers are caught between a rock and a hard place: if they obey the law they may very well lose their stock of grouse and in turn their house and livelihood; or conversely, if they break the law, they may be imprisoned or heavily fined, then sacked by an embarrassed employer who wishes to save face.

An answer may be found in a new venture which starting in 2008 to resurrect the Langholm moor which has been in a state of limbo since the Joint Raptor Study ended in 1996. Interestingly the harrier population fell, after keepering was discontinued, to similar levels of pre-1992, the grouse never recovering and at least four keeper's jobs being lost. The new venture intends to employ a headkeeper and assistants with a view to bringing the moor back to its former glory – *and* support birds of prey. I am sure all fair-minded keepers will wish them luck because they may need it!

The hen harrier frequents moors and uplands, including marshland, flying low, quartering the ground in search of prey which includes birds and mammals, with voles and meadow pipits a main source. It is said that hen harriers prefer grouse moors with a high percentage of grass to heather, which is ideally suited to voles and meadow pipits. This possibly explains why they caused so much devastation at Langholm: the hen harrier numbers increased as the vole population peaked, then had to find an alternative food source (grouse) when vole numbers crashed. The hen harrier is a striking bird and its most distinguishing feature is the white rump above the tail. This is present on both male and female but the female is brown with black tips to her wings and the cock bird is blue grey with black wing tips. The bird is buzzard/goshawk size but is more streamlined than a buzzard and has a more lanquid flight than the goshawk.

Four to five white eggs are laid in early May, with incubation starting immediately, leading to staggered hatching. Incubation takes thirty days and the chicks take a further 5–6 weeks to fly. During incubation the male supplies the female with food, delivering it in spectacular fashion: the hen leaves the nest, flying up to her mate, who transfers the food in mid-air with one or other bird flying upside down at some point. The hen then returns to the area of the nest, eating her share, then continues to brood her eggs. The nest is always on the ground in rank heather, rushes or young forestry and an experienced observer can find its location on any area of ground, as the site always seems to have a certain number of similar criteria.

The irony of the hen harrier nesting on the ground is that it is very vulnerable to predation from foxes so that the areas in the uplands where it would be safe for them to nest are limited to grouse moors. The answer is surely to keeper suitable areas which are not used for grouse shooting and manage them for hen harriers, giving the financial incentive of lottery money to land-owners who host successful nests. Harriers on grouse moors could be live-trapped then released in these areas and everyone would be happy. If only it was that simple! Either way, an answer must be found to this problem as it is a festering sore to game-shooting interests which will be scratched by our opponents on a regular basis forever, unless a solution can be found. I believe that this is possible, with goodwill on both sides and some adult dialogue but I will not hold my breath till it happens.

The kestrel

The kestrel used to be the most common bird of prey in the British Isles but this is probably no longer the case. The reasons for this are not known but one suspects that changes in farming practices have not provided the habitat that would allow this species to thrive. They are at home in mixed arable, hedge and rough pasture whereas the trend in the last thirty years has been towards a monoculture of grass, spruce forest or winter plough.

This development has coincided with an increase in more powerful birds of prey, such as buzzards and goshawks, meaning that kestrels are harassed at nesting time, leading to poorer breeding success. This would explain why they are often seen hunting the rough margins next to motorways, as they are tolerant of human activity, certainly more tolerant than either the buzzard or the goshawk.

The kestrel spends a large proportion of its time hovering over its hunting area in quest of small voles and mice, although he will also take birds especially the young of species that nest on the ground. It is not, however, a great threat to game, being too small to attack birds in a release pen or adult birds, although some grouse and partridge keepers maintain that the bird can be damaging to the young chicks of these species. The male, as in all birds of prey, is smaller than the female, with a blue-grey head, brown chest with black spots and a blue/grey tail. The female is dark brown on the upper wings and back with black spots, the breast being a lighter brown, again with black spots. Nests are built in hollow trees, old ruins, cliffs and vacant crows' nests, with kestrel eggs being laid in late April. Incubation takes four weeks, with the chicks fledged a month later.

The peregrine falcon

The peregrine is the largest falcon breeding in the British Isles and is reputedly the fastest flying bird in the world. It catches its prey either by stooping on it from a great height and at great speed or surprising its quarry in level flight. Its favourite quarry is the pigeon, either racing or wood, but it will also take wildfowl, especially teal. Grouse are taken and this is the chief area of conflict with game interests. They do not, however, seem to breed in close proximity to other pairs of peregrines and this means that there is not a cumulative build-up of birds concentrating in one area, such as happens with hen harriers and buzzards, who seem tolerant of other birds nesting nearby.

Some keepers, to accommodate peregrines on their ground, keep a loft of straggler racing pigeons on the moor, which are released to fly every day at the same time. The peregrines become aware of this time and take, it is hoped, their dietary requirements for that day from the flock, so taking pressure off the grouse stock.

The peregrine almost became extinct in the 1960s when the use of organochloride insecticides in seed dressings became common. These insecticides entered the food chain through pigeons and other birds which ate the dressed seeds, then became prey to the peregrine, causing egg thinning and hence low productivity.

These substances were banned in the 1970s and since then the peregrine has steadily recovered to over 2000 birds resident in the British Isles. The bird itself is fast, using many pigeon-like wing beats interspersed with short glides. The upper-parts are bluish with white closely barred under-parts, white cheeks and a black hooded head. He is bigger than a sparrowhawk but more elegant and smaller than a goshawk.

The peregrine loves open country where his keen eyesight and supreme speed can be used to the best advantage. Although it occasionally nests in a tree, making use of a disused raven, crow or buzzard's nest, the favourite nest site is a rocky ledge on a cliff or quarry. There are even peregrines nesting on buildings in city centres, living off the feral pigeons which abound there. 3–4 brown or orange eggs are laid in April, with incubation taking 29 days.

The young birds fly at six weeks of age. Scottish wild peregrines, especially, are greatly prized by overseas falconers and attempts are made every year to steal eggs to supply this trade. It remains to be seen if this can be curtailed. As the population expands the number of nests that cannot be protected will increase, leaving some vulnerable and there are always some people who are willing to take a risk for shining gold.

The red kite

Prior to 1989 the red kite was near to extinction, with only about twenty pairs left breeding in Wales. In 1989 a programme of reintroduction was started with chicks sourced from Sweden, East Germany and Spain. The young birds are kept in large cages at remote locations in north and central Scotland as well as the midlands and southern England. Human contact is kept to a minimum so that the birds retain their fear of man as far as is possible, then released after about a month when the birds are fully fledged. The birds are provided with food for a period in the vicinity of the pens, until eventually they become self-sufficient. The birds are fitted with a radio transmitter which sends out a signal which can be received by an operator, who can then track movements of the birds.

As well as this, the birds are fitted with plastic markers attached to their wings which are numbered and coloured so that each individual bird can be identified wherever it travels. This ability to track the released kites has had an unfortunate or fortunate consequence, depending perhaps on your viewpoint. Any bird which has been poisoned, deliberately or otherwise, can be traced with the subsequent furore unleashed leading to keepers accused, rightly or wrongly, of being responsible.

The red kite poses no threat to a reared bird shoot for he is chiefly a scavenger and does not seem to be drawn to pheasant poults in a release pen. He will, however, take young birds of other species such as lapwings, pigeon and rooks, taking the latter two from the nest. The bird may therefore be a nuisance on a wild partridge beat where stocks are low, especially in a poor breeding year. I do not see kites becoming established on grouse moors, as they seem to prefer mixed woodland and low ground agriculture, although they may hunt them from time to time, especially in the autumn if the moor carries a good population of rabbits.

The bird is slightly larger than a buzzard, with a more lanquid lazy flight. The most striking difference in flight are the crooked wings and forked tail of the kite. The colouring also differs: rusty red with dark upper parts and a prominent white-ish patch on the underside of the wing. The classic kite nest is in the fork of an oak tree but they will also use old nests of buzzards and crows in larches and spruce trees. 2–3 white eggs are laid in mid-April taking 31 days to hatch, the young birds flying two months later although the parents continue feeding their young for a further three weeks.

An interesting addition to some kites nests of twigs, grass and sheep's wool are pieces of silage sheet, old plastic shopping bags and other man-made fabrics.

The reintroduction of the kite to areas of Britain where it was absent has been a tremendous success story, with the number of these spectacular birds rising from 40 birds in the late 1980s to probably over a thousand today. Poisoning will always be a limiting factor on this species, as it is chiefly a scavenger and it is therefore imperative that this practice must stop. It does the profession of gamekeeping no service to be accused of this practice on a regular basis: our enemies must relish our weakness and the ammunition that some provide them. We must move on, with employers providing resources to make illegal practices unnecessary if we are to survive and succeed in the future.

The short-eared owl

The short-eared owl is the owl most frequently seen hunting during daylight hours over moor, rough pasture and marshland. He sometimes takes young grouse, with many keepers disliking the species enough to describe this owl as the 'flying fox'. His flight over the area that he hunts is low, punctuated by periods of hovering or gliding, the wings giving the impression of being long and narrow. Close up, the distinguishing features which separates this bird from owls of similar size (barn, long-eared and tawny) are the staring yellow eyes and the fact that this owl is unique in hunting throughout the daylight hours.

The nest is made on the ground in cover such as grass, rush or heather, as well as in young forestry plantations, with 4–8 white eggs being laid. Incubation starts immediately so that the chicks are hatched over a period of days, starting 24 days after the first egg is laid, the older chicks being more successful. The young birds are fully fledged after 35 days and in years of food abundance, such as peak vole times, two broods may be raised.

The sparrowhawk

The sparrowhawk is another controversial bird of prey. Some say that his successful recovery from the low point in the 1960s has corresponded with a decline in the numbers of certain farmland birds. Others, however, claim that habitat change is the chief reason for a drop in the numbers of thrushes, sparrows and grey partridges. What is agreed is that sparrowhawks are flourishing, probably due to the huge increase in spruce woods making up a large part of the re-forestation since the second world war. There are now over 70,000 sparrowhawks in Britain which, it is estimated, kill one thousand birds, ranging from finches and sparrows to pigeon and grey partridge, per hawk per year. This means that sparrowhawks kill seventy million birds every year, a quite staggering statistic.

A sparrowhawk on a wild partridge manor is bad news but it is illegal to interfere with it in any way. The partridge keeper must therefore do all in his power to provide cover in the way of wide hedges or, failing this, wigwams of brash built round a feeder making it impossible for the hawk to surprise a partridge when feeding, especially in the depth of winter and early spring, when birds have paired and escape cover is at a premium.

The sparrowhawk can also be troublesome at a pheasant release pen, especially the hen bird which is bigger than the cock and capable of taking quite large poults. Again, escape cover and sheltered feeding areas, combined with deterrents, will reduce predation to a tolerable level.

The nest is usually in a wood, preferably a spruce tree, although a larch with the nest built next to the trunk can be used. 4–6 eggs, white with brown speckling, are laid in May, with incubation taking 34 days. The young birds fly at five weeks of age then are dependent on their parents for a further month.

The tawny owl

The tawny owl is probably the most nocturnal of the British owls, hunting after dark, chiefly in woodland, for small mammals and birds. Its propensity to attack newly-released pheasant poults, resulting in mass kills, is the problem that most keepers will have had with this bird. They also disturb young birds which have gone to roost, causing them to flutter to the ground where they are vulnerable to attack from foxes, cats and other predators. As has been stated previously, good ground cover can reduce these losses, as can deterrents, which should be positioned just before poults are taken to the pen, so that the owls do not become accustomed to them. The deterrents, which can be flashing lights, reflective compact discs, scarecrows or string stretched across the rides, should be moved regularly to have the best effect. This does not have to be done for long to negate the predations of tawny owls, as the poults are generally too large and 'street-wise' to be taken by a tawny owl after about two weeks of the release date. Perches, which the owls could use before swooping on the young birds, should have plastic bags placed over them or, in the case of the release-pen posts (used to hold up the wire netting) six inch nails hammered into the top so that perching is made difficult.

The call of this owl is distinctive and can be heard after nightfall, the classic owl hooting often being the only evidence that they are present in a wood. This owl nests usually in a hole in a hollow tree, with 2–4 eggs laid in late March/early April. Incubation takes about a month and the young flying at five weeks old. Caution should be used when approaching an occupied nest. The parents have been known to attack the faces of human beings who have ventured too near a nest, causing severe injuries, including blindness. Where tawny owls are numerous, poults should be released in covered pens until they have grown too big to be predated or held back on the rearing field and released as older (and bigger) poults.

There are other birds of prey present in the British Isles, but the ones I have featured are the main ones to affect a keeper's livelihood. The whole question of birds of prey is a contentious one which, I stress, can be used by our enemies to blacken our name but I feel that the time is ripe for the shooting community to wrest birds of prey from our opponents and use them for our own benefit.

We are too slow to advertise the vast numbers of birds of prey which thrive on shooting estates because of the habitat and food source which we provide and seem almost terrified that anyone should know about this. If the RSPB have a rare bird land on one of their reserves for a day, they immediately tell the world about it, while a shooting estate with an osprey, red kite, golden eagle or sea eagle is sworn to secrecy. We must become more media-friendly and tell the great story that we know to be the truth to our advantage. Then, perhaps, shooting will have a secure long-term future.

CHAPTER FIVE

Various Vermin

The fox is the main threat to game on any type of shoot, and birds of prey can be a problem but are totally protected. But there are other creatures which can be a problem and these need to be controlled where this is allowed.

Carrion crow

The first predator which would come into this category is the carrion crow, sometimes called the corbie or hoodie. One of the most intelligent birds on the planet, the carrion crow is the ultimate survivor and any unkeepered part of the countryside can be recognised immediately by the obvious 'hoodie' nests adorning, it would seem, every second or third tree. Any bird unfortunate enough to select such an area to nest would be doomed to failure, for if the carrion crow did not find the nest itself, he would almost certainly steal the chicks after they were hatched. He is endowed with excellent eyesight and any attempt to ambush him with a gun can be very difficult unless great care is taken to attain complete concealment.

Winged vermin day

On arriving on an estate to take up the position of gamekeeper, the reader should assess the population of carrion crows. If there are many present, a good idea is to invite potential beaters to a winged vermin day. Baits such as hare and rabbit carcases, road casualty pheasant etc, should be saved to provide an attraction to corvids. Hides should be built and decoy eagle owls placed nearby. The dummy eagle owls are normally placed on a post overlooking the bait and, often in conjunction with decoy crows and magpies, are an irresistible draw for members of the corvid family.

Guns can be used singly or in pairs and should wear full camouflage, including face masks and gloves. Semi-automatic camouflaged guns are the ideal weapon for this purpose and if several different decoy sites are used, a good bag of crows can be attained.

As nightfall draws nearer, the guns can be moved to the woods where previous reconnaissance has shown that crows choose to roost. This can be good sport and the end result will be a reduction in your crow population and an opportunity for you to make contact with people who might help you in the future.

Carrion crow traps

Large cages with funnel-type entrances in the roof can catch carrion crows all the year round, especially if decoy birds, ie. other carrion crows are kept in them. The decoy birds must be provided with shelter, roosting, food and clean water, so if you cannot make a commitment to the decoy's welfare, do not undertake this practice. Baits should be placed below the funnel: rabbits, hares, pheasants, pigeons eggs or any other attractive food you can think of. The construction of these traps will be described in a subsequent chapter and they are well worth the expense and effort. They mop up birds all the year round, especially in hard weather.

As spring comes round and the weather becomes warmer, the carrion crows pair up and start to build nests. This is a remarkably swift operation and it feels as though nests appear overnight. Isolated hardwood trees are a favourite site, although carrion crows will nest in woods or in thorn trees close to the ground on a hill. There are even recorded instances of them nesting on the ground or on the top of a dry stone dyke. When the territory becomes apparent, the Larsen trap becomes

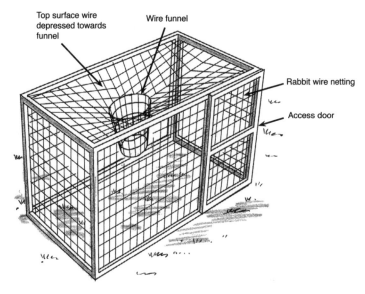

Top surface wire depressed towards funnel

Wire funnel

Rabbit wire netting

Access door

The crow cage trap

most effective. A trap set near a nest site will almost always catch the pair, often within hours of being set. The Larsen trap is basically a cage with three compartments, one for the decoy, two to catch the territorial pair. I will describe their construction and deployment in following chapters.

The elusive ones

The previous measures should have reduced your population of corbies considerably, but there will be individuals and pairs who decline to play ball and have to be dealt with by other means. Two, three or even more guns can approach a difficult nest at dusk, slowly converging until there is no safe exit route for the hen hoodie. If she flushes, she should be dealt with: the semi-auto is useful should a difficult shot be provided. The nest can be approached at certain stages of incubation and the hen will not flush despite shots fired past the nest, shouts or hands clapped. In such circumstances, if you are sure that the bird occupies the nest, the only alternative is to shoot the centre of the nest using heavy shot. You may kill the bird on the nest or force her to flush. However, if she is not at home she will nest again and perhaps, as she will be more wary the second time, you may not find her so easily again.

The attention that you have given to your crow population will have made them more wary and sophisticated, therefore it may well be that the few survivors can only be accounted for by decoying birds to baits as described earlier and hiding 50–100 yards away using a .22 rim-fire or centre-fire rifle to account for them.

A scarcity of carrion crows is a prerequisite for a wild partridge, pheasant or grouse shoot, the keeper spending more time on this task than perhaps a pheasant keeper on a reared bird shoot. That said, every keeper should control carrion crows to the best of his ability and resources, as the benefits accrued to the bird population by that practice cannot be overestimated and this is one of the most compelling arguments for predator control.

Times past

Employers should realise that it is much more difficult for the modern keeper to control crows than it was in years gone by. In times past, eggs dosed with strychnine or some other freely-available poison could be placed over the full extent of the shoot, wiping out the crow population in a short time. A difficult nest could be dealt with by climbing to the nest, breaking an egg and administering poison. The hen bird on returning to the nest could not resist the yolk, even though it was one of her own.

Another ploy was to place 'Cymag' (cyanide powder) in the bottom of the nest below the eggs with the addition of a little water. The hen, on returning sat on the eggs, inhaled the gas and succumbed in a very short time.

Trapping was also easier and effective, a favourite being the gin trap set on a purpose-built peninsular jutting out into a pond or a lake. A bait was set at the end of the peninsular so that any bird or animal trying to approach the bait would have to be caught. An added refinement to this method was a weight attached to the trap chain, the weight placed in such a way that the struggles of the victim caused it to fall into the water taking corbie, fox or other predator to a watery grave.

One last point to remember: never underestimate this bird. If you account for the hen at a nest, be aware that the cock bird will bring another hen to incubate the eggs so try to get him at all costs.

Set out the dead hen as a decoy near the nest then shoot the cock as he approaches to investigate. A hide, and camouflage clothing, are obviously an advantage. If you fail to get the cock bird, make sure to destroy the nest.

The magpie

The magpie is a striking black and white corvid which, perhaps, is not as intelligent as the 'hoodie' but makes up for this by his sheer brass neck. For a keeper to have a number of magpies on his beat is a sure sign that he has been negligent of his duties. They are easily trapped using Larsen traps or decoys, since they are unable to resist any dead animal. Perhaps because they are smaller than a buzzard, carrion crow or kite, they feel that they must be the first on the scene.

They are often shot at pheasant shoots as they are not strong flyers, choosing to take the shortest route from cover to cover whereupon they can be easily intercepted. If there are a large number of these birds and a flight line can be found on a windy day, good sport can be had and much good can be done. Again beaters, potential or old hands, can be recruited to drive strips and hedges where the birds are known to frequent to standing guns and if you will forgive the pun 'kill two birds with one stone'.

Like its cousin the carrion crow, the magpie loves to remove the eyes from stricken animals, sometimes while they are still alive. I remember being shown lambs which were quite blind, yet still running around crashing into obstacles as they went about their business, their eyes having been removed by corvids when they were newly-born.

Their technique when hunting differs from the carrion crow who floats over an area before perching near a potential food source, using his keen eyesight to alert him to any such source. The magpie tends to methodically beat out a wood, copse or hedge, meticulously searching for nests, eggs or young of any birds unfortunate enough to choose that area to breed.

Her own nest is a domed structure made from sticks and can be difficult to find, often in the centre of a thick hedge or spruce plantation. They are prolific breeders: broods can be seven or even eight, but mercifully the young magpies are easily trapped, as stated previously. A circular multi-catch trap with the decoy in the centre compartment will mop up the entire brood in a short space of time.

The jay

The jay is a bird which causes me mixed emotions. On the one hand he undoubtedly raids the nests of other birds for their young and/or eggs. On the other hand he can be a useful alarm to a keeper, his call alerting him to any two or four-legged intruder who has ventured onto his patch. I would therefore suggest that a keeper on a reared pheasant beat, who is perhaps troubled by foxes, stray dogs, cats or trespassers may wish to spare this bird, valuing his sentinel qualities above the damage that he does. Again the keeper must weigh this up himself; he must decide.

The jackdaw

The jackdaw looks like a miniature hooded crow, black with a grey neck and about the size of a magpie. He tends to feed gregariously which can be the main reason for keepers and farmers to control him. Any feed in pheasant hoppers, sheep feed in troughs or poultry feed will be scavenged by these birds as flocks descend and any available food is hoovered up in a short time. Their droppings add insult to injury and the keeper does the local community great service by controlling this noisy pest. Cage and Larsen traps, baited with grain, eggshells or bread will account for many. Pre-baiting, ie. feeding outside the trap or leaving the cage open, can help to make a big catch, with live decoys making them even more effective.

The jackdaw nests colonially in hollow trees or buildings with ruins a favourite, especially the chimney. Again, invite beaters if you have a good stock of these small crows and good sport can be had as they flush from a hole in a tall tree or out of the top of a chimney.

The rook

The rook is similar in size to the carrion crow. The adult rook can be distinguished from its cousin by his large grey beak, with no feathering on the base of the bill. The juvenile rook is harder to tell from the 'hoodie', the difference being that the latter is black in plumage while the young rook's plumage has a bluish tinge. If you are still in doubt, smell the dead body of the carrion crow. It has a distinct smell which instantly identifies him for what it is.

The rook is popular with many country dwellers, the sound of a rookery in the breeding season being quintessentially springtime in rural

England. The owners of large country houses whose adjacent land plays host to a rookery can be superstitiously protective of this bird, believing that bad luck will follow its destruction.

The damage

Keepers on a wild partridge manor abhor the bird, blaming it for depredations on partridge nests, especially in dry springs and summers when ground cover can be sparse. He can, like the jackdaw, descend on pheasant hoppers, sheep feed and poultry feed, consuming huge quantities of food. He can also strip fields of corn at the time of ripening, so it is obvious for good neighbourly relations, at least, that his numbers should be controlled where he is a pest.

Large cage traps are the most effective form of control. The gregarious nature of the bird's feeding habits mean that once one bird enters the trap, many others will follow. Again, evening flights in roosting woods will also reap dividends. Some people advocate the sport of shooting 'branchers', ie. young birds that have moved onto the branches adjacent to the nest. This usually takes place in May and a high-powered air rifle and shotgun are commonly used. My own view is that this is shutting the door after the horse has bolted but if this takes your fancy, then so be it. I have always been of the opinion that control undertaken before breeding is far more cost-effective, indeed over-all effective, than a mopping-up exercise after the event.

The raven

The raven is the largest corvid in the British Isles and is totally protected. It can be difficult to spot the difference between a raven and a carrion crow without some yardstick to measure the difference in size. The other most striking difference is in their call, the carrion's being a harsh rasping call, repeated often, especially if food or an enemy is spotted. The raven's call is low croaking, similar to someone lightly tapping two hollow sticks together.

Although he will nest in trees, he prefers a site on a cliff or crag. 4–6 eggs are laid in February or March with three weeks incubation and the chicks fledged six weeks later.

THE MUSTELIDS

The Stoat

The stoat is the artful dodger of the animal world. Bold to the point of cheeky, he shows little fear of any other creature, a fact which can be his undoing. If a stoat is disturbed at a kill, do not think that your chance to shoot him has gone if he runs off and hides in nearby cover, such as a hedge, dry stone wall or log pile. If you are patient and do not move, he will re-appear, often after quite a short period of time, providing the opportunity of a shot. Be quick, however, as he possesses lightening fast reactions and when he realises you are there, will retreat back to cover, giving a very sporting shot ! It is far better to be concealed and take him when he is stationary, perhaps on his hind legs surveying the situation. A .22 rim-fire rifle with a silencer can give good sport also, the stoat being a small target, even at short range. If you miss him, however, the game is generally up and he is unlikely to show himself again.

Like the fox, the stoat can be called by sucking the fleshy part of the hand between thumb and forefinger imitating a rabbit in distress. This will be more successful if you have not alarmed him in some way prior to calling but when it works, he may approach you at great speed, so be ready.

The stoat is one of the most athletic and agile of animals, capable of climbing quite tall trees to pursue young birds and eggs. He is also a great predator of young red squirrels, as well as ground nesting birds and their young. His favourite food is, however, rabbit, and stoat numbers seem to be inextricably linked to the rabbit population. Stoat numbers crashed after the 1950s outbreak of myxomatosis which killed in the region of 99% of the nation's rabbits.

The stoat would appear to hunt like a hound, ie. by scent, selecting a single victim and ignoring all others until he has accounted for it. It is said that a rabbit, on realising that it is being pursued by a stoat, almost freezes with fear and allows the little killer to spring onto its back, administering the *coup de grace* by a bite to the neck. My own view is that at least some of these instances could be attributed to the stoat attacking the rabbit and making an unsuccessful bite on the neck. As anyone knows who has killed a number of rabbits, it is quite easily disabled by any injury to the nerve in this part of the body. I have seen rabbits caught in snares which seemed to be paralysed and I am in no doubt that this was the reason.

I was once present when such a rabbit caused a controversy which gripped the nation. Perhaps an exaggeration but anyway, that part of the nation which competes at trials for spaniels.

Old Tom, probably the most disarming and generous man I have ever met, was running a field trial on rabbits for spaniels in the district where he worked. Tom walked over the ground a week before the trial and was disappointed with the show of rabbits, so being anxious to provide a day befitting the standard of handler who was expected to attend, decided to catch a number of rabbits from adjacent ground, using knotted rabbit snares. Knotted rabbit snares, as the name implies, have a knot formed in the wire in such away that the noose cannot close, allowing the rabbit to be caught alive. The live rabbits were duly collected and distributed over the trial ground to augment the existing population.

This practice may or may not have been successful but anyway the trial was in full swing with game coming to hand nicely. Then high drama (if you are a spaniel nut)! A handler, who the field trial world held in awe and fear, came on a rabbit lying on a piece of bare ground, alive but seemingly stunned. His dog picked up the live rabbit and delivered it to his handler. A gasp was heard from the crowd, as in spaniel trials, a dog which catches unshot game is generally eliminated but in this case the revered one suggested to the young judge that the rabbit was wounded and not quite right. The young judge duly skinned the rabbit and found no damage, so the revered one was eliminated. Well not quite: he was allowed to continue in the trial, won it, proceeded to open stakes and won the spaniel championship, much to the chagrin of his enemies. The uninitiated would argue that the dog must have been a good one or it would not have been subsequently successful. They would be correct in their assumption but totally naïve as to the nature of field trial politics.

The fire was fanned when old Tom, quite unnecessarily, let the cat out of the bag. Tom could only be accused of one fault, a tendency to loquacity; he meant no harm but was probably the only man who ever competed at trials who did not have a side to him, nor held a grudge. That said, if old Tom had been judging, the revered one would have been out. I have related this seemingly irrelevant story to illustrate, albeit in a long-winded manner, how a rabbit which has suffered nerve damage to its neck, gave all the appearance of being in a daze or, as some people would describe it, 'stoated'.

The stoat is a major killer of game. It is equally a menace on a grouse moor, partridge manor, wild or reared pheasant shoot. It will hunt a hedge like a spaniel, climbing likely bushes in search of bird's nests, in season, and the chances of game breeding successfully where the stoat thrives are non-existent. His ability to climb is quite astounding.

I remember feeding pheasants one morning at a release pen when a stoat appeared from cover heading directly towards the pen at right-angles to the perimeter wire. He proceeded to scale the six-foot net effortlessly to gain entry to what, I had previously thought, was a vermin-proof fortress. This sort of incident is guaranteed to give a keeper nightmares for weeks and sharpen his desire to control this little menace.

The most widely-used weapon against the stoat is the tunnel trap. On a well-keepered beat a keeper will run a network of traps, usually fenn or similar, at the junction of dry stone walls, where they meet a stream: on bridges, in hedges, at gateways etc. I will enlarge on this subject in the chapter on traps and trapping.

In the north of the country, stoats turn white in winter. This seems to occur after the first sign of hard weather, although with the present mild winters it means that the usually well-camouflaged little predator becomes quite conspicuous when snow cover disappears. This is perhaps not such a disadvantage as it would at first seem, as the stoat tends to be more active after dark in the winter months. During spring and summer the stoat can be seen at any time of the day out hunting.

The female stoat has her young in April using a nest site in a dry stone wall, rabbit burrow or under a sheet of corrugated iron which has been left lying on the ground. A large litter of up to twelve kits is produced with the parents feeding the young till they are self-sufficient. Then the parents force their offspring to disperse and find new territories of their own. Up to this point the whole family will roam together in a pack, attacking any threat, even it is said, human, that presents itself. When the stoat is feeding it will tackle almost any prey, including rats, and is able to carry prey much heavier than itself. When alarmed the stoat emits an unmistakable odour, which I can only liken to the smell produced by a certain brand of bubble gum, the stench a certain sign that a stoat frequents the area. In summing this section up, I would say that a lack of attention to stoat numbers on any shoot can lead to disappointing results by the end of the season. Ignore this game little predator at your peril.

The weasel

The weasel is much smaller than the stoat, the other difference being the lack of the black tip to his tail which is the stoat's main characteristic. He is not as common as the stoat and does not present such a threat to game, although he will still predate the young of game birds and for this reason can be a pest on a wild bird shoot.

The mink

Most people are aware that the present wild population of mink are descendants of farm bred and reared mink produced for the fur market. Some of these escaped and adapted quickly to the British countryside. They were helped in this by a number of factors. The first was that at the time of the rapid increase in the number of mink farms, ie. the 1950s, the number of gamekeepers was probably at a low ebb, with the gamekeepers that were employed being more heavily employed in rearing game with less emphasis on predator control. The second factor was that, at the same time as the mink was starting to colonise new territories, the otter was declining, due to the environmental effects of pollution. The third factor was that the mink is omnivorous, eating shellfish, mice, rabbits, birds, voles, waterfowl, vegetables, berries, carrion: in short just about anything that can be eaten.

Whatever the reason for the mink's success there can be no doubt that he has been successful in establishing himself as part of the British natural fauna. Forty years ago many naturalists were calling for the complete eradication of this creature in Britain, because of the devastation he could wreak locally on waterfowl populations. Today, apart from eradication attempts on islands with vulnerable bird populations, the policy can only be containment with the population now estimated at 100,000 plus, perhaps a conservative estimate.

The natural colour of the mink is dark brown with a white patch on the chest, although they can be grey, yellow, white, black and white.

Some of the yellow mink suggest cross-breeding with ferrets but I am not sure if this is possible and it may be a natural colour of farmed mink and the result of a throwback when it occurs in the wild. The male can weigh 7lbs but the females are only half that weight. Males can reach two feet in length.

Mink have their young in April and May, litters numbering 4-6. The young are able to breed at one year of age, another reason for this creature's profligacy. A good terrier which has had a previous encounter with a mink can be extremely useful in detecting mink breeding sites, which are usually near water in an old rabbit burrow or similar. An occupied site will have evidence of occupation in the way of kills near the entrance and well-worn runs leading to it. At one time the holes could be gassed but this is now illegal, so alternative measures must be used.

Snares can be set on all access runs to the den. Alternatively, a position could be found overlooking the site and the keeper can wait for the parents to appear, accounting for them with a .22 rim-fire plus sound moderator.

The ideal policy, however, is not to allow any mink to breed, keeping cage traps operating from the autumn through the winter and spring to catch new arrivals from other areas. The old keepers' adage of nipping any trouble in the bud before it can flourish is as true of mink as any other predator.

The otter

The otter is a fortunate animal because it is almost universally popular. Otter numbers have been severely reduced by the pollution of waterways with similar chemicals to those which caused problems to peregrine falcons. Fish, the prime food of the otter, were contaminated, leading to these chemicals entering the food chain. The results of this were, as in the case of the peregrine, a lowering of fertility and a subsequent fall in otter numbers.

Ironically, this fall in numbers was first noticed by otter hound packs, who realised that they were not finding otters so easily or in the same numbers as previously. The otter gained full protection in the 1970s and this, coupled with a reduction in pollution, has led to an increase in numbers.

The present population in Scotland is said to exceed six thousand while the numbers in England are estimated to be less than five hundred.

The method used to count otters is to check bridges over rivers and other likely sites for droppings called 'spraints'; a system which I am sure underestimates the numbers. I have worked in areas where otters were present and have found that the only reliable way of checking for the presence of this animal is after snowfall. The distinctive round footprints and trail left by the tail are unmistakeable and I wonder if the lack of snow cover in England for any length of time has contributed to the low estimate of numbers in England. Certainly they are very elusive and are seldom seen, even where they are relatively common.

The otter can produce litters in any month of the year and at one time the lack of otters was blamed by some 'experts' on predation by mink on young otters. I very much doubt that this is the case as the otter is three or four times as large as the mink and by no means the cuddly animal portrayed by some. Many naturalists who decided to rear orphaned otter cubs found out the hard way just how punishing the otter bite can be: even a young otter is capable of biting off a man's finger!

Any terrier which is game should be kept away from otters as their bite can crush the skull of a small dog with ease. The otter can measure over forty inches from nose to tail and weigh twenty five pounds or more, heavier than a dog fox, a fact reflected in the size and ferocity of the otter hound, the animal used to hunt them. There are tales that these hounds occasionally killed and ate kennel men who were charged with looking after them, which I feel is probably an exaggeration.

However, I did once speak to a huntsman, who came from a long line of otter huntsmen, who was attacked, when a youth, after entering the kennel unaccompanied. His father, on hearing of his narrow escape, gave him the whip used to control these hounds and told him to go back into the kennel to 'exercise his authority', otherwise he would never have been safe from them! In the past, otter control, other than by hounds, was undertaken using gin traps set at the entrances to holts or at baits beside the river. Snares were also used where the otters slid from the bank into the water and these 'slides' are another indicator that they are present, as the repeated use of one route to access water produces a well-worn shiny run.

Otters and duck

The main conflict between the gamekeeper and otter occurs where reared ducks are released onto ponds, either to augment the wild population or for direct shooting. These ducks, normally mallard, are released directly onto ponds, often without any sort of containment, the ducks' liking for water keeping them in situ, as well of course as the fact that they cannot fly for several weeks after release.

If otters are present in this situation, they will almost certainly become a serious pest, harrying the ducks and killing many. Their usual modus operandi is to dive below the unsuspecting ducks then attack them from below, pulling them under water, before taking them to the bank to eat. As can be imagined this causes the duck to become nervous and unable to settle, often travelling some distance from water to escape their tormentors, leaving them vulnerable where they are unable to fly, from dogs, cats, foxes, stoats and mink: in short, a complete disaster. The otter is totally protected, so the keeper must either decide to forget reared ducks or completely protect the pond, using electric fences and weld mesh grids at inlets and outlets. Otters are surprisingly bold and where deterrents are used, they are likely to be ineffective, a fact which I find puzzling, as the animal appears to be shy and reclusive: the otter is best summed up as a contrary animal.

The pine marten

The pine marten has the appearance of a large stoat with a bushy tail. They can reach thirty inches in length and weigh up to three and a half pounds. The pine marten is a woodland animal by choice, although it can exist on rocky moorland. Its prey includes small birds, rodents, invertebrates, fish, berries and squirrels, being capable of catching the latter by pursuing and catching them in the trees. It is also a great nest robber, including the nests of birds of prey.

The pine marten is fully protected and the only measures a keeper can take if he suffers pine marten predation at one of his release pens is to protect it thoroughly with electric fencing, which must include a live top wire as well as a turnover of the top netting. When control was legal, baited traps were effective and in North America special marten sets using conibear-type traps are particularly effective: these consist of nailing bait 6ft from the ground, to a tree, then using wire netting or branches to guide the marten to the trap, the bait being covered so that it does not attract a bird.

The pine marten breeds in late March or April and the litter is produced in rock crevices and nest boxes designed for birds, especially owls, or old magpie nests. The present UK population is thought to number less than four thousand animals.

The polecat

The wild polecat is the ancestor of the domestic ferret; indeed escaped ferrets are thought to breed with wild polecats and the offspring are indistinguishable from pure wild animals. They are apparently protected from trapping but can be shot legally. Four or five young are born in April or May, with the possibility of a second litter. They do not climb well but can squeeze through an incredibly small space, making them a threat to any captive-bred game or poultry. Pens must therefore be very secure if polecats are present.

Historically, the polecat was very vulnerable to the gin trap set for rabbits, as any polecat in an area will sooner or later investigate occupied rabbit burrows and fall victim. Most of the mustelids will respond to a call imitating a rabbit or other creature in distress. This can be successful after dark. The eyes of the polecat are surprisingly bright and the bobbing movement of them will cause the lamper to wonder what on earth is approaching until he becomes accustomed to the sight.

I have a feeling that the protection status afforded to the polecat could change at any time, so it would be advisable to glean advice from the National Gamekeepers Organisation or BASC before embarking on a control programme.

The badger

The badger is a controversial animal at the present time. Many people born after the second World War have been inspired by the multitude of wildlife television documentaries beamed into a large percentage of the population's homes. The badger is the ideal actor in these productions, with his black and white snout and 'ham' characteristics, ideal credentials to gain a place in the urban viewers' hearts. Badger groups have recruited members eager to support a cause and protect this animal from any threat, real or imagined.

Badgers and TB

In the meantime, laws were passed to give the badger complete protection and it is thought that 2009 UK badger numbers are almost 500,000, more than the UK population of foxes. This is obviously a success story but as in all things, there is, in my opinion, a catch: tuberculosis. In the south-west of England, where badgers are most common, tuberculosis has become a great problem in dairy cattle with herds having to be culled to stop the spread of this disease. The herds are then replaced and become re-infected. Many blame badgers for this. Trials were undertaken involving areas being cleared of badgers in rotation and tests were done on cattle in these areas. The purpose was to ascertain whether or not a cull of badgers would lead to a reduction in the incidence of TB in cattle. The results were deemed to be inconclusive and a widespread cull was not undertaken, although a similar trial in the Republic of Ireland did lead to a cull being instigated. It will be interesting to see how many of these heavy populations of badgers are involved in road accidents or how much money is spent on compensating farmers who lose their cattle, before a government grasps the nettle and allows at least a limited cull in areas where there is an over-population of this, admittedly, attractive and interesting animal.

Badgers and game

Badgers can cause a keeper problems. For example, a badger on a wild partridge beat will miss nothing while searching a hedge for worms and invertebrates, taking the eggs from a nest or the sitting hen if he is lucky. He can be guilty of forcing his way into pheasant pens and causing havoc, and the only measure guaranteed to avert this is the electric fence. Apart from this the badger does not cause too many problems on a reared bird shoot. Care must be taken not to use any snares on fences as they are likely to catch badgers where they are common but on open runs they should be able to push below the snare if it is set six inches from the ground. If you are unfortunate enough to catch a badger in a snare, use a forked stick to hold him down by the neck and cut the snare using top quality wire cutters, taking the entire snare off. A badger caught in a snare is one of the scenarios (another is the poisoned carcase of a rare bird of prey) which causes great harm to the reputation of the keepering profession and provides our enemies with ammunition. Care should be taken to avoid this situation. Interestingly, the method used to catch badgers in the TB trials was cage traps baited with peanut butter, which apparently was very effective.

How to identify a badger sett

When using terriers to search fox earths, make sure that they are fox earths and not badger setts, the latter characterised by the larger entrances, more earth removed, smoother well-worn runs leading away from the holes and the absence of prey remains around the entrances. The final definitive indicator of the badger is the presence of latrines some distance away from the sett. Their latrines are scrapes into which the badger defecates, their droppings being far looser than the fox's typical 'billet'.

The main food of the badger, if available, are young rabbits but badgers will also consume mice, rats, voles, frogs, slugs and hedgehogs, the classic sign of the latter being the spine-covered skin lying minus the edible body. The keen nose of the badger allows him to detect rabbits below ground. When this occurs he will dig straight down to the nest and consume the whole litter of young rabbits. These vertical digs into rabbit holes are a good indicator that badgers are hunting the area but it is not 100% definitive, as foxes can use the same technique.

Cubs are born in the first three months of the year and they remain dependent on their parents until they are over a year old, at which stage they will disperse to set up new territories. This dispersal, coupled with full protection and a lack of natural predators, means that the future of the badger is secure in this country.

The wildcat

The Scottish wildcat is a formidable creature, a terrible fighting machine when cornered and, pound for pound, one of the most efficient predators in the world. He has long been held in awe by keepers and when any keeper tells of an encounter with the 'Scottish tiger', a hush descends on the audience. One wildcat, in the days when they were present throughout the UK, is reputed to have killed a man on the Yorkshire moors. More usually, prey includes rabbits, blue hares, grouse, young deer and lambs, the latter two often having their heads removed and brains eaten.

At one time it was thought that there was a danger to the wildcat from hybridisation with the domestic cat but recent studies have shown that this may not be as big a problem as was once feared. This should not be a surprise as the wildcat favours habitat in remote locations where it would be unlikely that even the most resourceful feral domestic cat could survive. Most feral cats still have some, albeit tenuous, contact with humans, especially in periods of hard weather – a common occurrence in the Scottish highlands.

The wildcat is always brindle in colour with a large flattened head and a blunt bushy tail. They are almost three feet long and weigh up to eleven pounds. Kittens are born in May, with occasionally a second litter. The female rears the kittens herself as the male wildcat has the unfortunate habit of sometimes killing the young kittens, a trait shared by other felines, thought to be caused by the desire of a male cat to bring the female back into season by killing her young.

The wildcat has total protection now but in the past they were controlled by gin traps on bridges, peninsular traps by water and by using baits and snares on known routes. Cairn terriers were bred to hunt cats in the crags where they hid during daylight hours and at breeding time, bolting them to be shot by waiting guns. The present population is thought to be less than 4,000 and there is little prospect of the wildcat being taken off the protected list.

Feral domestic cat

The feral cat is a great menace on any shoot, causing as much damage as the fox. It is bold yet cunning, meaning that he cannot be discouraged from raiding a release pen (apart from an elaborate electric fence) and it can be very difficult to account for. Of course the keeper must be sure that the cat is feral and not the wandering pet of some local who is quite unaware of his pet's nocturnal hunting expeditions. The cat is unique in that no matter how much damage it does, his owner is not liable for its depredations but conversely, if the keeper kills the cat, the owner can have him prosecuted.

This has caused many, sometimes, humorous situations where the keeper and cat owner have clashed. A famous postcard from before the war portrays the keeper talking to a housewife in the village with his gun under his arm, unaware that his flat-coated retriever had just retrieved the lady's cat, shot previously, and is standing proudly presenting it to his unsuspecting master.

In a similar vein I remember one rather dim-witted keeper, on being asked by a man if he had seen his cat, responding, 'Was it black with white feet and a red collar?' The man replied hopefully, 'Yes, that's Towser!' The keeper then replies, stoney faced, 'No, I've never seen him.'

Feral cats were previously kept down by rabbit catchers, pre-myxomatosis, when gin traps were still legal. Since the banning of the gin trap, the feral cat has had a much easier existence. The cage trap specially designed to catch cats is the most effective means of controlling them. Baits normally used are fish, rabbit guts, game or cooked chicken carcases.

Many farms have a colony of semi-wild cats which are fed occasionally but normally fend for themselves, tolerated because they keep the population of rats and mice under control. The fecundity of the cat is legendary and 'farm' kittens are drowned, when found, to keep the population under control. The female cat who has lost one or two litters in this way will decide to have her kittens deep in the woods in future, often in the spring and summer months when the farm rats have moved out to the woods and hedges to breed. Young rabbits are also prolific at this time of year and the kittens will thrive on them as well as game birds, the sitting partridge being a particular favourite of the female feral cat feeding kittens. These kittens reared away from human contact will obviously grow up to be wild and can grow to an impressive size, much larger than their home-reared cousins

How to spot feral cat territory

Crows, jays, curlews and pheasants all give their alarm call, the crows banding together to mob the cat as it hunts its territory. The cat uses any available cover to traverse the ground using hedges to move from one wood to another. The keeper should always look for signs of a cat kill on his beat, the classic evidence being the skin of a rabbit having been peeled back and the flesh gnawed away.

Cats can appear at any time of the year, as if they had been parachuted in, but what has probably happened is that owners, on finding their cat was pregnant again, have driven their cars out into the country far from home and dumped the unfortunate animal. Another source is the cat left after someone has moved house, cat owners seemingly having little conscience about leaving their pet to fend for itself. Feral cats will always keep appearing and the keeper, as in all things, must never be complacent and be for ever on guard for them.

The hedgehog

The hedgehog is one of the most instantly recognisable animals. His spiny coat is unique to him, with no other creature in the British Isles remotely resembling him. He feeds on slugs and other invertebrates, eggs and carrion often well decomposed. His fondness for bird's eggs caused controversy in Scotland when he arrived in mysterious circumstances to an island in the Outer Hebrides. The alarm was raised when it was found that the hedgehog population was severely predating the nests of rare birds on the island. Scottish Natural Heritage authorised and funded a cull which proved to be costly and only partly effective.

As can be imagined, the animal rights brigade had a field day, organising stunts such as transporting hedgehogs back to the mainland with full publicity. The original animals were imported to the island by people who wished to control slugs in their garden, completely ignoring the fact that the wildlife of the island had evolved for centuries free of this creature. The hedgehog had no natural enemies on the island and took full advantage of the situation, breeding twice a year with 4-5 young each time. In a relatively short time the Outer Hebridean hedgehog population numbered in the thousands, hence the necessity of a cull.

The hedgehog is a good swimmer and can move surprisingly fast when he needs to, but his main defence is always to curl into a ball using his quills as protection. Hedgehogs partially hibernate in cold weather, usually December to March, but can wake up if a warm spell occurs. They normally hibernate in a nest made from leaves, straw or dry grasses in the root of a hedge or deep in a disused rabbit burrow or hay shed. The hedgehog's liking for eggs is the main reason for him being disliked by keepers but it can also kill pheasant poults if he gains access to a pen before the birds are able to roost, as well as pulling their heads through the netting outside the pen at ground level, then consuming the head.

Hedgehogs were always controlled in the old days by gin traps at rabbit burrows or by digging a pit and putting a dead rabbit in it, the hedgehog falling in and being unable to climb out. Cage traps also caught this animal, as well as the common tunnel traps. I once owned a German pointer who hunted hedgehogs with vigour, locating every one in a field, despatching them with one bite, then retrieving them to me. Incidentally, if your dog is keen on hedgehogs, make sure you use some form of flea treatment as per recommendation on him as the hedgehog is one of the most flea-infested creatures on earth.

The hedgehog is now protected and the keeper must take steps to avoid killing this animal when tunnel trapping for other species. The simplest method is to fit 2-inch square weld mesh to the ends of the tunnel. This will deny access to the hedgehog, yet allow stoat, rat, even mink to gain access.

The mole

Pound for pound the mole is one of the strongest animals on the planet, moving huge amounts of earth to the surface while constructing the network of tunnels which he needs to secure his main food source, the earthworm. I have included the mole in this section because the banning of strychnine for use in mole control has meant that moles will become a bigger problem to land managers in years to come. Keepers may be asked to help and therefore I have decided to describe control measures, should they be needed.

The old days of mole control

Mole control using strychnine was relatively simple, exploiting the fact that moles have a voracious appetite and earthworms are their favourite food. They travel their runs every day, pulling worms, which have half entered the tunnels, fully into the underground passage, they then hold the worm in their paws, drawing the worm through their mouth to clean it before devouring it. If the mole is not hungry or has caught a surplus, he will bite the head of the worm and push it into the wall of the tunnel for use on another occasion.

The first step in using strychnine to control moles was to acquire worms. This could be done by following the plough, gathering the worms as they were unearthed and placing them in a bucket. The numbers required are quite large: a 200 acre farm maybe needed 500–1000 worms depending on the severity of the mole infestation. The second step was to obtain the strychnine, which was done by applying to DEFRA for a licence to purchase the poison. A DEFRA official would then carry out a check to make sure there was a mole problem and also to check that the user was a suitable person to possess such a poison. This included a home visit to check security, as the poison had to be under lock and key at all times. Because I was a gamekeeper when I applied for a permit, I was treated with particular suspicion, no doubt fuelled by the bad press associated with gamekeepers and poison at the time, one official conducting an unauthorised search, such was his suspicion and prejudice.

Once you had your worms you had to store them. Plastic barrels or dustbins would be used. They had to be clean and free from contamination and smell, the worms spaced in layers of straw, sphagnum moss, cardboard, hessian etc. They had to be protected from frost and the lid drilled with small holes to allow air to circulate.

Mole-finding equipment

To locate the mole runs, the equipment you needed was a dibbler. This could be a custom-made metal rod with a teardrop end and handle, easily made by any blacksmith, or in its simplest form, a walking stick with a metal reinforced end. You needed a small container with a lid which was easily removed and a pair of tweezers which could be made from fencing wire. A pair of gloves was the final requirement, made from a natural material, and they had be comfortable and free from smell.

Before dosing the worms they needed to be cleaned: the simplest way to do this was to place them in a container filled with damp sphagnum moss and leave them for 24 hours. This made the worms free of any smell which could deter the mole from taking them. You removed the worms after the cleansing period and placed 25 in the small container. You then measured an amount of strychnine which would cover half of your little finger nail using a knife or similar implement. N.B. This knife or other tool had to be kept, with the strychnine, under lock and key and was always labelled in some clear way, as should be all utensils and containers which come into contact with strychnine.

As a further guide as to how much strychnine was used, the recommended dosage was one gram to 250 worms, so from this it can be calculated that 25 worms would need one tenth of a gram. The worms were stirred gently to allow them to absorb the strychnine. The interesting thing to note is that the strychnine did not kill the worms but merely seems to make them hyperactive for a period after the strychnine was administered. Strychnine is highly toxic and, be in no doubt, a small dose will kill you stone dead; a death, apparently which is a horrible sight to behold with limbs thrashing and the spine going rigid between convulsions. It is probably this that caused the banning of the substance completely. I feel that moles will become such a problem following this ban, however, that this section has been included because a new poison may in future be found and the techniques used to control moles using strychnine could be adapted to this new substance.

The worms were left for one and a half hours, using this now-banned strychnine method, before they could be used and during that time they would produce a lot of liquid. This was poured off or the worms would drown and become unattractive to the mole. The surplus liquid had to be poured into a deep hole well away from watercourses as it was very toxic.

Many mole catchers use a different technique which allows the worms to be used after 20-30 minutes. This involved squeezing the worms behind the head with a pair of pliers. This seemed to immobilise the worms and allowed the strychnine to be absorbed more quickly. A third technique was used, especially where the worms gathered were large, which involved cutting the worms in half and those half worms were able to be used immediately. The drawback to this method was that a large amount of liquid was produced, entailing more time spent emptying the container.

The advantage of dosing small numbers of worms at a time was that they remained firm and attractive to the mole which obviously made the control campaign more likely to succeed. Do not be tempted to exceed the dosage rate of strychnine as it is very bitter and the mole will taste it and reject the worm.

The next step was to place the worm where it would do the most good, or harm, depending on your viewpoint. In a field with a moderate infestation, molehills will encroach from the perimeters of the field, such as a wood or hedge, into the centre. If you go to the molehills nearest to the middle of the field, you will observe the most recently formed molehill, the soil either being darker in the case of a very recently made molehill or lighter where the wind has dried it. This operation was best carried out in drying conditions.

A time of heavy rainfall with the runs flooded and worms plentiful near the surface would make the operation unsuccessful. You probed the molehill which you considered to be the newest with your dibbler. Practice would tell you when you had found the run, as the earth gives way suddenly. Remove the dibbler and place a worm, using the tweezers, in the hole, sealing it either by lightly kicking it or placing a stone or small sod over it. Check for main runs near the hedge, wall or woods, using the dibbler. Main runs are usually larger than the feeder runs and are used all the year round. The feeding runs in the field become redundant in the summer as the moles retreat to the woods or damp ground in search of worms. The main runs are usually situated where they are not disturbed and will be betrayed by bare earth flattened where the mole has repaired a tunnel which has collapsed. If you found a main run and you had a good supply of worms, excellent results could be obtained by placing 3-5 worms together, as these main runs would be used by more than one mole.

If time allows, flatten all mole hills, so that a check can be made a week later revealing where moles are still working at a glance and further treatments could be administered. Severe infestations will take several treatments to remove all moles, the best results being obtained where neighbouring woods and rough ground are treated also.

Mole traps

Traps can be of the scissor or barrel type. Scissor-traps are used on deeper runs; the barrel on surface runs. Locate the run as described previously using a dibbler, then carefully cut a section of turf exposing the run. The hole should be of a size which will just accommodate the trap and no more. Make sure that no earth has fallen into the tunnel on either side of the opening as this will cause the mole to push earth into the trap and set it off. The floor of the run on either side of the trap should be flattened and smoothed by hand (gloves should be used but not rubber gloves), then the set trap placed in position. The turf that was removed to create the hole should then be used to seal the trap in, making sure that the working parts are not restricted in any way. Coloured pegs should be placed by the traps so that they can be found easily when checking them.

If traps are going to be effective, they will normally have caught a mole after 48 hours, so a trap on a feeding run should be moved after this time if it has not worked. A main run may continue to catch moles for weeks if it is in a good spot, especially if the infestation is heavy. Where the mole has pushed soil into the trap or even pushed the trap out of the ground, it is probably because air entered the run where the trap was not sealed properly and the mole has instinctively tried to block the source of air or light.

Gas can be used to cull moles but will be expensive and ineffective.

The pellets can be administered, using a specially designed dispenser, into the runs, using the methods described previously. The amount required will be described on the container. This is a viable option where there is a light infestation and areas of molehills small. It would probably require traps, especially in main runs to reduce the mole population when used in conjunction with the gas.

The rat

There are a number of methods to control rats: hunting with terriers, lamping using an air rifle or four-ten, ferreting, traps, snares and gas but I will only describe one technique, as the problem is such a huge one (there are estimated to be over fifty million rats in Britain at the present time) that I feel that the most effective method is the only one that should interest a gamekeeper.

My reason for adopting this stance is that gamekeepers can create a rat problem if they are negligent in controlling rat numbers on their beat. Because of the amount of feed that keepers distribute through the woods in wintertime, rats can survive in greater numbers and breed more often than they would have done had there been no keepering.

Poison

The busy keeper has little time to indulge in sport such as terrier hunts and ferreting for rats, which can be enjoyable but ineffective and I therefore would advise that they forget such measures and concentrate on the most effective method, ie. poison. The important thing to remember when using poison for rats is to ensure that only the rat can access the bait. To do this, place the poison below sheets of corrugated iron, placing heavy stones on top to make it impossible for the sheets to blow away. If this is impracticable, use tubs which have a secure lid and partition the interior so that the bait can be stored on one side then drill a hole 2-3 inches in diameter in the opposite side. The tub should be placed under shelter with stones restricting access to the entrance by birds and domestic animals. The area should be searched regularly for dead bodies and these should be buried or incinerated. Some poison can be purchased in sachets and these can be pushed down rat holes which appear near hoppers etc. It may be necessary, after a few days, to move the hoppers some distance away to force the rats to take the poisoned bait. Where rats are reluctant to take bait, it may be necessary to use an alternative base such as pasta which is reputedly a favourite of rats. At the end of the day the rat will not take your poison if there are ample supplies of a more attractive food available to it.

If a rat eats a bait which makes it unwell but does not kill it, it will never touch that bait again. Any bait with an unusual smell or taste will be left untouched for long periods before it will be touched, as will a foreign body such as a tub or poison hopper.

Wax blocks can also be used. These are cylindrical blocks of wax, impregnated with poison which have a hole drilled through them so that a length of wire can be pushed through, allowing the blocks to be hung above ground in a tub or box. They are attractive to rats who love to gnaw on the hard wax but are unattractive to birds and therefore may be useful in some locations.

Some rat poisons are anti-coagulants while others work in a different way. It is recommended that a rotation of types of poison is used to avoid the rats building up an immunity or resistance to one particular poison. It is also advisable that sufficient bait is placed down and it is checked regularly to ensure that it never runs out, as if a rat does not eat sufficient amounts of the bait he may develop a resistance to that particular poison.

Cannibal rats

The rat, to add to his other foul habits such as spreading weil's disease through his urine, is a cannibal and I remember a keeper describing how he sat at a refuge dump, shooting feeding rats with an air rifle. The survivors, on encountering the dead bodies of their relatives, excitedly dragged the corpses back to the holes to devour them in comfort. This was, in the past, exploited by some keepers who on encountering a severe infestation would toss a rabbit or bird, laced liberally with strychnine, into the midst of the colony. Before long a number of rats had taken the bait and succumbed, being subsequently consumed by their brethren and so on, the toxicity meaning that the rats were eliminated in a short time. (Strychnine is so called because it kills nine times, hence the name strike nine).

Caution

Be extremely careful while handling dead rats, whether they have been poisoned or not, as they carry many different diseases such as salmonella and weil's disease. Gloves should always be used, especially when removing them from a tunnel trap, as a cut or graze suffered can allow infection to enter the blood stream with serious results.

Tunnel traps will mop up stray rats questing through the woods and hedges in the springtime but poison must always be available. The problem of rats is just too serious for them to be allowed to gain a foothold. A pair of rats is reputedly capable of producing a population of one thousand in one year.

There is another method of dealing with the rat which, although not strictly a control measure, can remove a problem, especially where the source is on land over which you have no jurisdiction. This can occur where a food source such as hoppers or where a patch of maize have been placed just over the march. If no control is exercised, the rat population will rise and the surplus invade your land, raiding your feeding points before returning to their home burrows to rest up in the daylight hours, then returning the next night.

One solution, which is highly illegal, is to first live trap a rat in a cage, then either remove it using welding gloves or drop it into a stout bag (I know which method I prefer). Once the rat is in the bag, a liberal quantity of waste engine oil, creosote, or 'Renardine' is applied to the unfortunate creature before it is taken home to its own burrows and released.

On release the rat, no doubt unable to believe his luck, will enter the holes, anxious to be re-united with his family. When he finds his companions the reaction he receives will not be what he expected for he is no longer one of them, he is a stinking creature who is leaving a smear of unpleasant oil throughout their home. The resident rats immediately evacuate to other holes, anywhere that is free from the appalling odour. The smelly rat cannot understand their attitude and follows on, contaminating more holes until the rats leave completely, still followed by the increasingly lonely, smelly rat until they are long gone from the area. This method can clear an area of rats for six months or more depending on the strength of the oil used.

Rabbits

The rabbit has been native to Britain since the 11th century when it was introduced by the Normans to provide a cheap, readily available food source. This was the role of the rabbit up to the time of the 19th century when it became a sporting animal.

The rabbit increased in numbers at that time, taking advantage of the growth in driven game shoots and the reduction in the numbers of predators. The rabbit always maintained its position as a food source however, never more importantly than during World War II, when it must have helped to avoid malnutrition when the country was at her lowest ebb.

Myxomatosis

After the war Britain remembered her debt to the rabbit by introducing myxomatosis which wiped out 99% of the population. The rabbit was thought to cost the country millions in damage such as crops, grass and trees eaten. Was the country better off after myxomatosis? Possibly, although few statistics take into account the numbers of rabbit catchers, game dealers and possibly gamekeepers who lost their jobs, as well as the loss of a source of cheap free-range meat denied to the less well-off.

In praise of rabbits

It is difficult for people who have no sporting instinct to see any value in the rabbit but for a normal person, the rabbit is a splendid creature. He can provide sport for the ferret, the lurcher, the terrier, the rifle, the shotgun and the spaniel. His value to bio-diversity cannot be overestimated: buzzards, kites, stoats, otters, polecats, wildcats, goshawks, foxes, badgers and pine martens use the rabbit as a prime food source and to eliminate the rabbit will change the countryside completely.

This is not to say that the rabbit should not be controlled: it should be, especially where cereals are grown and extensive planting of trees is undertaken. This requires labour which many estates and the government have been reluctant to provide but in the present climate this labour should be provided to control rabbits manually rather than by spreading a virus such as myxomatosis or the new RVHD.

The new rabbit disease

Rabbit Viral Haemorrhagic Disease, or RVHD to give it its common acronym, has a devastating effect on rabbit numbers. It has many advantages over myxomatosis, the main one being that its victims tend to die out of sight in their burrows, with any that die in the open giving no visible sign of having any disease – they give the appearance of having just died of natural causes. The percentage of rabbits killed is similar to that when myxomatosis was introduced and recovery is very slow, many people speculate that if RVHD is used over a large area, the rabbit will never recover.

The keeper and the rabbit

What does the keeper do when he arrives on a new estate that has a good population of rabbits? The first thing is to patrol the fields after dark either on foot or using a vehicle. Assess, using a spotlight, the number of rabbits actually on the ground. Remember, if there is a good stock and you do what most keepers do when arriving on a new place, ie. kill every fox and stoat as well as other predators, the rabbit population will explode, so do not forget to cull as many as possible before they start breeding.

Rabbit control: lamping

The quickest way to kill numbers of rabbits, where there is a good population, is to lamp them from a quad bike or four-wheel drive, using a .22 rifle with a sound moderator. If the rabbits have not been controlled using this method before (which is unlikely) good bags will be obtained and this should be continued until it becomes less successful and new methods must be tried. The best nights to lamp are dark and moonless with a wind. The shooter should try and intercept the rabbits between their feeding grounds and their burrows, quartering the ground, preferably into the wind, like a questing spaniel. Shot rabbits should be left until you have cleared the field and collected afterwards. This is a pest control operation after all.

Ferreting

Stage II in your campaign is to gather as many guns together as you can, providing they are good shots. Ferret handlers should be enlisted and promised the bag if they provide ferrets and operate them. The guns reward is the sport. Gas pellets should be carried and where a bury is too difficult or time-consuming to ferret, it should be gassed, with the guns concentrating on the easily ferreted holes. This is because you are in a race against time before the rabbits start to breed, at which point they will refuse to bolt. They may refuse in any case so you should leave a man with an electronic locator to dig the ferret and rabbit out, and move on to a new set of burrows.

If possible you should cover the whole estate, identifying problem areas which will have to be returned to and at the same time learning much about your new beat. Fox droppings, badger hair, the smell of the stoat will all tell you a story. Where it is impossible to ferret or gas the burrows, it may be advisable to stink out the rabbits using diesel or Renardine. This can be done by stuffing toilet paper into spent cartridge cases, then pouring the chosen repellent onto the toilet paper. Using rubber gloves the cartridges should be placed deep into the holes, leaving one clear so that the occupants can use it for an exit, and left for a week to ten days, after which the rabbits will lie out in nearby cover or move to the nearest unoccupied (and smell-free) burrows which should be ferreted as a matter of course. The rabbits which are lying out should be hunted, using dogs such as terriers or spaniels and shot when they flush.

After these methods have been exhausted you should return to lamping, remembering that the survivors will be much more wary now but the important fact is that one rabbit killed now is worth ten killed at the beginning of the campaign. The final step should be to gas any burrows which still hold rabbits although snares can be used to pick up survivors provided you are careful not to catch pheasants.

Drop traps

If the rabbit population is so large that these methods have to be undertaken every year, it might be worthwhile installing a network of drop traps. These must be used in conjunction with extensive lengths of rabbit netting. This may be already available if the estate has rabbit-netted the fence next to a wood to prevent rabbits from encroaching onto adjacent arable fields. Other sites are next to hill or rough ground and improved fields. If netting is not already installed, it can be fixed to an existing fence using a special gadget which clips the net to the fence. The bottom of the wire should be pinned down or buried under the ground.

The catching box is usually 2ft–3ft square and 2ft deep with a lid which is pivoted in the centre so that when a rabbit steps on one side it falls into the box. When not in use and when it is first installed, the lid is fixed so that it does not flip, allowing the rabbits to become accustomed to passing over the trap door. The box must be buried so that the top is level with the ground and a number need to be placed 50–100 yards apart along the fence, depending on the infestation.

The trap works by channelling the rabbit population through holes in the net which guide the individual rabbits over the trap door. This is obviously achieved by placing the fence between the rabbit burrows and their preferred feeding grounds. Once the rabbits are passing over the trap door and a well worn run shows that the gap in the fence is accepted as a main point of access, the traps can be set.

Killing trapped rabbits

The traps should be emptied at first light in the morning and any rabbits caught must be killed at once. The most humane way of doing this is to pick them up over the back just in front of the hind legs with the left hand and, placing the right hand round the rabbit's head in front of the ears, pulling upwards with your middle fingers under the chin. This will kill the animal instantly.

Another method used by ferreters is to hold the rabbit over the back behind the head and pushing the chin back using the heel of the hand. This is normally used when the rabbit is in a net and great care must be taken that the rabbit does not draw his claws down your arm using his free back legs. Any wounds caused by this can become infected and cause trouble for weeks.

Once the box traps have caught, they become even more effective as the smell created by a number of rabbits in such small confinement is fascinating to such a sociable animal. A word of caution: before putting your hand into the box, check that another species has not become trapped. Stoat, mink otter or cat can inflict nasty injuries when cornered, so check first.

Run the traps for 2–3 days then fix the trap doors for a week or so, before repeating the catching process. The beauty of this system is that once it is in place, it requires no skill to operate and an inexperienced assistant can set and check the traps, allowing the head-man to attend to fox control or other more pressing matters.

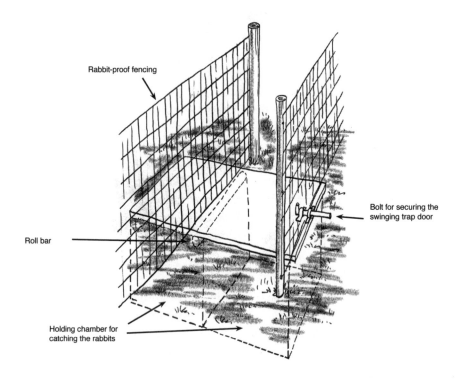

Rabbit-proof fencing

Bolt for securing the
swinging trap door

Roll bar

Holding chamber for
catching the rabbits

*Drop trap for catching rabbits. The flip-lid is secured for several days using the
bolt. This allows the rabbits to get used to a firm surface. Then, the keeper can
release the bolt and the trap becomes active.*

The rabbits should be gutted as soon as possible, then hung on
poles to air in pairs, hind legs interlocked. They can then be sold, the
income hopefully eventually covering the cost of installing the net and
boxes. This is achievable because where rabbit numbers are large, so are
catches. But the main benefits will be derived from a reduction in rabbit
numbers.

The methods I have described apply to a keeper arriving on an
estate where labour and finance are available. On an estate where forestry
and/or cereal production is important, the keeper's tenure may be short-
lived if he is unable to control the rabbit.

Rough shooting

On other estates the rabbit may be something of an asset, providing sport to augment pheasants on rough shooting days, for example. These days are let on a daily basis under the supervision of the gamekeeper and usually 4–8 guns walk in line working their own dogs, shooting any game that they flush. The pleasure of working their own dogs is one of the main attractions that draws sportsmen to this version of the sport, plus of course the fact that it is more affordable, allowing sections of society to participate in sport on keepered estates that would be denied them on financial grounds if they had only driven birds to consider. Some estates are proud of their bio-diversity, the rabbit adding to this as he provides food for so many rare species and he also provides a 'buffer' food source between the predator and game birds.

A keeper often has to control rabbits around the gardens of the big house. The rabbit will eat expensive shrubs and flowers, as well as ruining the appearance of a finely manicured lawn by scraping and digging. A control programme will have to be instigated, which will have to include quite a large area surrounding the gardens, as rabbits will travel a surprising distance to savour a favoured tit-bit. Wire cages baited with carrots can be effective and again pre-baiting is advised; shooting, where safe, using a point .22 or shotgun; plus ferreting or gassing all known holes in the area.

Snaring

A cheap alternative is to snare. This has become less popular in recent years for a number of reasons, one being that snaring is most effective where rabbits are travelling some distance from their burrows to their feeding grounds, crossing rough pasture to access these grounds. Where this happens, lines of snares crossing the rough ground will account for a good percentage of the rabbits. The snares should be 4 inches off the ground and well pegged, with five being set left handed, five right handed and so on, to make checking easier. They should be checked at first light, mid-day and dusk if time allows. The advantages of snares are that they are cheap, they can be used after the period when rabbits will not bolt using ferrets, the inaccessible burrows do not have to be cleared to deal with them by gassing etc, and they are relatively safe to use compared to gas, shooting etc. The disadvantages are that they must be checked regularly. There are fewer rough fields now than in years gone by and they cannot be used where farm stock, or people walking dogs, are present – and a skilful operator is required to set them. However, I do feel that the young keeper can learn a lot by setting rabbit snares and a headkeeper can also learn a lot by observing how an assistant goes about his task, when his skill and conscientiousness can be measured.

Where an estate homes tenant farmers, the keeper must realise that they have legal rights to take ground game. This will not present problems where the keeper controls the rabbit population but when he does not, it can become a bone of contention. For example when a tenant farmer is in dispute with the estate or when a rent rise is being negotiated, the fact that the farm is over-run with rabbits, making farming impossible, can be used as a lever by the farmer and he may exercise his right to put on his own rabbit catchers to kill the rabbits. If these people are honest and reliable there will be few problems but if they are poachers who use their time on the ground to plan further illegitimate expeditions at night after pheasants or deer, a nightmare scenario develops for the keeper. This can be done deliberately by the farmer, who, if he is of the mischievous sort, will take great pleasure at the chagrin of the keeper. This is more likely if the keeper is unpopular with the farmers, another reason why the keeper should take time to build bridges with the tenantry. However, some people never forgive or forget a transgression and the keeper may plough a hard furrow to improve relations with some of the farmers. The keeper should take great care not to give the tenants cause for complaint as any indiscretions he may practice will inevitably be brought home to him should some dispute occur in the future, as surely as chickens come home to roost.

CHAPTER SIX

Traps and Trapping

The development of the trap should not be underestimated in the history of the human race. Man is the only mammal I know which sets traps to catch prey or protect from predators.

The pit

The earliest trap made by man was probably the pit, which was a deep hole dug perhaps 10ft or more in diameter and 10ft deep, covered with sticks and leaves to camouflage its presence and placed on the paths that approached the camp or village where humans had a permanent base. Wolves were a target and such traps were used until quite recently in Europe, with well-documented stories of late-night human travellers blundering into the pit and finding it already occupied. Interestingly man and wolf usually spent the rest of the night facing each other, with neither being prepared to attack. An added 'refinement' to these traps

119

was to drive stakes into the floor of the pit and sharpen the tops, the aim obviously being to impale any unfortunate creature which fell in, saving the trapper the task of despatching it himself. In modern times the pit was still used, albeit in a much reduced form, for such as hedgehogs. Here a hole was dug and rabbit guts were placed in the bottom. Pits were sometimes dug near regular fox-breeding earths, the sides lined with stone to make them permanent. The purpose of this was to place the vixen in the pit after she had been shot, leaving the cubs in the earth to join her. This method was used at earths where it was dangerous to use terriers, and has since been revived because of modern restrictions on the use of gas and terriers to kill cubs – it is probably the most humane way of dealing with cubs, apart from waiting at the earth and shooting them as they appear using a .22 rifle and a sound moderator.

Another adaptation to the pit has been used to catch mink. A length of plastic pipe 4–5 inches in diameter and at least 3ft long is buried vertically near a stream or pond frequented by mink. The pipe can protrude 6 inches or so above ground but is surrounded with stones or earth up to the level of the top of the pipe. Bait such as fish, rabbits or game is dropped into the pipe, which must have smooth sides to its interior walls. The mink will enter the pipe but cannot escape.

The snare

The snare was probably developed after the pit, the early versions using animal sinew or plant fibres to form a crude running noose. It would be unlikely that such a snare would hold its victim for any length of time, so it is presumed that primitive man drove animals such as deer to pre-set snares which held them just long enough for the hunter to despatch his quarry, probably using a spear. Whilst on the subject of primitive man, modern poachers still use similar techniques, driving deer to snares or nets, with men being placed close to the devices so that they can kill any creature caught using a knife before they have a chance of escape.

Snares have become more sophisticated as the materials available became more suitable for the purpose. Fine brass wire, twisted by a machine (or sometimes home-made by suspending a length of single wire from a hook and spinning a metal wheel of about six inches in diameter) was widely used to catch rabbits and hares. The snare ran through an eyelet used to run shoe laces through and was normally 6–8 strands in thickness. The favourite wood for making teelers (which are the sticks which keep the snare in position) is hazel, roughly ½ inch in diameter and 5–6 inches long. One end is split to accommodate the snare, the other is pointed to enable it to be pushed into the ground. The snare is attached to the anchor peg by string, preferably nylon, which obviously must be strong enough not to be broken or bitten through by the rabbit. The anchor peg is normally made from ash but larch can be used if ash is scarce. The string is made into a loop with a diameter 14-16 inches and fed through the hole formed when the strands of wire are twisted together. A notch is cut in the anchor peg to allow a double loop to be made in the string then secured by the notch, although some trappers drill a hole in the peg then feed the string through using a knot to prevent the string slipping through.

Most professionals use a system which uses a wire teeler. The advantages of this are that the teelers never rot or dry out which would cause them to lose their grip on the snare; and they are less prominent being thinner than the wooden version. The snare should be about 18–20 inches long when laid out before being formed into a loop. The loop so formed should be 3½–4 inches in diameter. On open runs the snares are set at the height of your hand and between the depressions formed when the rabbit travels a route on a regular basis. Before setting a rabbit snare, the trapper should spend time observing rabbits travelling their runs, noting the height of his head as he moves along and it is only by watching and learning that the trapper becomes proficient in this art.

Deer snares

Deer have been snared by poachers for as long as man claimed game for his own property. They were also snared, quite legally, to protect forestry interests until the 1960s. It is now a serious offence to set snares for deer but it still goes on, profit being the prime motive, although a deer offered for sale which has been procured using a snare is quite unfit for human consumption, not having been bled sufficiently soon after death to provide top quality meat. This is perhaps the reason why venison has had such a poor reputation as a food in the past, a fact which has happily changed in recent years.

Mink snares

Mink can be snared using snares made from nylon-covered steel trace such as is used as sea fish or pike fishing line. The breaking strain should be over 100lbs, the heavier the better, with a swivel placed halfway between the snare and the anchor peg or drag. Teelers can be similar to the ones used for rabbits and the snares of similar size. Pegs or weights should be long and heavy enough to ensure that the mink cannot escape. Swivels can be home-made using fencing wire. The sets can be at the end of baited pipes, on peninsulas running into water or even at the entrance to a likely burrow. Make sure that a bird cannot access the snare as it is illegal to kill any bird using a snare. Rats and stoats can be caught using similar methods and these snares.

Fox snares

Fox snaring has been covered in the chapter on foxes but a new technique is being developed which takes advantage of the latest electronic callers which have become common in the last few years. A caller is set up in a wood or other rough cover, preferably where runs already exist

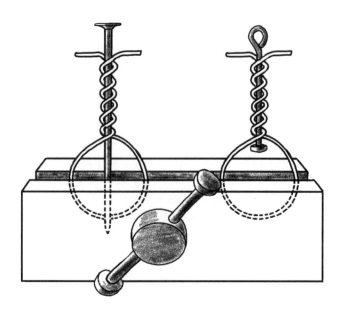

The home-made swivel for use on snares

or narrow points have been created using branches, Rylock or a water barrier. All access routes to the caller should be covered by snares, with the caller activated at nightfall and allowed to operate all night before being switched off. These callers have many different options, so a different call can be tried every night, and are activated by remote control, meaning that the trapper does not have to approach the trapping site. Without his scent in the area, he is more likely to succeed. This is a modern refinement of the 'midden' where offal and game were buried in an area and the snares set on the runs created or already present.

The dead fall trap

The next trap to develop was probably the dead-fall trap. This consisted of a heavy weight, either a tree trunk or stone, suspended above a bait which was attached to a trigger or placed on a run used by game. An animal travelling the path tripped the trigger, causing the weight to fall on it. Some weights were suspended by ropes or chains. A more refined version was the Figure Four or Samson trap, as it is called in the north of England. The trap consists of a stone slab which varies in size and weight depending on the quarry for which it is intended. The trigger mechanism consists of three lengths of wood which form a figure of four with notches cut to enable the framework to support the slab. One of the pieces of wood is baited at the end, which protrudes under the slab; the intended victim pulls at the bait, resulting in the whole affair collapsing on top of the unsuspecting creature. This trap was a favourite of gamekeepers on the Yorkshire moors where the stone naturally occurs in flat slabs, so that the raw materials are freely available. The pest species accounted for by this trap ranged from weasels and stoats through to cats and even foxes, especially cubs. Alternative methods were used in other parts of the country, such as forming slab boards into a flat, pallet-like structure, the trap being set first before being weighed down with stones placed on top. This trap was humane, did not deteriorate in the weather and blended in with its surroundings. Many hill keepers swore by the Samson and used it even after more modern metal traps were invented and became widely used; indeed as a novice keeper I remember accompanying my headkeeper, a grizzled veteran of first class grouse moors in Yorkshire, who bemoaned the quality of the stone in the south of Scotland, saying almost daily that he wished that he had access to a lorry so that he could bring a load of good Yorkshire stone up north.

Cage traps and gin traps

The first cage traps were probably made from saplings of willow or similar, formed into various shapes depending on their purpose. Cylindrical catchers with funnel type entrances at each end were used to catch fish, umbrella-shaped cages would be used to catch birds, either by propping them up and using a figure four or other trigger, or suspended by a string to a trigger directly beneath, the bird activating the trap and being captured alive. These type of traps would have been used extensively to catch birds but the capture of mammals would have been difficult until the invention of metal, which in turn made the construction of the gin trap possible. The gin trap is possibly the most easily-recognised trap in the world. Different designs were capable of taking animals from the size of a mouse up to wolves and even man himself. The fur trapping industry in North America created a great demand for an easily transportable, simple and effective trap that would be quickly set and highly versatile. The growth of game preservation and the huge numbers of rabbits that were gin-trapped meant that there was a thriving market in the British Isles resulting in firms growing up in the English

The Samson trap - now outlawed but once widely used

midlands which concentrated on producing traps as their main source of income. There is little doubt that the gin trap was cruel, especially when used in large numbers to catch rabbits but it was very effective and extremely useful for specialised tasks such as accounting for foxes at dens. Its banning in the 1960s-1970s meant that gamekeepers lost a tool which has never really been replaced. An interesting side effect of the widespread use of gin traps was that foxes became extremely wary of metal objects, especially chains, a fact which many keepers exploited near their release pens by hanging chains and placing old traps in the vicinity of pheasant re-entry holes, Charlie being so understandably frightened of these devices that he would slowly dig a small trench towards a suspected trap until it was uncovered. Perhaps even more interesting is the fact that foxes do not seem to have nearly the same aversion at the present time, showing how adaptable they are to a threat or danger and explaining why they are one of the great survivors in the animal world.

The 'Imbra' and the 'Juby' traps were developed after the banning of the 'gin' as a straight replacement, specially designed to trap rabbits in their burrows. The mechanism was similar to the gin trap in that a trigger plate was used to release sprung jaws to catch its victim but the jaws were angled so that they caught the rabbit no matter which direction it approached the trap. The jaws were curved so that they enveloped the rabbit round the neck or ribs, killing it very quickly. The disadvantages were that they were difficult to set and conceal, with more work needing to be done to the sides of the burrow to accommodate the trap, while at the same time the treadle plate still had to be covered with fine sieved soil and rolled flat as in the setting of the gin.

The Fenn rabbit trap

This was a further invention which tried to solve the problem of providing a humane rabbit trap which was easily set and effective. The Fenn was probably as successful as any in fulfilling this aim and is very useful in dealing with problem burrows which keep being re-occupied after previous incumbents are culled. The trap is similar to the Fenn Mark Six but the jaws are round rather than square, curving again as in the Imbra and Juby to envelope the rabbit when it stands on the trigger plate. The jaws are designed with a gap, so that it is impossible for an animal to be caught by the leg only. The setting of the trap consists of placing the trap inside the mouth of the rabbit hole (the sides may have to be widened to accommodate the trap) and the plate is again covered by finely-sieved soil (some trappers cut squares of newspapers or thin card to fit between the jaws of these traps and gins to cover the plate, preventing the problem of soil or debris piling up beneath the plate and stopping it from functioning properly).

These traps all tried to replace the gin but never became widely used, probably because the rabbit population crashed after myxomatosis or because fewer people were prepared to go to the trouble of setting large numbers of traps, involving carrying and digging without any great reward. Simpler ways of killing rabbits, such as shooting at night using a lamp and shotgun or .22 rifle with sound moderator, either on foot or using a four-wheel drive vehicle or quad bike, became more attractive. Where severe infestations existed, the use of gas, cymag or similar, became common; the fact that a whole area could be treated in a single day being the obvious attraction.

The gin trap was versatile, in that it was capable of catching from rats and weasels up to foxes and otters. No trap has been able to approach this versatility, as witnessed by the number of successors to the gin which are only able to account for a small range of prey species. The most successful of these traps has been the Fenn trap. This trap was the most widely-used and accepted by gamekeepers after its introduction. It is made in five sizes, mark 1, 2, 3, 4 and 6 as well as the Fenn rabbit. The most widely-used by gamekeepers is the mark 4, although most keepers keep a few mark 6s handy for mink. The mark 4 deals easily with stoats, rats and even mink if the tunnels are not too high. The ideal set should leave only ¼ inch to the top of the tunnel to allow the trap to jump. Too much headroom above the trap could lead to the stoat or other creature being thrown clear of the trap, allowing the jaws to close, missing their target. The traps must be set inside a tunnel away from domestic livestock or inquisitive dogs.

Good positions are where a stream passes under a dry stone wall, over a bridge, where two hedges meet, round a pond, on top of a wall, either side of a gateway, in a dry drain pipe, in the outside furrow of a ploughed field and in a tunnel leading from the side of a thick wood or cover out to a bare field.

All traps can be more effective if a small drop of rabbit's blood is placed under the trigger plate. Similar results can be obtained in the spring by substituting a piece of fresh eggshell for the rabbit's blood. When a trap has been successful and accounts for a stoat, it's urine should

A Fenn trap set in a hedge with 'wings' to guide your quarry over the trap

be squeezed onto a rag or paper, which can then be cut into pieces to allow them to be placed beneath the trigger plates of other traps on your beat: a deadly draw for other stoats.

Types of tunnel

Tunnels can be fashioned using old waste drainage pipe, stones or bricks, slab wood or rabbit netting. Standard 7 inch sarking or roofing board can be utilised to construct portable tunnels which are useful when placed on the outside of pheasant or partridge pens. These tunnels can be any length but are usually 2–3ft long and are basically four lengths of 7 inch board, two of which form the sides. The base is cut into two pieces leaving a 6 inch gap which allows a Fenn trap to sit at the same level as the rest of the floor, making it more attractive to a prospective client. 2 inch weld mesh or a square piece of board with a 2 inch hole drilled in the middle, form the ends of the tunnel, while the fourth board rests on top to become the lid. A weight, such as a brick or stone, should be placed on the lid to ensure that the trap does not throw the board up when it is set off.

127

The advantages of this trap and tunnel are that they are portable (the trap is stapled to the tunnel) and only target species will be caught, meaning that they can be set round pens without the danger that a pheasant poult or partridge will be caught. If necessary it is easy to camouflage these tunnels by covering them with brash, stones, logs or sods, with the added refinement of netting 'wings' to guide target species into the tunnels. In a hedge these wings stretch to the outside of the hedge and taper towards the tunnel in the centre. Logs or stones can be used for the same purpose and are perhaps more aesthetic.

Special traps

The BMI magnum and Victor conibear trap have been an innovative and interesting addition to the gamekeeper's armoury. They were designed to answer the call for a trap to catch predators such as mink, marten, grey squirrels, skunks, stoats, rats, muskrats and beaver in a humane way for the American fur trapper. The magnum/conibear was the answer, killing its victims quickly without any danger of the victim's legs being caught.

The design is ingenious, consisting of two rectangular pieces of steel rod, hinged at the centre of two opposite sides and joined together by a rivet. A sprung arm draws up the sides of the rectangle in opposite directions, causing the rectangle to reverse its position under pressure. The trap is activated when the trigger is disturbed, causing a cam to dislodge a notched piece of metal which holds the two rectangles together.

The trap can be baited by attaching bait to the thin wire which is attached to the cam, or it can be set on a run, the victim setting off the trap as it brushes through the trigger wire, which is flexible and can be bent to any shape required. The wire should be moved slightly, before placing in position, so that it swings freely, ensuring that any animal touching it sets the trap off with minimal contact.

In North America special plates can be purchased which grip the jaws of the trap when it is set keeping it in a rigid position. These plates can be replicated or felt nails can make a suitable alternative. The traps come in many sizes up to fox and otter, being set in the open in the North American continent but in the UK they must be set, as per other traps, in tunnels.

The Lloyd trap was similar in concept to the gin. The spring and treadle plate were identical; the difference was in the jaws. In the gin, the jaws shut tight with serrated teeth ensuring that any animal caught had no chance of escape, the foot being the usual part of the body caught. In the Lloyd trap the jaws were shaped to close over the body of a stoat or rat and crush the ribs resulting in a quick kill. The jaws were shaped in a similar way to the Magnum or Conibear traps meaning that any animal caught by the foot would escape unhurt. The Lloyd never became very popular, for no apparent reason. It was gin-like so keepers would have been familiar with the mechanism and it was robust, so perhaps the problem was the fact that it only caught from one direction, as the spring ran in the same direction as the tunnel.

The Fuller and Kania traps are similar and were developed chiefly for grey squirrel control, although stoats, mink, rats etc could also fall victim to them. The traps consisted of a metal box with an access hole large enough to admit a grey squirrel. Inside the box a treadle plate, on being depressed, allowed a metal bar under tension to catch the squirrel or other animal against the inside of the box. These traps would be baited with whole maize inside the box and a tunnel had to be used to deny access by non-target species.

The Sawyer trap was similar to the Imbra or Juby but was used to take stoats, rats, grey squirrels. It is no longer manufactured but is still legal to use, providing it is placed in a tunnel. At the same time as these traps were being introduced to try and replace the gin trap, some trappers adopted a different course by constructing wooden see-saw box traps. These traps could be virtually any size but were usually 2ft long with one end 3–4 inches square sloping to 5–6 inches at the other end. The floor of the trap is a see-saw which is locked shut when an animal enters the box and passes over the point of balance, the other end of the box being covered with weld mesh to give the animal the impression of a straight-through tunnel. These traps were often set in pairs in gaps in walls etc with each trap facing in the opposite direction. The advantages of these traps were that they were cheap to construct, with many allegedly impecunious land-owners becoming almost deliriously happy at the prospect of the estate joiner knocking these up during slack times or even more desirable, a handyman/keeper salvaging scrap wood to construct them for free as opposed to purchasing shiny new Fenn traps at a seemingly exorbitant price. Oh what joy! The main disadvantage of these traps was that catches had to be emptied into a sack so that they could be despatched, a mink obviously creating an interesting dilemma.

All of these metal traps have one thing in common, they use the power of tempered steel to exert the strength necessary to make the traps effective. Before this technology was available, gamekeepers and trappers had to use other means to achieve the same results.

Hanging snare

One of the simplest examples of this is the hanging snare. This was constructed by selecting a sapling which, when bent over to the ground reached a position near a suitable run used by a fox for example. A peg was driven into the ground which had a notch cut near the top. A piece of rope was tied to the top of the sapling and a peg similar to the one driven into the ground was attached to the other end of the rope so that the two notches could lock together, holding the sapling in the bowed

The hanging snare

The baited hanging snare

position. A snare would be attached to the top of the tree and set on the run. When the snare caught its intended victim, its struggles freed the pegs resulting in the animal being lifted off the ground. This had two advantages: the captured animal had no leverage in its struggles so was less likely to escape or break the snare or, in the case of an edible catch, it was safely hung above ground away from any scavenging predator. Adaptations to this trap used bait and a trigger with the snare lying around the bait so that an animal pulling the bait would be caught round the neck or body, then swung into the air.

The majority of the previously described traps have been used to catch mammals; the following will concentrate on devices which have been designed to catch birds.

BIRD TRAPS

The Larsen

The main target of these traps are carrion crows and magpies and the most popular version is the Larsen trap. As I have said previously, the Larsen trap was invented by a Swedish gamekeeper to catch goshawks but was adapted for use in Britain to catch corvids. The trap in one form is approximately 3ft square by 20 inches high. There are three compartments, one taking up half of the box, the other two taking up the other half. The decoy's compartment is the largest and must contain a perch and some form of shelter. Food and water must always be available, dry dog food being the easiest way of feeding the decoy and water is best dispensed using a purpose-made drinker.

The original trigger on the catching compartments consisted of two lengths of 1½ inch broom shank which were held together and placed between the set lid and the frame of the trap to keep it open.

When a crow alights on the split broom shank, the trigger collapses and the lid slams shut, trapping the crow in the catching compartment. Newer versions use a trigger which is attached to the frame of the trap. The trigger has a notch or screw which catches the lid when it is set keeping it open, until pressure is exerted on the end of the trigger which extends into the catching compartment. This version is probably more reliable and easily set, being easily adjusted to ensure that both catching compartments do not close at once, when one is activated.

Siting the Larsen

Prominent positions are most successful for siting a Larsen, as the resident crows cannot stand to see a rival bird on their territory. Other sites can be tried near water, either ponds or rivers and of course near a carrion crow's nest. Some Larsens have a side entry as well as a top but these can be a nuisance on low ground as inquisitive pheasants will keep being caught in them. A perch, in the form of a post driven into the ground beside the trap, can help to encourage reluctant birds to come close to the trap, although in some cases this means that the bird merely sits on the post and calls without entering the trap. A difficult bird can sometimes be tempted by breaking an egg on the lid of the trap and placing another in the catching compartment. Moving the trap if it is not successful is recommended, although a good site can kill regularly throughout the breeding season, especially if there is a good supply of non-territorial crows in your area. If a corbie is still at large after all your efforts to tempt him into the trap, the only course of action is to build a hide and shoot him with a rifle.

Larsen traps are portable, which is one of their main advantages and they can be moved to mop up incoming crows which have arrived from neighbouring land but they are labour-intensive. The decoy compartment is small and the trap must be moved to keep the bird clean and healthy. Because of this, most keepers build a large multicatch trap on a good site which has proved successful using larsens. These can be any size, the minimum being 10ft square by 6ft high. A funnel is placed in the roof of the trap to allow the crows to enter. This funnel is usually 3ft

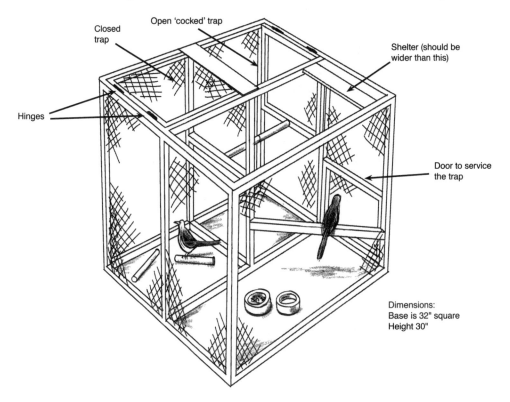

The Larsen trap with the call bird on the right and a new victim on the left. The compartment furthest away is still primed and ready for action.

in diameter at the top tapering to 2ft at the bottom, which is 9 inches off the ground. I have found, however, that they can be cylindrical, 3ft in diameter and 2ft off the ground, especially if the cage is larger than the minimum 10ft square.

My own design would involve selecting a site over running water, such as a small stream, then constructing a cage 12–24ft square covered in soft pheasant pen netting on the roof, with two 8ft posts supporting the funnel. The door should be large enough to allow easy access and a hopper or tub available to allow several days' supply of dried dog food to be accessed by the decoy bird or birds.

The advantage of this system over the Larsen is that any crows caught have access to food and water immediately and only a cursory check need be made to ensure that food has not run out, leaving a busy keeper to run more traps in the same time.

Letterbox trap

There are other versions of this trap: all have their advocates but perhaps the most popular is the letterbox or ladder trap. The illustration shows the construction of this trap. It is important to remember to place 6 inches of wire net at each end of the ladder to prevent escape by the crows. Some trappers fix lengths of plain wire to the sides of the ladder, hanging to the ground about 15 inches apart, the theory being that this helps to prevent escape. Although these traps can be very effective, I feel that they are more difficult to construct and when the occupants have to be removed, the design makes moving about in the trap difficult for the keepers. I would recommend the funnel type every time.

Sheep-netting multi-trap

Another type of multi-catch trap is constructed in the same way as all the others, except the roof is covered in what is described as sheep netting. Sheep netting is not now manufactured as far as I know, although someone out there may be able to find a source. Sheep net was used prior to the introduction of electric fences to partition turnip or rape fields so that they could be strip-fed by sheep. The net is light so that it can be easily moved and has circular holes of between 4–5 inches in diameter. Do not confuse this net with Rylock which is the commonly used fencing material at the present time. The important thing with this type of cage

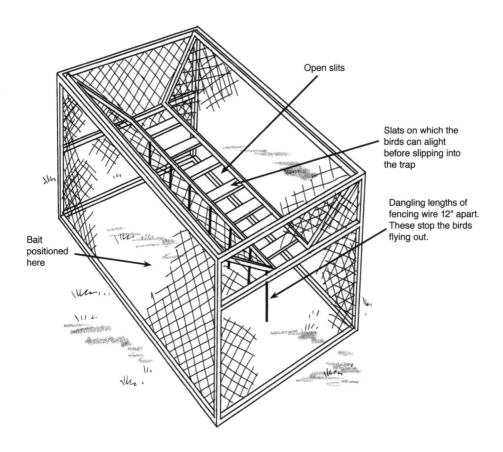

Open slits

Slats on which the birds can alight before slipping into the trap

Dangling lengths of fencing wire 12" apart. These stop the birds flying out.

Bait positioned here

The letterbox trap

is to overhang the top net with a 9 inch fringe of rabbit netting all the way round to prevent the crows from climbing up the inside of the wire net and so escaping through the sheep net. I have personally never seen this trap work so the only advice I can give is to stick with what you know will work, as it is a lot of work to construct a large cage, only for it to be ineffective.

When using the multi-catch traps to catch rooks and jackdaws it may be advisable to make ground-level funnels, as some crows will walk round the outside of the trap to gain access, especially when there are a number already caught. The funnels are best made from weld mesh or, failing this, scrap Rylock covered with rabbit net. This is because birds already caught will crush funnels made from rabbit net alone. The funnel

135

entrance should be about 12 inches wide and 9 inches high, extending about 15 inches into the cage and tapering to about a 5 inch hole. A fringe of weld mesh shaped in a semi-circle should protect the 5 inch hole to stop the crows from exiting there. Straw is a good attraction for crows and should be coupled with wheat, flaked barley or sheep mix. The roof of the trap should be removed, if possible, until good numbers are visiting. This is not strictly required and good results can be had by just baiting the traps and waiting for a crow to enter. Once this happens more will follow until you must remove some of the occupants. The best time to do this is last thing before dark when, hopefully, any survivors have gone elsewhere to roost. Make sure to provide water for the captive birds and leave some in the cage as decoys, until the trap stops catching.

First find your decoy

The Larsen and the various multicatch traps for carrion crows all require a decoy bird to be effective. Many keepers keep corbies all the year round in large aviaries so that when the catching period in the spring-time comes round, they have a number of decoy birds readily available. If you know such a keeper you may be able to borrow a bird from him but if all the keepers in the district rely on someone else to provide decoys, you may wait a long time. In the old days keepers used an old weak gin trap with the jaws padded, often set near water with eggs or a half rabbit as bait, sometimes set in the conveniently shaped site between the roots of a large hardwood tree. If the bird was retrieved soon after it was caught, there would be little damage (regular checking was essential) and it could be used immediately. A small cage can be constructed about 3ft square and 2ft high with one side of the top covered with a six inch strip of netting. A door similar to a large Larsen trap door is fixed to the side opposite with a trigger located in a similar way to this trap. The cage should be set in a likely spot and camouflaged with branches etc and baited with eggs. This should provide you with a decoy, although it may take time, especially if carrion crows are not plentiful.

Illegal pole trap

The most famous illegal bird trap was the pole trap. This, as the name implies, was a trap placed on the top of a pole about 6–8ft long. The site was usually a on a ride where a sparrowhawk or goshawk would hunt, searching for available prey. Other sites were in hedges, near ponds and overlooking rabbit warrens. The trap used recently was usually the ordinary Fenn trap, which may or may not have been camouflaged. In days gone by, when pole traps were legal, purpose-built traps were made specially for this purpose. These were beautifully designed little circular traps which used a curved piece of tempered metal to power the trap. These fitted perfectly onto the top of the pole and was therefore more easily concealed from prying eyes. These traps were hugely effective but unselective, with blackbirds, thrushes and virtually any song bird falling victim to them. The main targets of these traps would be sparrowhawks, buzzards and goshawks: in short all birds of prey, and were undoubtedly a major factor in the severe reduction in the number of birds of prey in the British Isles in days gone by. This trap is now completely illegal and anyone convicted of using one would be liable to a large fine or even imprisonment.

Flip-over trap

Another bird trap was the flip-over trap. This was a semi-circular shaped net which was attached to a frame, sprung so that it swung over and caught a bird which had activated the trigger. This trap came to prominence on one of the investigative television programmes. The aim of this programme was to expose the killing of birds of prey by the game shooting industry. One landowner, unaware that he was being filmed and recorded by a secret camera, described how he had purchased one of these traps in good faith, having been persuaded of its legality by the vendor. The landowner demonstrated the trap in what looked like his front parlour and one can only imagine his dismay when he was unveiled as the unwitting star of this programme of deception. A police wildlife officer was discovered who was convinced that the trap was illegal, as well as being disgusting and barbaric, or words to that effect. The trap may be illegal, although why it should be, I do not know, as it catches alive and would be useful for trapping hard-to-catch hoodies using eggs as bait. I would advise anyone not to take the risk until there has been a test case to prove or disprove its legality.

Butterfly trap

The butterfly trap also came to the attention of the general public during a television programme. The programme was *The Wildlife Detectives* which highlighted the work of police wildlife officers in Scotland. During one of the investigations followed by this programme, a 'gamekeeper' admitted to having a 'butterfly' trap set in one of his release pens. These traps resemble a letterbox or ladder trap when set, the top section folding inwards when the perch is activated. I have to admit that this trap was new to me and I was impressed by its ingenuity. The problem with this trap from the legal aspect was the decoy live pigeons placed in a compartment on the floor of the trap, goshawks and sparrowhawks presumably the target. This was only one charge to be laid against this 'keeper', a rather hapless character and as the programme progressed the evidence accumulated by the wildlife officer was overwhelming. There was a disquieting aspect to this case, however. The 'keeper' was not, at least on camera, read his rights or advised to seek legal or other advice before the search of his buildings was undertaken. The police wildlife officer was accompanied by what appeared to be members of the Ramblers Association, who were not introduced or announced to the keeper, again at least not on camera. As the programme unfolded the 'keeper' became more and more agitated, culminating in him trying to run down the camera man with his quad bike. This desperate act did not, however, lead to viewers turning against the keeper: I am sure that even the most rabid 'twitcher' felt, like me, that this little man was being used to procure a 'sensational' piece of investigative journalism. I feel that this backfired and many people must have yearned for the old-fashioned country bobby who would have dealt with this situation by issuing a warning that if the culprit did not stop his activities, there would be trouble. But then there would have been no television programme!

Black's patent

This illegally set 'butterfly' trap was a descendant of the 'Black's patent' hawk trap. I presume from its name that a Mr Black must have patented the design, although many keepers risked prosecution by copying the original. The trap was about 4ft high with 1ft legs. The bottom compartment housed decoy sparrows, which had to be fed and watered. The catching compartment was clumsy, compared to, for instance, the Larsen trap system but was effective, the trap being, reputedly, deadly on sparrowhawks.

Another variation on a similar theme used a cylindrical piece of wire netting 3ft 6 inches high with a funnel 1ft in diameter tapering to

6–7 inches at the bottom fixed to the roof of the trap which was made from larger 2 inch mesh. The trap was baited with grain to attract small birds which enter and leave through the large mesh until a sparrowhawk appears causing panic amongst the small birds, leading to the sparrowhawk entering the funnel in pursuit of them and becoming trapped.

Pheasant catcher

The last bird trap which I shall describe is the pheasant catcher, used by keepers to obtain breeding stock for the furnishing of laying pens at the end of the shooting season. The simplest design is a small cage 3ft square by 2ft high with funnels on opposite sides made from weld mesh. Many were made from rabbit netting on a wooden frame but modern versions were constructed wholly from 2–3 inch weld mesh. A soft net is normally strung on the top to form the roof of the trap.

Some traps use a hinged entrance which consists of four vertical rods hinged on a horizontal one so that as a pheasant puts his head through the (3 inch) gaps between the rods and pushes forward, the rods lift, allowing him access to the cage, the rods falling down back into place once he has fully entered. A baffle should be placed on either side of the entrance to prevent birds already caught from escaping. These can be made from wood or weld mesh.

Most keepers use four 10ft pen sections adapted to form a large catcher. These can catch large numbers of pheasants at a time, which obviously is an advantage if the keeper has to contain hundreds of hen birds for egg production. A gated section should form one of the four sides and soft nylon net should form the roof. The door should be left open and the net left off while the trap is pre-baited for a number of days before being set. A landing net will be required to catch the pheasants which should be immediately placed in purpose-made crates.

Some keepers use these catchers for a different purpose when neighbouring shoots feed the marches to try to lure their neighbour's birds to their side to shoot them. These roving syndicates can be quite sophisticated, beguiling gullible farmers and land-owners to let their sporting rights in exchange for money, favours and invitations to shoot. Once ensconced they release birds (the bare minimum usually) then without conscience commence to do all in their power to entice the keeper's birds away. In this situation the keeper must hunt the birds away from his neighbours at every opportunity, while at the same time setting

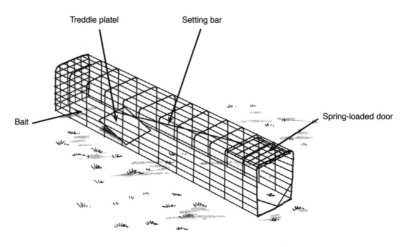

Treddle platel   Setting bar

Bait

Spring-loaded door

Single entry mink trap

catchers near the offending march, using his advantage of being on the ground every day (and often night too) to make sure that he gains more birds than he loses.

Summary

Live trap cages were developed to provide an acceptable alternative to the traps such as gins which were deemed unacceptable to the greater population. Traps of similar concept had been utilised for years prior to this, made from stone slabs. These were used to catch otters, badgers and occasionally foxes, often at dens but occasionally baited. The chapter on foxes describes such a trap which was often used at crag holes where it would have been dangerous to use terriers.

Many parts of the country have the remnants of these stone slabs which were set on riverbanks to catch otters. The advent of wire weld mesh meant that traps could be built which were portable and light, yet strong enough to hold any creature.

The range of live trap cages designed for different quarry runs from rat to fox with versions for mink, squirrel, rabbit, cat, otter and badger in between. The latter two creatures are obviously protected but during recent trials to investigate the connection between tuberculosis and the badger population, cages were used quite successfully to trap badgers.

This method was the only acceptable way for the government to sanction a cull.

My opinion

My own view is that cages are probably more inhumane than an efficient spring trap or snare set in the correct way. Many creatures, including foxes, injure themselves trying to escape from cages, especially if the mesh size is greater than 1½ inches. Much depends on the trapper, who may feel that, because the cage is deemed to be humane, he does not check it as soon as possible after first light. Less skill is required by the trapper to operate cages, a factor which is attractive to an employer who may

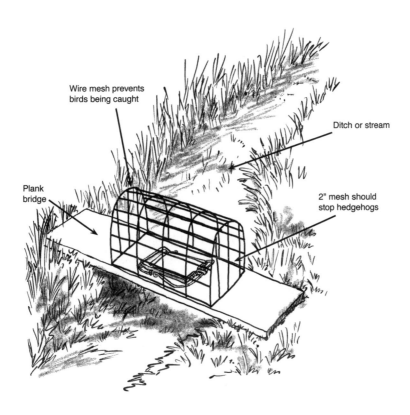

Fenn trap housed in a wire mesh cage on a plank bridge.

wish to cut labour costs by deploying inexperienced or less knowledge-
able operators when some cull has to be undertaken, especially if such a
cull is on a large scale. Interestingly, while on the subject of humaneness,
the trap used to trap wolves in most countries, for the purpose of radio
tagging, is the toothless gin.

Mechanisms and springs

The number of different mechanisms and designs to activate these cages
are numerous and ingenious. One of the earliest was the Legg multi-
catch, designed to catch rats and grey squirrels. This consisted of three
cages approximately 2ft x 8 inches by 8 inches each. These are connected
to form one structure, the middle cage having a door which leans inward
so that it can only be opened one way. Bait is placed inside the trap and
the rat or squirrel, on investigating, pushes the door open, sliding under
until the door falls shut behind, leaving him with no escape. Pre-baiting
is recommended with the door jammed open until the bait is being taken
freely before being set and a good catch ensured.

The Fuller continual catch is similar but has two entry doors and a
tray is placed on the ground first, filled with bait, then the trap fits neatly
inside the tray. It is recommended that the trap is firmly pinned down
so that an animal does not overturn it to access the bait. The trap can be
attached to a larger cage or can be fixed to a metal drum or other suitable
container with a mesh lid. The beauty of these traps is that in a situation
of high infestation they continue to catch without having to be reset and
with pre-baiting can make significant inroads into pest populations.

The catching of rats in such traps has always held a special fascination for me and, judging by the number and variety of old traps found
lying around farms and buildings, a great many other people also. The
rat is such a cunning creature that the catching systems have to be fool-
proof, or the rat will merely by-pass them or give them a wide berth
completely. Some cages used a funnel which gradually inclined so that
the rat dropped onto a platform which inclined in the same direction,
but was pivoted so that when the rat tried to exit back through the funnel
from the platform which sloped downwards towards it, the platform
tilted, preventing escape.

One of the most satisfying traps was the barrel trap. This consisted
of an open-topped barrel with a plank of wood reaching from ground

level to allow the rat to reach the top of the barrel. Across the top of the barrel a plank is fitted with the middle section pivoted so that any animal walking on it falls into the barrel as the plank tilts. Cooking fat or lard was often smeared onto the tilting board, both as a bait but also to make the chance of the rat gripping onto the wood and making good his escape, impossible.

Some people used grain as bait by smearing treacle on the board and pushing grain into it so that the bait was always available after the board tilted and swung back into position. Another version used a plank fixed to extend 6 inches into the barrel with another similar plank placed on the opposite side, leaving a gap of 4–6 inches in the middle. The second plank is balanced so that the rat, on springing across to land on it, falls into the barrel. The balance of the plank, caused by the pivot being more than halfway along its length, brings it back into position after every catch, the pivoted plank being greased to ensure success.

Single catch traps are all similar in that they are made from weldmesh and formed into cages of varying sizes. The differences are in the mechanisms that close the door and in the method used to hinge the door. For instance some trappers use a treadle plate to activate the door while others prefer a trigger with a bait attached, claiming that the treadle plate is too often stopped from working because of leaves, or other debris finding its way under the plate.

The earliest designs consisted of a cage with a sliding door entrance, a metal rod jammed into a hole in the door, keeping it open when set. A string or wire led from the rod to a treadle plate or bait hook so that when the target species either stood on the plate or pulled the bait, the rod was pulled out of the hole in the door, allowing it to fall shut, trapping its victim.

More recent designs allowed the door to swing inwards and a hook in the roof of the trap catches the door, keeping it open. Again a wire connects the hook and plate or bait. The door is usually sprung and falls shut against the frame of the cage so that it cannot be pushed open. A length of wire rod shaped to fit inside the cage is hinged so that it falls against the inside of the door, preventing any animal caught from pulling the door open. This mechanism is used in many double entry traps, ie. traps which have an entrance at each end of the trap. This design is very effective and can be set on runs or bridges as well as the more conventional cage trap sets.

Many cages now have a door which closes inwards, the theory being that some quarry entering these cages can jump backwards on releasing the trigger, be it a treadle plate or baited hook, and squeeze through the closing door of the early designs which either fell vertically down or swung outwards. The new design pushes any creature inside the cage further into the trap. Another plus point of this type of mechanism is that the door and mechanism is fully housed inside the cage so that an animal trying to reach the bait can only set off the trap mechanism from within the trap itself.

Fox cages

The most interesting of these cage traps is the fox cage and, as I commented in the chapter on foxes, many are sold up and down the country, a fact which would suggest to me that foxes are more numerous than they used to be and also less wary of man and subsequently easier to catch. This obviously does not apply to well-keepered areas such as the Yorkshire moors, where one would imagine a cage trap would lie set for years without claiming a victim. These cages are generally 6ft long by 3ft x 3ft with the catching door swinging inwards towards the catch. Some cages have the entry at the end of the trap in the orthodox position, while some position the door on the side at the far end of the trap from the trigger.

I remember being shown a trap in the 1970s which had been made by a pest-controller/keeper. This was large, about 10ft square at least and was made from heavy weld mesh and positioned on a hill frequented by foxes. The bait was always a dead sheep and the door slammed shut vertically, being guided by metal channels. This trap was quite successful, probably because of its size, which made a fox less wary of entering and also because the winters in that part of the world, at that time, were severe and foxes needed to scavenge carrion to survive.

My own preference would be for a larger trap of 10ft x 4ft x 4ft with a double entry system. This could be constructed of part timber and part weld mesh, both to reduce costs and to make it more attractive to a fox. If this trap was placed near roads or paths in forestry and covered with brash, bracken etc, especially on a natural passing place for foxes such as next to a stream or pond, then baited both inside and outside the trap, it would be more likely to succeed.

The small size of the commercial fox trap has more to do with economy, both in construction and delivery, than efficiency. Baits can be deer gralloch, rabbits, game, cooked chicken carcases, parts of a previously killed fox or it is even possible to buy ready-made lures which are supposedly guaranteed to draw a fox to an area.

In a large permanent trap such as described, it would be advisable to sink a pipe below the treadle plate so that bait could be placed out of sight. Bait can also be fitted directly to the trigger with the addition of a pigeon's wing or rabbit skin, including the tail suspended from the roof of the trap by a wire which includes a swivel, so that the bait moves enticingly, a great way to catch big cubs in forested areas.

These are my views on traps, for what they are worth, and any young keeper can spend hours devising new systems and trying them out, gaining valuable experience of his quarry as he progresses. This is desirable for his future career, as no gamekeeper can truly be said to be worth his salt, unless he is a proficient trapper.

CHAPTER SEVEN

Rearing and Releasing

The first decision a headkeeper or shoot owner must make is whether his shoot would be most successful as a totally wild bird shoot or whether it should depend wholly or partly on reared birds.

Wild shoot

A wild bird shoot must be of sufficient size to allow several days' shooting, as the wild bird cannot be so heavily shot as the reared one. This means that in many parts of the country a beat would only be shot once for both cocks and hens (in poor breeding years hens might not be shot at all) with subsequent days, cocks only. It really depends on how many days the shoot owner needs. If he wants, say, 6–8 days a year and has an estate of over 3,000 acres with suitable habitat, it would be perfectly possible, given the correct keepering effort, to provide that number of days. A stand-by could involve releasing cock poults of a suitably good flying strain in bad years to ensure that shooting was viable every year.

The advantages of this system would be that costs would be considerably reduced as no birds would be bought in, in good years. The disadvantages are that the potential for letting days is greatly reduced and it is impossible to predict the size of the day with any accuracy. Birds would possibly fly better, although the modern strains of reared birds

146

perform far better than their forebears. The habitat and farming practices would have to be sympathetic to game preservation, which is seldom the case in the modern countryside, most keepers having to make do with what they are presented with.

Predator control must be a priority on the wild bird shoot: every hen is like gold dust and to lose a percentage before and during nesting time is obviously going to severely hamper the provision of a shootable surplus that shooting season.

New legislation which gives the general public access to land makes wild bird keepering even more difficult, due to increased disturbance both by them and more damagingly, their inquisitive dogs, so you can see that the areas which can provide wild bird shooting, pheasant or partridges, are severely limited compared to years past.

However, if you are a keeper on such land, it would be a privilege to cultivate it as a wild bird shoot. The satisfaction gleaned from providing shooting from purely wild birds surpasses any that you may experience from a reared bird shoot, so my advice would be to go for it, especially if your boss is enthusiastic and supportive, for there may be disappointments before you reach your goal.

Reared-bird shoots

The majority of keepers will have to provide shooting from land which is less than ideal for this purpose. This is where the reared bird comes into its own as, providing there is roosting cover and a reasonable acreage, any piece of land can produce shooting with hard work and financial input. In many ways this is where a keeper is really required, as an estate with perfect habitat, surrounded by other keepered estates, can provide shooting by merely releasing poults and feeding by hopper, with a few nights lamping for foxes to check that there has not been an invasion of these after release. It is therefore a fair assumption that the vast majority of shoots will rely on reared birds to provide shooting in the British Isles.

The next question to be asked is how will these birds be sourced and which species will be most suitable for the conditions prevalent on your particular estate. The keeper who has just commenced employment on a shoot should meet with his employer or employers at the first opportunity to ascertain their requirements and aspirations for the coming season and beyond. Some employers can be quite coy on this subject, a fact which I have always found difficult to understand. Perhaps they are afraid that the new keeper may ask for more funds than are available to fulfil his employer's dreams. Another theory proposed by one keeper, somewhat bitterly it has to be said, is that every employer longs to discover a keeper who can make a silk purse from a sow's ear at very little cost, producing game out of a hat!

Your employer will tell you the basic retinue for the coming season. For example he may want 20 days with 5 days at partridges at the beginning of the season, leading into the cover shooting proper, with days to average 200 birds per day. The five days at partridges will yield 1,000 birds so you now know that you will have to release 3,000 partridges. The remaining days at pheasants will provide 3,000 birds, so again you will probably need to release 9,000 poults. These calculations are based on a presumed return of 33.3% which will probably cause many keepers and shoot managers to raise a few eyebrows but it should be remembered that this is probably the average result achieved by a keeper in his first season on a new shoot, if the truth is known.

The early days at partridges will need to have at least six drives dedicated to partridges with perhaps five release points in each drive. The fifteen pheasant days could be covered by fifteen drives with probably seven or eight release points. If this programme is to is to be started from scratch on land which has had no pens built on it previously or if existing pens are no longer fit for purpose, there is a heavy work-load ahead if everything is to be ready for the arrival of poults in July, especially when one considers that the shoot is unlikely to have been well-keepered previously if it requires so much attention.

Costing: poults versus day-olds

In these circumstances it would be advisable to buy in poults with the option of rearing when pens and predators are under control in the future. Where all other factors are equal, the question of poults versus day-olds or egg production is basically a question of cost. 3,000 partridge poults cost about £10,000 and 9,000 pheasant poults would cost roughly £30,000, bearing in mind that partridges can vary in price from £3.50–4.50 and pheasants £3.10–3.80. This basic cost of £40,000 to provide birds for the shoot between July-September must be compared with rearing from day-olds.

The cost of a day-old chick is £1.20 for partridges and £1.00 for a pheasant, on average. The cost to feed chicks to poult is 50p per bird, gas and electricity costs are 30p. It can therefore be seen that a saving of up to £1.50 per bird can be made, although it must be remembered that the keeper's time is not included in this figure, nor is the depreciation of rearing sheds, heaters and other equipment which must be calculated to give a true figure of savings made. Extra labour may have to be employed at busy times, such as bitting or releasing, so that the true saving may be less than £1.00 per bird, especially if the percentage reared falls below 95%.

Another factor which must be considered is the fact that a keeper tied to a rearing field may not have time to attend to vermin control prior to release, and the release pens themselves may not be prepared to the standard required, again due to lack of time. This lack of attention to detail may result in a lower return being attained which again would affect the calculations and the actual amount of the savings made.

If the shoot does not own the land, it may have to rent the rearing field which would be another additional expense, which may not have been anticipated. It is therefore worth carefully considering before embarking on a rearing programme, bearing in mind that in some estates in the north or west of the country, it is far more difficult to rear a high percentage of poults and this must also be taken into consideration. At the end of the day it probably depends on your employer and the number of birds required.

If he requires more than 8,000 then some at least should be reared, less than that and poults would be the best option. If finances are really tight, then you will have to produce as many as you can as cheaply as possible, a situation where a keeper really earns his corn.

Blueprint for rearing 10,000 birds

We will assume that you have to rear 10,000 birds, so I will endeavour to describe how best to do this. The most cost-effective way to start is to catch wild hens and produce eggs yourself. This assumes that there are hens present on the shoot, survivors of previously released birds. Check that the birds are of suitable quality to be used as breeding stock: perhaps they did not fly well or were affected by disease. If this is the case then it would be folly to catch up these hens and it would be better to cull these birds and buy in hens from a reputable source. Finding that source may be difficult, as there are many unscrupulous dealers out there who will sell the unsuspecting game bird rearer poor quality, fully in the knowledge that the purchaser will not know how poor the hens were until well into the shooting season, perhaps eight months later.

Housing laying hens

We will assume that you have acquired good quality birds. The next step is to house them properly so that they will produce many good quality eggs. Probably the best system for a small number of hens, that is, less than 150, would be 10ft x 6ft moveable pens containing one cock and six hens. Brash should be provided to give the birds privacy and obviously food and water should always be available. The advantage of these pens is that the ground is always fresh. Fighting between cocks is avoided as there is only one cock in each pen and the eggs are safe from crows. The disadvantages are that they require more ground, the pens have to be moved and egg collection is more time-consuming because the keeper must enter each pen to collect the eggs.

Most estates use one large pen, which is usually open-topped but some are covered by large meshed net to protect from corvids.

The birds must be brailled, using purpose-made brails which are available from game suppliers, to prevent them from flying out of the pen. The ground chosen for a laying pen should be well drained and sheltered. Cover, such as brash and shelters made from corrugated iron or half-cut 50 gallon drums should be provided to allow hens to escape from over-amorous cock birds. There are no hard-and-fast rules as to the size of these large open-topped pens but the general opinion is that most are too small for the number of birds housed in them. As a rough guide however, a pen of half an acre would be sufficient to hold 200–300 hens.

The birds should be wormed using flubenvet and innoculated against any disease which is liable to threaten and affect egg production and/or the health of the chicks produced. These diseases can be a perennial threat but some occur as a one-off so the only way to guard against them is to consult your veterinary surgeon and other large-scale game rearers for advice as to best practice.

Hens should be fed carefully to ensure that they do not become too fat. Pre-breeder pellets are the best ration to ensure this. These pellets should be fed until three weeks before the first eggs are expected, say the first week in March then subsequently fed the standard pheasant breeder pellet until the end of the laying season. Eggs should start to be produced by the end of March, with each hen laying 30–40 eggs, some strains such as the Michigan blueback laying more than this.

EGG PRODUCTION

Partridge

Partridge egg production is more difficult with the birds having to be paired in raised pens with weld mesh floors. The actual sexing of partridges, both red legged and grey, is quite difficult. Red leg cocks will have spurs while, in grey partridges, the hen has two horizontal stripes on her shoulder feathers and the cock tends to have a dark horseshoe shape on his breast, although this is not infallible. If conditions are right, partridges can produce an abundance of eggs, 50–60 per hen, but it may be difficult to achieve these perfect conditions. My own view is that the keeper would be better advised to source eggs and incubate them himself, rather than embark on the very difficult and specialised task of the production of partridge eggs.

Mallard

The production of mallard eggs should be avoided, unless the shoot intends to specialise in duck shooting. The reason for this is that the chances of cross-contamination between laying pens, incubators and rearing field are so great that few if any game farms rear duck and other game on the same site. A keeper can hardly be expected to succeed where the game farms have failed. Salmonella, the main problem in this scenario, is very difficult to eradicate once present and can result in huge losses, with any birds that do recover from this disease unlikely to perform adequately during the shooting season. This is not to say that I am against reared duck *per se*, I am not and feel that there are many shoots up and down the country that could benefit from having more ponds created and stocked with reared duck. On flat land which provides ordinary pheasant and partridge shooting, duck can provide better quality shooting, if done well. Fewer beaters are needed so days can be planned at short notice when, for instance, your employer has unexpected guests. A wet and windy afternoon can produce sport for such guests that they will remember for years and this is an avenue that the shooting world has not yet fully explored.

Once you have the eggs they must be washed using a proprietary brand of egg wash. A purpose-made egg washing machine is a good investment, as it is more efficient and time saving. The eggs must then be stored in trays in a cool building. Great care should obviously have been taken not to damage them when collecting and they should have been gathered at least twice a day. The trays should be tilted once a day if the eggs have been kept over a week but ideally eggs should not be more than a week old if they are to be set in an incubator.

Most people know that at the start of artificial rearing of game birds broody hens were used, both to hatch the eggs and rear the chicks. I will not describe the techniques involved as they are well-documented but I will comment on the fact that it was back-breaking and time-consuming work, although the quality of the birds and the returns were far superior to the results from modern methods.

Incubators

Incubators are nowadays far more sophisticated than earlier models which were usually designed for hen eggs. These machines often took a year or two for the operator to gain the best results so I would suggest that the keeper recommends to his employer the purchase of a modern machine and receives full instruction in its operation. A pheasant's egg takes 24 days to hatch with most incubators being unable to successfully hatch the eggs without the transfer to a purpose-made hatcher on the 21st day.

This means that you will need both an incubator and hatcher. The number of poults that you require determines the size of incubator. For instance, if the shoot intends to release 10,000 poults you will need to produce 11,000 day-olds and in turn 11,000 day-olds will need 13,000 eggs produced from 350 hens. If you are intending having six hatches then you will need to set just over 2,000 eggs per week, so you now know that you need an incubator with a capacity of 6,000–7,000 eggs and a hatcher that can deal with 2,000 plus eggs.

Eggs are normally set on Fridays with the transfer to hatchers on Thursdays, hatching taking place on Tuesdays. There is no hard-and-fast rule to this but most game farms set on Fridays and hatch on Tuesdays, the reason presumably being that all labour-intensive operations take place away from the weekend when help may not be available. Eggs should be set pointed side down. Any mis-shapen or unusual eggs are best discarded so that the ones set are as uniform as possible. Approximately a third of the incubator will be filled each week until the first transfer to the hatcher takes place on the 21st day, the space created being filled by the fourth set of eggs. If all goes well, the chicks which have hatched will be ready to be transferred to chick boxes on the Tuesday following. They may not all hatch at the same time and any weak chicks should be left in the incubator for a time so that the chicks in each individual box are of a similar strength, being left in the boxes for several hours to get on their feet before being placed under brooders.

Brooders

These brooders can take many forms, and are fuelled chiefly by electricity or gas. Electric hens are basically a plastic cover strung over a wooden frame with an element sandwiched between the plastic cover and an insulated lid. Adjustable legs at each corner allow the 'hen' to be raised up as the chicks grow. These brooders need to be housed in a fairly draught-free insulated building as the heat generated is a contact type with no space heat being created. It is advisable to have a back-up generator handy (many estates have this so that the incubator can be kept running in case there is a power cut when eggs are being incubated) as well as some form of heater to raise the ambient temperature should you experience unduly cold weather when chicks are small and at their most vulnerable.

Electric hens are not so popular as they were in the past, probably because the rearer cannot see under the brooder to check that everything is OK. There is also the feeling that they do not produce as hardy a poult, a fact that I would dispute. Corrugated paper, which can be purchased from a game supplier in rolls, should be placed under the electric hen. This gives the chicks a good foothold as they push upwards to the heat as well as retaining some of the heat produced by the brooder and the chicks.

Care of the growing chicks

As the chicks grow they will still try to push under the brooder so it must be raised when they show difficulty in doing this up to the age of 4–5 weeks when it is advised that the brooder is either removed or lowered to the floor. A back-up heater may be advisable to see the birds through the first two or three days after this, especially if the weather is cold. The corners of the rearing shed should be rounded off with chick boxes to prevent poults gathering in the corners and smothering each other.

Previous to this the chicks should be contained by hardboard surrounds, two feet high, which keep the chicks close to the heat, as well as food and water. Chick crumbs should be provided in trays when the chicks are young as it is important to get them feeding as soon as possible. A good idea is to use trays of plastic in a colour which contrasts to the colour of the chick crumbs, so stimulating the chick to feed.

Watering the chicks

In the old days, water was provided by small drinkers with pebbles or pieces of hose placed in the trough to prevent the chicks drowning. Nipple drinkers have been invented which are activated by the chick pushing a metal rod housed in a red plastic valve system. This allows the water to flow down the chick's throat and hopefully less water ends up on the bedding, a fact which goes a long way to avoiding disease, as the ideal conditions for bacteria to flourish are heat combined with damp. These nipple drinkers are fixed in a row so that any number of chicks can be serviced at a time, the whole system being fed from one water container. The drinkers will have to be raised as the chicks grow and may have to be augmented with conventional drinkers after four weeks, especially in hot weather, as the birds may not be able to access enough water from the nipple drinkers alone. Plastic mesh can be purchased to be placed under drinkers and feeders so that the chicks are kept clear of soiled bedding and damp stale food. If this is not done and soiled bedding and food not removed it can result in chicks forming balls on their feet which can be difficult to remove.

Bedding

The type of bedding used is up to the personal preference of the rearer and there have been many materials used from pebbles to wood shavings. My advice would be to use good quality, dust-free shavings from a reliable source, avoiding shavings from a joiner's shop for instance, which may contain insecticide from treated wood, with disastrous results. No matter which bedding is used, it is up to the rearer to maintain excellent standards of hygiene if he is to produce top quality, disease-free birds.

Fitting bits

At three weeks of age the birds will have to be fitted with 'bits' to prevent feather pecking. To do this, the birds need to be moved into a small pen so that they can be caught easily. Some people use a shelter pen attached to the brooder hut. Three people are probably the minimum number for this operation to run smoothly, although if labour is available the more the merrier, if they are competent. A pop hole should be made so that bitted birds can be 'posted' back into the brooder hut with the minimum of effort as you may have to deal with 2,000 in one day. The bits are administered using a purpose-made dispenser available from game industry suppliers and are simple to use. Two catchers should be able to keep a continuous supply of birds to the bitter with the minimum of stress to the birds. Some keepers try to cut corners by not bitting or delaying until pecking actually occurs. This is folly as here is an area where prevention is definitely better than cure.

Health of birds

Good husbandry is the key to successful rearing. The successful rearer will spend time checking his charges to ensure that all is well. Loose droppings, often yellow in colour, are a sign that all is not well and advice should be sought from a veterinary surgeon if you are not certain of the cause yourself, as a delay in administering medication may have disastrous consequences. Prior to its banning, Emtryl was used to prevent blackhead, hexamita and trichomonas and was an excellent cure-all for these and other common ailments. Nowadays alternative medicine must be obtained, either contained in the feed or administered directly into the drinking water, by prescription from your vet.

Poults 'snicking', a condition caused by 'gapes', a parasite present in the poult's wind pipe, must be treated with feed medicated by the drug 'flubenvet'. A supply of this medicated feed should always be available as this ailment can occur at any time, especially after wet weather, the condition being connected to the presence of earthworms.

Good quality feed should be used which will contain medication at a preventative level to reduce the chances of disease taking hold. If you feel that your poults may be at higher risk, such as stress brought on by bitting or severe weather, it is possible to have the levels of these medicines increased with the necessary authorisation from your vet. Any feed containing medicine must be sold only with a vet's authorisation and your feed supplier must be furnished with your vet's details (address and phone/fax number) before a transaction can go through.

Gas brooders

The rearing of pheasants using gas is similar, apart from the fact that the gas brooder is suspended above the chicks and therefore can be observed more easily. The correct height is determined by the behaviour of the chicks. They should be evenly spread with perhaps a small circle clear in the centre immediately below the heater. Large powerful brooders can be hung higher as they will heat a greater area, the thermostat keeping the heat at a constant level despite changes in the ambient temperature. The conditions in each shed should be checked at least every hour for the first week in case there is a malfunction in the brooder or in case the chicks are obviously distressed, which will manifest in the unmistakable sound of them cheeping plaintively, a sound which the rearer dreads like a cold hand gripping his heart.

Gas can be provided from a central tank and distributed by a series of pipes to the rearing sheds or by individual gas cylinders which can service each shed. The important thing to remember and gauge is when the gas will run out, as this would obviously be disastrous, especially if it happened during the night. Most systems have an automatic change-over valve to transfer from one cylinder to another, should one empty; the empty one being, hopefully, replaced immediately. When purchasing gas brooders, always look for one with a built-in thermostat. This is especially important in the north of the country where the ambient temperature can plummet in the middle of the night. Many rearers will try to dispose of old heaters without thermostats at a seemingly bargain price but I would advise against such economy, as it is almost certainly a false one.

The rearing shed

The size and type of shed are many and varied, some estates converting existing stone buildings and others buying custom-built sheds at great expense. The conversion of static buildings can be a success if they have some form of insulation and a system of dust extraction is installed; the disadvantage is that the outside runs will be used every year with no respite and the ground can become stale. This can be avoided to a certain extent by building runs on both sides of the building and using them in alternate years. Another option is to rear the birds indoors in these buildings, which have the advantage of being cool in very hot weather with no extreme of temperature either way, then move them to smaller sheds on a rearing field at three weeks, after they have been bitted. The sheds to house three-week-old birds would not need to be so sophisticated as sheds which would house birds from day-olds to six or seven weeks of age. The build-up of bacteria from day-old to six weeks would be avoided as the birds are being removed to fresh conditions at three weeks; the only disadvantage is probably the extra cost of buying or building the sheds.

The original rearing sheds were about 8ft x 6ft by 5ft 6 inches high and made from ³/₈ inch plywood with a gas heater supplying the heat. These had no insulation and were difficult for large keepers to enter or exit. They usually had a shelter pen of 10ft x 8ft attached, so that chicks could be allowed onto grass as the shed became stale. The shed was floored with plywood and shavings or, if no floor was used, gravel was put down. These contained 150–200 chicks and were perfectly satisfactory, although labour-intensive and time-consuming. Gradually sheds were made larger, up to 16ft square to accommodate 500–1,000 chicks with a large shelter pen covered with a Perspex roof and clear plastic sides that can be removed in hot weather. Materials have become more sophisticated, with insulating board being used to save energy and also to stop the wild variations in temperature which could occur in the old sheds.

The Rupert brooder

Some older readers may remember the little gem that was the 'Rupert' brooder. These were small-domed, circular brooders about 4ft in diameter which looked as if they had come from a different planet. A box attached to the totally galvanised metal construction housed a paraffin heater which had not to be overfilled. This, of course, often happened, especially if the brooder was not totally level, the box filling with paraffin and igniting, the resulting flames and smoke erupting through the pipes which circulated the heat through the brooder and emerging out of the chimney at the top. The chicks meanwhile, if they were lucky, made good their escape into the small run which was attached to the front of the brooder, although many would have taken on a rather blackened, singed appearance. The obvious improvement was to convert to gas which was an improvement, as the gas flame did not blow out in the wind as the paraffin one did. Originally it was recommended that 100 chicks were placed in this brooder in the centre of a 30ft x 30ft pen with a wigwam of branches built over the 'Rupert' to provide shelter.

I remember rearing using this method during a most foul summer and having a complete disaster. Horizontal rain and low temperatures combined to kill a large percentage of the birds.

In later years, the suppliers suggested changes to the use of these brooders with the 'Rupert' being fitted halfway into a shelter pen, in effect an admission that no research had been done to find problems when the 'Rupert' was used in practice, especially in the harsher north. I often wonder, when surveying the haggard, war weary faces of some older keepers, how much this was owed to rearing for a few seasons with 'Rupert' brooders in the north of the country! In the 'Rupert's' defence, they are ideal for rearing 2–300 birds and produce absolutely top quality poults.

The runs

The runs attached to the rearing sheds are made from pen sections. These are usually 10ft x 5ft–6ft with the bottom half covered in corrugated iron or board. A soft net of nylon pheasant netting covers the top. This should be fairly tight so that poults flying up do not become entangled. This can be achieved by placing poles of 7ft in the pen to support the net. An added advantage is that it keeps the net clear of the heads of 6ft keepers who need to service the pens.

Runs should be long and fairly narrow, ie. 20ft wide, to facilitate driving birds back into the sheds or shelter pens at night in the period before the birds are fully hardened off. This should take place from 4 weeks on, the exact timing being dependent on the weather, a warm settled spell obviously being desirable. If the weather is unseasonably cold or wet it may be necessary to switch the gas heat back on to prevent birds piling up on top of each other at night. If the weather is good the heat can be switched off for short periods from the age of 3 weeks, the aim being to gradually harden the birds before they are released to the wood.

Release

Once the birds are 6 weeks old they are ready for release, providing they have been off heat for at least a week and the weather forecast is good. Keepers with a heavy rearing programme cannot afford to be choosy about release dates and tend to get birds to the wood at the earliest opportunity providing the weather is not very wet. To help in this, some keepers shut the birds in to keep them dry so that they can catch them without the fear that the birds will lose feathers if they are wet.

Wing-clipping poults

If the birds are going to an open-topped pen, they should be wing-clipped and their bits removed. Some keepers do not wing clip, stating that a poult which is free-winged will take care of itself should a fox, cat or even a dog enter the pen. My own view is that if this is going to be a problem, the chances are that any birds which fly out of the pen to escape a fox will be mopped up by other vermin on the outside of the pen, or failing this, starving before they find their way back to feed, not having had time to acclimatise to their new surroundings.

It is a simple task to wing-clip poults properly. Open a 6-week-old poult's wing and you will see a number of primary feathers on the outside of the wing which are a different colour to the rest. The sheaths of the feathers where they grow out from the wing will be different and new feathers that have not fully grown will be seen. The outer primaries which are about to fall out are the ones which you should clip, leaving the poult unable to fly for a week to 10 days.

Red-legged partridge rearing

The rearing of red-legged partridges can take the same course as rearing pheasants, although they are better reared in smaller units of less than 500 birds. A single electric 'hen' is ideal for rearing 250 partridge chicks which are, if anything, simpler to rear than pheasants, with no need to bit at three weeks or wing clip at release.

The outside rearing pens should have curtains of scaffolding mesh or similar hung 3ft down from the roof of the runs and about 10 yards from the ends of the pens to prevent the young partridges from flying from one end of the pen to the other and crashing into the hard wire on the outside of the pen and breaking their necks. Red-legs can be kept in rearing pens for longer, up to 12 weeks old if conditions and space are adequate, before being released to outside pens on the shoot. This is because they are far less prone to feather pecking, although standards of hygiene must be high if disease is not to be a problem if partridges are held back.

Building release pens

Release pens must be built and ready to accept poults weeks before they are actually needed, for to leave this job to the last minute is to invite problems due to corners being cut to construct pens in too short a time.

The first requirement when building a pen is to select a suitable site. This should be in a quiet location away from disturbance from walkers, farm traffic and away from public roads. Farming and forestry operations should be anticipated so that unforeseen disturbance is avoided: for instance it would be a disaster for forestry contractors to arrive with the intention of felling a wood which housed a release pen full of newly-released poults. This may seem to be an unlikely occurrence but I can assure the reader that this has happened on more than one occasion.

Another nightmare scenario would be poults which had recently vacated a release pen jugging out in standing crops such as wheat, barley or silage. The high speed nature of modern farm machinery means that these birds are liable to be chopped to pieces, especially if the crops are cut, as is now commonplace, after dark. If there are poults roosting on the ground in such a crop, they must be disturbed in late afternoon and evening to persuade them to return to the pen or at least the wood where they will be safe from the farm machinery. The obvious solution is to situate your pens away from such dangers and also to ascertain from the farmer or farm manager the rough date when he expects to bring in his crops. Once these dates are known, birds can be held back or bought later for deployment in such pens which are placed in a vulnerable situation. However, bad weather can postpone harvesting by weeks and birds will have to be put in these pens, with all the resultant risk involved. It is therefore more satisfactory, especially for the keeper's peace of mind, to situate your pens away from danger.

Once the pens have been constructed and are vermin-proof, they should be hunted through with a terrier and/or spaniel to ensure that you have not enclosed a litter of fox cubs – yes this has happened! – or stoats. Any suspicious holes, including rabbit holes, should be gassed and the operation repeated just before birds are placed in the pen.

Release pens should contain ground cover such as brambles or rhododendrons to provide escape cover for poults so that they can avoid birds of prey. They should also contain young trees such as larch which will provide low roosting cover that can be utilised by young birds newly arrived in the release pen. The sooner the poults start to go up to roost the better, as they are then relatively safe from predators at night.

The pens should receive sunlight for as much of the day as possible, with trees outside and inside the pen providing shelter from wind and rain. Shelters 6ft high should be built where the birds can be fed in bad weather, trough-type hoppers being preferable to hoppers which distribute the food on the ground, these latter promoting disease conditions.

Water can be accessed from a stream which flows through the pen providing it is fresh and free-flowing and does not dry up in high summer, but the sides of the water should not be steep. Contrary to perceived opinion this is healthier than water sourced from a tank as it is being constantly replenished, although the disadvantage is that it is not possible to administer medicine in the birds' water supply, the preferred method for many medicines and this may be a deciding factor weighed against the saving in time and labour from not having to carry water to the pen.

The alternative is to provide water via purpose-made drinkers which are suspended above the ground and supplied from a 100–200 gallon tank. These will have to be filled by a bowser of similar size, a petrol-driven water pump being necessary. Access to the pen should be provided by a track of some sort so that water and feed can be taken in bulk and stored using a Landrover or similar.

Pen size

Once the site has been chosen, the size of the pen is the next consideration. A pen for 1, 000 birds could be 350–400 yards in perimeter; a pen for 500 birds 200 yards round. The first thing to do is select places where the corners could be situated. The pen does not have to be square but can follow the natural topography of the ground: a circular shape indeed would be quite suitable as it would avoid the corners of a square or rectangular pen.

Let us assume that you are going to build a pen 300 yards in perimeter. For this you need fifty 8ft poles, 3 inches in diameter which will have to be driven by a tubular mallet which sits over the pole and is driven using the attached handles. A pinch bar will be needed to break the ground first, facilitating the driving of the poles.

The gates should be large, as being able to enter the pen with a vehicle is a great boon when delivering feed to hoppers situated inside the pen. These gates should 8–10ft wide and made from 3 x 1½ inch rails. The main gate should be measured and your first two poles driven, using the cylindrical mallet. They should be as vertical as possible and driven until they are 6ft 6 inches high. The next pole, at a corner or where the pen turns in some way, should be driven and so on until you have the basic shape of the pen laid down, using perhaps 8–10 of the poles. String should be strung between poles, or even before they are driven, to check that the course of the perimeter net does not encounter an obstacle which will make the building of the pen difficult.

The rest of the poles can now be driven in using the string as a guide to keep the poles in line and tidy. The posts at the gate, at corners and other places where the pen will have extra tension must be braced, or the tightening of the plain wire will cause them to be pulled over. This can be done either by digging a small trench and placing a flat stone at its end, then resting a pole against it and lowering it until it touches the gate post. Cut the brace pole vertically so that it fits snugly against the gate post and fix using a 4 inch nail, or alternatively a short post can be driven into the ground to replace the flat stone. Perimeter poles which may be pulled in can be braced by attaching a length of plain wire to a short post outside the pen, as can corner posts.

Once the perimeter poles and gateways are in place, you must string thin high–tensile plain fencing wire round the pen at ground level, 3ft and 6ft 6 inches high. To do this purchase sufficient rolls of such wire which may be 300–600 yards long, therefore for a pen 300 yards in perimeter you will need at least 900 yards of wire.

You will require a special device which allows the plain wire to unwind in a manageable way. This spins on a short stob with the wire enclosed by a frame that allows the wire to be pulled straight for any distance. The correct end of the wire to be pulled is normally marked by a label. As the wire is taken round the pen it should be stapled to the occasional post at the appropriate height. The steeple should only be hammered in a short way as the wire must be able to move freely to be tightened.

Take the wire about 100 yards, depending on the post which will have to be braced, then having first wound the wire round the gatepost and secured it using staples, pull the wire using a wire strainer which can be purchased from an agricultural supplier. When you have reached the required tension, hammer the staple home on the braced post so that the wire cannot slip loose, then cut the wire, leaving enough surplus to be wound round the post, another staple securing the end with any spare wire being wound tightly round the tensioned wire. Radishers, which are fitted directly onto the wire then tightened with both ends already secured, are an alternative which have the advantage of the wire being adjusted for tension after the pen has been built.

You should now have a pen of 300 yards perimeter with the required gateways and three tight wires at ground level, 3ft and 6ft 6 inches. The next step is to attach rabbit netting to the tensioned wire. This net is supplied in 50 metre rolls 3ft 6 inches high and therefore you will need to purchase 12 rolls to clad this size of pen. Unclip the net so that the end is free, then fix this end to the gatepost, allowing plenty of overlap. Roll the net out on the ground until it is fully unwound, then clip the top to the 3ft high wire using a purpose-made tool which clips wire to net, an indispensable item for anyone building any number of pens and again available from game or agricultural suppliers.

At each post, pull the net to tighten it as much as possible, then staple the top of the wire to the post to hold it in position. The bottom of the net should be pushed in with the surplus net forming a lip which should prevent a fox or dog digging into the pen. Any areas where there is a gap should be covered with extra net. The clipping tool should be used to attach the bottom of the net to the wire at ground level and the net stapled lightly to the posts.

The top net is fixed in as similar way, being clipped to both middle and top wire and again stapled lightly to the posts. The netting does not have to be very tight, although it will look better if it is, but a slightly slack net is preferable because it is more difficult for a fox or cat to climb.

The lip at ground level will have to be pinned down, as well as a strip being placed on the ground at the gateways to stop a fox or dog digging in there. The easiest way to do this is to use wire pins made from 10 inch–1ft long lengths of plain soft wire bent to shape. A roll of suitable wire should be purchased and taped round so that the coil is restrained.

An angle grinder is then used to slice through the roll producing a large number of lengths of wire in a short time. The pins should be pushed home alternately next to the plain wire and the edge of the netting about 6–9 inches apart.

The doors can now be fitted. A good idea if the pen will be driven out on shooting days is to provide large doors to enable birds to run out of the pen in the desired direction. Such strategically placed doors are more trouble to build at the time but are most worthwhile in the following season when they merely need to be shut as opposed to major work entailed where the net is pulled up or even holes cut in it which are the usual alternatives. The uprights of the gates can be formed from poles cut to 6ft 6 inches, a hinge system created by driving the piece 1ft 6 inches into the ground next to the doorframe. A hole is drilled in the top of this post and a 5–6 inch nail with the head cut off is placed in the hole. A similar hole is drilled in the upright of the door, this being placed over the nail so that the door can swing, a wire loop retaining the top of the door to the door frame.

Electric fence

An electric fence should be built round the pen, unless the shoot is in the enviable position of being totally fox-free. The same high tensile wire should be used, the ideal being three wires six inches apart supported by purpose-made stanchions with short posts and insulators being placed at the corners where there is tension. One set of wires should be strung about 2ft from the perimeter of the pen. This will protect poults which have flown out from inside the pen then returned to the pen but have been unable to gain entry. These poults will often 'jug' out next to the wire on the outside of the pen and are extremely vulnerable to predation from foxes.

A single wire can be run at right angles to the pen out 20–50 yards spaced about 20 yards apart. These wires will deter a fox from circling the pen outside the original electric fence, although many keepers believe that once a fox has received a shock it will never come near the pen again. This is difficult to prove or disprove but there can be no doubt that, on most shoots, electric fences will improve returns. Having said that, most keepers still place snares on paths and runs approaching their pens as you cannot be too careful where the red menace is concerned.

Further protection

Pop-holes or fox grids should be placed every 50 yards round the pen. These can be 18 inch-long cylinders of wire netting 4–5 inches in diameter and about 4 inches above the ground. This will allow young poults to get back into the pen but the drawback obviously is that undesirables may use them also. For this reason, for the first week or so after they are opened at least, they should be closed in late afternoon, especially if you think that a number of birds have still not started to go up to roost. Fox grids can be bought and are, as the name implies, a grid about 2ft wide by a foot high with rods 3½–4 inches apart, the theory being that poults can enter but foxes can't, a theory which I suggest you never put to the test – and build that electric fence!

Alternative release technique

Some keepers use 10ft x 10ft pens made from four 10ft sections to release. The technique to release, say, 500 poults, would be to erect five 10ft x 10ft pens in the selected release-pen wood. The pens would obviously be covered by a top net and 25 poults placed in each, food and water provided. Outside the pen, similar hoppers and drinkers would be placed so that after a week some birds could be released. As with the large open-topped pens an electric fence is desirable and should protect the poults in the vicinity of the pens.

After a few days all the pens will be empty and should be immediately re-filled and the process repeated until all the birds are released. This system has the advantage of being flexible: the pens can be moved every year to a new site, it is less expensive, the poults are not restricted on stale ground for such a long period and, if required, the sections can be removed so that no signs of birds having been released are left for guns to see during the shooting season.

In days past most keepers fed birds using a regular hand-feeding programme, the birds being accustomed to coming to feed on hearing the keeper calling or whistling. The regime was strict, with each feed being timed to the minute and the amount carefully measured so that the birds were never over-hungry or over-fed. The birds were fed twice or even three or four times a day, especially if adequate labour was available. One wonders if this was totally necessary and the reasons for such demands perhaps came from a headkeeper who could check on his undermen easily if he knew the exact time they would be at a certain pen and could watch and catch out any dilatory keeper.

Hoppers versus hand-feeding

Nowadays many shoots use hoppers exclusively, especially large commercial shoots where keepers may be shooting 4–6 days per week, with hoppers being filled whenever the keeper has a spare day, or night. Returns from hoppers and hand-feeding vary considerably from shoot to shoot. Some shoots achieve perfectly acceptable returns from hopper feeding, while keepers on other estates swear that only hand-feeding will be satisfactory on their particular patch.

My own view is that it all depends on the quality of your woods and the proximity of alternative cover. On an estate with good, warm, game-holding coverts, with game crop available and bare uninviting ground surrounding these, hoppers will be successful. However, if woods are draughty and unattractive, hand-feeding will be necessary, with the birds kept sharp for two or three days before a shoot and not fed on the day of the shoot so that they hang around to be fed and hopefully are intercepted by the keeper and his beaters.

A compromise between hoppers and hand-feeding can be arrived at by feeding hoppers plus a light feed of game mixture. This is a mixture of seeds which is usually soaked in aniseed or similar and can be purchased from game feed suppliers. It is also expensive and must be used sparingly, perhaps mixed at one part mixture to five or six parts wheat. As the shoot day approaches, let the hoppers empty so that no feed is present in them perhaps two days before the shoot day, then treat feed as you would in a hand-feeding scenario. After the shoot, refill the hoppers with just enough to see them through to the period just prior to the next shoot.

Partridges are normally released in 10ft x 10ft pens in a similar way to the method described for pheasants, although some shoots build larger pens 30ft x 30ft with a top net and gradually leak a few birds 20–25 at a time, leaving some birds in the pen for as long as possible, as this undoubtedly helps to hold the released birds.

It is best for a number of release points to be situated in each drive, so that a steady stream of birds go over the guns. The pens should be spread from the start of the drive and should not be placed too near the guns so that birds will fly forward and land in cover which should not be situated closely in front of the gun stands. These birds are more likely to get up in ones and twos than when flushed from the vicinity of a pen situated near the guns. If the pens are too near the guns, the birds will tend to go over them in one large flush. The pens should be placed so that when the keeper approaches them to feed, the released birds flush in the direction that they will be driven on a shooting day, otherwise difficulties may be experienced, with birds going back over the beaters' heads on the shooting day proper.

Partridge feeding

Feeding of partridges is usually done by hoppers, small grower pellets being popular as opposed to straight wheat. The game mix with wheat can be scattered near the pens daily or even every second day, some keepers using a spinner which is fixed to a quad bike. This is a way of scattering a large quantity of feed in a short space of time. The spinner is battery powered and has been developed as a result of the demand from large commercial shoots which must distribute large quantities of feed in as short a time as possible. With all types of feeding, the keeper should check that all the feed from previous visits has been eaten. If it has not, there may be a problem: a fox or bird of prey may be disturbing the birds on the feed, they may have strayed or it could be simply that they are being over-fed. This obviously should be corrected either by missing a feed or reducing the amount of feed, possibly both, experience being a great help in making such decisions.

General care

The keeper must do all he can for his charges, providing for all their needs, feed, water, grit etc. He must also ensure that his birds are not disturbed in any way. This may lead to a clash with dog walkers who cannot understand why they cannot hunt their dogs through your woods containing hundreds of birds which you have spent hours, days and weeks protecting from weather and predators, rearing them from day-olds. It is a basic rule of pheasant keepering: 'keep your woods quiet'. The same applies to partridges, although they will return to the pens, especially if there is a call bird, more quickly than a pheasant after disturbance.

Duck-release

Ducks are usually released to ponds at 6–8 weeks old and it will be a further eight weeks before they can fly strongly enough to leave the pond. The secret of successful shooting using reared mallard is to source suitable duck for release. Some suppliers are only interested in selling a large number of ducks and are not bothered how they perform on shooting days. It is important therefore to source from reputable game farms which supply pure-bred mallard from a strain which is known to fly and possess much of the wild bird's qualities.

The first time I tried reared duck I did my homework and did everything to the book, well aware of the horror stories which are told whenever reared duck are mentioned. The results were appalling. The ducks would not leave the water and those that eventually did circled round the ponds and would not leave the vicinity. My employer was understandably not happy with the duck and it took all my powers of persuasion to convince him to try duck the next season, albeit on a greatly reduced scale. I tried a different game farm and treated the ducks as before but this time with brilliant results. High and sporting, these duck flew far into the distance along with wild wigeon, teal and even geese which they had attracted to join them on the large pond which was their home. Guns who had turned their noses up at reared duck had to admit that they were difficult and sporting birds and a great future was predicted for duck shooting on my estate. Unfortunately this did not happen. As the reader will find out, perhaps to his cost, in the shooting and keepering world, everyone remembers tales of a disaster rather than a triumph and I was saddled with the tag of being the keeper of the ducks that would not fly, so duck shooting was discontinued on the estate after three or four seasons, wrongly in my opinion.

Duck feeding

The feeding of ducks is an important factor in ensuring success. Two or three days' feed should be put down at a time, with the supply never being allowed to run out. This will stop the ducks from approaching the keeper looking for feed, which is undesirable. Contact must be kept to a minimum otherwise the ducks will become over-tame.

Pellets can be fed from hoppers or troughs for two or three weeks, with some flaked and whole barley being added gradually until the birds are completely off pellets. The flaked barley is useful as it floats over the pond and keeps them occupied for long periods of the day. If by some chance (perhaps wild birds coming to the pond) the feed runs out, try to feed at another part of the pond so that the ducks do not associate you with the food. It is essential that the ducks retain their fear of man.

Dummy run

The ducks will start to fly at 15–18 weeks and will start to fly of their own accord, taking short flights around the pond. When you consider that the vast majority are capable of flying, it is the time to give them a dummy run of what will happen on a shooting day. Enlist the help of one or two colleagues and approach the pond from the direction you would on a shooting day. Wear fluorescent jackets or use fluorescent flags and try to surprise them. A gun should be placed where the guns will stand on a shooting day to salute the birds as they pass.

Hopefully the duck will lift and fly high and fast out over the gun stands. If this is the case you need only repeat the exercise once more before the first shoot. If they do not fly and merely swim to the far end of the pond you may have to stretch a length of sewelling between you and your colleague. Do not send a dog into the water before the shoot as the duck may learn that they can avoid a dog merely flying a short distance from one end of the pond to the other and your dog will exhaust himself trying to catch them. This should not happen, however, if you have bought wisely and followed my instructions, and you will find that reared duck are easy and rewarding, giving variety on a shoot and invigorating drives which have become stale.

Multi-variety drives

Multi-variety drives are loved by guns. They do not know what to expect next. A drive which normally held only pheasants can be revolutionised by the introduction of partridges and, if water is available, ducks. Many keepers keep partridges and pheasants apart because pheasants tend to raid partridge hoppers and so hand-feeding becomes impossible. The answer is to feed pellets in the hoppers and feed a game mix to both partridges and pheasants. Duck should be fed whole wheat at the water's edge with some in the water. This system, while not producing the best returns, provides shooting of variety that is well worth the effort and gives your shoot a signature which will be recognised far and wide.

A final note on the siting of release pens. Most people are aware of the technique where birds are released at one point, then fed some distance away so that they can be driven back to their home wood. Hand-feeding is advised in these circumstances as the birds can be whistled short distances each day until they are being fed in their new wood.

If it is impractical to feed from one wood to another (perhaps because disturbance of some sort keeps driving birds back to the pen) it is quite possible to put the pen in the drive itself. This will work better if one of the new strain of pheasant, such as French ring-neck, byzanty, Kansas, large Mongolian or Michigan blue-back is selected. All of these strains are wilder than the old English black-neck but of course there is always a catch, as returns are always lower with the new strains. These new breeds of pheasants are so wild that long before the end of the season they are running and flying out of the woods before beaters are even entering the wood. Some keepers say that it is a waste of time hand-feeding these birds as they are so wild that they will never come to feed after the first shoot, indeed this is a disadvantage of these new strains as they will desert a drive if a period of not less than two weeks is not left between shoots.

The old black-neck is placid, will tolerate much disturbance, can be shot every week if need be and will hang around in one wood while the next is being shot, so you have a choice. I like to adopt a 'horses for courses' approach, using French ring-necks where needed but having a percentage of black-neck crosses as insurance that there will be some birds at least.

Summary

In conclusion, the young keeper who has bluffed his way into a job and has doubts as to his knowledge and ability should be frank with an experienced keeper and admit that he needs help. Most keepers are willing to help, as they are basically softies under that gruff exterior (honest!). Where he has questions about the incubators or brooders which he has inherited, he should contact the manufacturer or game supplier to gain the information he requires. He should be meticulous in checking existing equipment and pens, as a small hole in wire netting allowing poults to prematurely escape can ruin the entire season. If all else fails and he works day and night providing his charges with all their needs, using common sense and stockmanship, he will surely succeed.

CHAPTER EIGHT

Shoot Day Management

You now have your birds on the shoot where you want them and you have your shooting dates. The most important thing to do now is to check that you have beaters to enable you to drive the birds over the guns.

Beaters

Beaters come in all shapes and sizes, all ages and all social backgrounds. If you have arrived on a shoot and have no contacts, the previous keeper perhaps having left under a cloud, you will have to start from scratch recruiting beaters. This can be difficult, especially if you have moved some distance from your last post and cannot take your team of beaters with you. If you have loyal beaters, some may travel huge distances to fulfil their obligation to you. It is a sign of a good keeper when he can count on beaters who will endure severe weather, long car journeys and often the wrath of their spouses to turn up on each and every shooting day on a particular estate. These beaters should be looked after, as they are like gold dust to the keeper, being able to be trusted with jobs such as stopping at corners of a wood or blanking in a hedge, from which birds escape, often without having to be told, sharing in the triumphs and disasters that occur on every shoot as if they were their own.

It is desirable to have at least five of these die-hard beaters on every day that you shoot, as they can take the outside and the middle of each beat. This will ensure that the line does not break (a large gap appearing in the line with one side falling behind the other allowing birds to escape). If your woods are large and you need to employ twenty beaters or more, these accomplished beaters will keep an eye on less experienced beaters when the line is out of sight of the keeper, especially if the cover is heavy.

The previous keeper, of course, may have taken his beaters with him, so you will have start from scratch if this is the case. However, make enquiries, find out if any of the regular beaters can be contacted and if so ask them for phone numbers of other beaters who used to beat for the estate. By doing this you may unearth other contacts until you have a manageable number of beaters available. Estate workers can be enlisted, and if they are interested they will almost certainly approach you and offer their services.

On some estates, especially in days gone by, estate workers were press-ganged into service. This was not very satisfactory as many objected to beating, especially if the weather was not pleasant, and they could be awkward to say the least. This often led to the keeper deploying them as stops, which at least removed them from the beating line, where their bolshie character often proved infectious to the other beaters. This scenario may seem strange to outsiders looking in on the traditional country estate but the perception of all estate workers being obliged to sing to the same hymn sheet, is a fallacious one: with internecine rivalries and jealousies being frequent rather than the exception.

Estate quarrels and beating

If this seems strange, the situation on some estates where a number of keepers are employed is even stranger! Rivalry between keepers can become serious and damaging, especially if the headkeeper is weak and/ or unpopular. This can lead to keepers assisting on other beats, deliberately missing cover or allowing birds to run out of a wood. The poor underkeeper on a shoot in which he is expected to run the beaters while the headkeeper stays with the guns will encounter bloody-mindedness as he tries to organise beaters; the rival keepers using their seniority to brow beat the underkeeper into cutting corners. These cowardly acts, which are usually only inflicted on a young inexperienced man, are to be condemned and are one of the reasons why estates do not employ numbers of keepers nowadays, preferring to let their land to syndicates or commercial shoots who take the responsibility of employing keepers.

As the season progresses you will find out which of your beaters are good, which are bad and which indifferent. If everything is going to plan, with no friction between beaters and no unpleasant incidents with guns or even yourself, it is best to carry on to the end of the season maintaining the status quo. You can always adjust things next season if you can find better beaters but always remember, beggars cannot be choosers and you may not be able to improve your beating force: sometimes you have to accept that nothing in life is perfect. However, if a beater is upsetting other beaters or the guns, he must be told that he is no longer welcome. Be sure of your case and do not go off at half cock without good reason for your action. It is best to face the man at the end of the day and tell him his services are no longer required. He may not be happy and will probably call you to the dogs in the surrounding countryside, but such is life, especially if you are a gamekeeper, who is seldom without a detractor of some sort in the district.

Poachers as beaters

The subject of employing poachers is a delicate one. The problem is that many beaters have done a fair bit of poaching in their time, and you would be showing them your woods (although they may have had a look themselves beforehand) which they could use to their advantage. The answer, I think, is to judge the man, not his past. If your instincts tell you to trust him, then go ahead, but if you have a gut feeling that he will be more trouble than he is worth, then avoid him like the plague. Remember that if you employ such a man and have to ban him later, he may be the type to take revenge, which will cause you much time and trouble to prevent.

Respect your beaters

Treat all beaters with the same respect, whether they are schoolchildren (who can make excellent beaters) or pensioners, again good beaters. Treat them the way you would expect to be treated yourself, making sure that any rebukes for not being in line, for instance, are justified and not excessive. The keeper has a difficult line to tread here, as he must gain the respect of the beaters but at the same time not alienate or, in some cases, frighten them!

One tip I can give is to enlist the help of one of your experienced beaters who is in on the act with you. Brief him in advance that he will receive a severe reprimand at the start of the second drive. This is best done during the second or third day, leaving two or three days between each deception. The other beaters will note that one of your trusted beaters has been chastised and will automatically take care not to incur your wrath for some time after this. Swearing and abuse, although understandable when things go wrong, should be avoided as it does the keeper no credit, especially to the guns who can often hear every word that the keeper utters throughout the day. A calm keeper who uses his authority in a quiet confident way will always command more respect than a keeper who curses and shouts his way through the day.

Pickers-up

Pickers-up are essential on any shoot as they obviously gather birds which have been shot. Most shoots wait till the drive has ended before commencing picking-up, although runners should be tried for immediately if the pickers-up dog can be trusted to follow that particular bird and deliver it to hand without being distracted by the shooting which is still going on.

The numbers of pickers-up can vary from shoot to shoot but normally there will be a minimum of four for a team of eight guns. This minimum would apply to a day of 100–200 birds. Where numbers are expected to be larger than this, it is preferable to have eight pickers-up, one to each gun. This means that a picker-up can count his gun's birds down, then aim for this figure at the end of the pick-up.

Many shoots, as well as employing pickers-up, utilise back markers, where this is practical. These men take up a position often 200 yards behind the line, picking-up pricked birds which have only been lightly touched or which collapse a long way behind the guns. This is only possible on grouse moors, partridge shoots or pheasant shoots where there is a large area of ground between the drives and, most importantly, a return drive is not intended, the ground to be driven on the second drive having to be left undisturbed.

There are usually more candidates for the role of picker-up than for beater. This is because there is more glamour attached to picking-up than beating: it is almost a class division. Many people like to tell their friends that they pick-up on Lord so-and-so's estate, this carrying a certain social kudos that beating does not.

It is often thought that picking-up is less physically demanding than beating but, as anyone will tell you who has done both, it is actually harder work to pick-up where the job is done properly. A good picker-up must be conscientious and do all in his power to pick-up birds which have been shot. This may take time, so a picker-up may have to be left behind to collect difficult birds, rejoining the team halfway through the next drive.

This means that he must know the ground well and may need to be provided with transport if the distance to the next drive is great. It may be necessary to allow him to use his own vehicle and pay him extra for the fuel that he will use, or failing this, the driver of the game cart can wait for him and bring him to the next drive.

I like to promote keen beaters who have suitable dogs to pick-up from the beater's ranks. It can affect morale if pickers-up are brought in over the head of an ambitious beater, so weigh up your options carefully, bearing in mind that a good beater is often harder to replace than a moderate picker-up. Field trial wannabees often use picking-up to gain valuable experience for their dogs and you must assess each one at face value. Remember that, unless they have rough and ready dogs available, they may be reluctant to allow their dogs free rein to hunt cover for fallen birds. They may also miss important days because they are attending field trials, which in the case of retrievers are held over two days. The danger may also be that a cabal of field trialers will turn your days into a mock field trial for their own ends, using their powers of persuasion to beguile your employer, especially when you are absent during a drive.

Field trials

While on the subject of field trials, it may be that your employer has been persuaded to host such a day, either because he is interested in dogs or feels an obligation to help in the promotion of gun-dogs or field trials. In days gone by, the majority of the competitors at field trials were ex-gamekeepers, professional trainers or amateurs from a shooting background. This is not the case nowadays, the average field trialer having only a rudimentary knowledge of shooting or game preservation.

Be prepared to be patronised as you have never been before, as every year trial ground is lost because of the lack of respect afforded to the keeper on shoots which have been generously donated and expensive birds provided for the pleasure of the field trial elite.

Retriever trials

Retriever trials are usually run on the lines of a walked-up day, the ground utilised being a crop such as turnips, sugar beet, kale or just rough ground. The estate, often the keeper, supplies the guns, who should be competent and 6–8 are usually required. Four dogs will be in the line at a time, with a judge or judges taking two at a time.

The line will be wide, including guns, judges handlers and their dogs as well as game carriers and sometimes spaniels and their handlers to flush birds. The line will proceed at a good pace so you will need a large tract of land if game is scarce. You are in charge of the line and whereever it goes, you are the steward of the beat. This means that, not just where the line goes, but the pace of the line is in your power. This is important, as often the line goes too fast and walks over game. No matter what anyone says, you are in charge. If there is an accident or the day is not successful, the buck stops with you and you will carry the can.

You will encounter judges, trial secretaries, stewards and field trial committee members, but at the end of the day they are but chaff before you and they must bow to your will. If this does not suit, then so be it, and you should not lose any sleep over what is, at best, a thoroughly enjoyable day and at worst a boring inconvenience.

Spaniel trials

Spaniel trials are run on different lines, with a maximum of four guns, two to each of the two dogs which run at a time. Sixteen dogs form a stake, with each run lasting 15–20 minutes and a minimum of 32 head of game should be shot. A redeeming factor for the keeper is that spaniel trials are best run on rabbits so precious birds do not have to be wasted. As in retriever trials, this is your responsibility, so do not be afraid to take charge and impose your will. The ground cover should be light enough for the dogs to be seen working and the game shot easily but not too light and bare that rabbits will not lie in it.

Rabbits should be stunk out as described in the vermin chapter, the only certain way of ensuring that they will be above ground on the day of the trial. The main mistake that keepers make when stinking out is to treat the holes too late, too near to the trial date. At least 10 days before is a general rule and two weeks is even better. Burrows surrounding the trial ground should be 'stunk out', the repellent used liberally so that even the cover above ground is affected, while the trial ground itself should be ferreted using a muzzled ferret or a young bitch, the holes being blocked after they have been evacuated. This will yield the best results and ensure that the trial is a success.

Preparation for the shoot

In the days and weeks leading up to the first shoot, walk the drives quietly and try to anticipate any problems which are likely to occur when the woods are actually driven. A piece of thick cover which would hold birds but could not be penetrated by even the keenest beater may need to be thinned using a power saw or hedge knife.

Stiles may need to be renewed or new ones built over walls or barbed wire fences, this applying to guns, beaters and pickers-up. Release pens should be checked in case birds gather in a corner and fly back rather than run to the flushing points in the wood.

Check that the cover in the woods still lends itself to the birds flying over the guns. This may seem obvious but the cover in a wood changes so rapidly from year to year that birds may gather at, say, a fallen tree, then fly out through the gap at the edge of the wood so created, causing the keeper much frustration which can be avoided if the cover is cleared and a stop or cover is placed to deter birds from exiting at this point.

The transport of beaters should be thought out long before the first shooting day. Some estates use a tractor and trailer with straw bales as seats. This may be satisfactory but the legality of such transport should be checked, bearing in mind that third party public liability insurance may only cover the estate if you can prove that you took appropriate measures to ensure the safety of beaters when they were being transported from drive to drive. Ex-army four-wheel personnel transporters are utilised by many shoots as a safe, cost-effective way of moving beaters. Check that you do not need a heavy goods vehicle licence if you are travelling for any distance on a public road. It may seem obvious but the driver of the vehicle which moves the beaters should be competent and experienced.

Shoot safety

Beaters should be offered safety glasses before every shoot, because some insurance companies may not cover a claim for eye damage where it cannot be proved that adequate precautions were taken to avoid injury. The bottom line is to check with your insurance and get it in writing if there is any doubt.

Other areas for concern are stiles, both for beaters and guns, which should be checked for rot before the shooting season. Treated rails and posts should always be used with a metal rod on top of the rails to ensure safety and any flat surfaces covered with spare rabbit netting and stapled down to prevent slipping, especially with older green wood.

Bridges should be built where necessary to allow beaters to access parts of a wood which would otherwise be missed or driven in the wrong direction, as well as facilitating the journey of the guns from their vehicles to their shooting pegs.

Pegs

Pegs should be placed well before the first shoot as any problems which might have been unforeseen can be remedied well in advance of the first day. I prefer short posts with plastic numbers fixed to them by felt nails, although some people use a heavy duty staple gun. The plastic numbers can be purchased or obtained free from a feed firm or game farm, who gain free advertising from their deployment on your shoot.

The pegs are usually 50–60 yards apart, although they can be wider apart or closer if you have a good reason for this. A straight line is preferable but in some circumstances you may have to bring the end guns round at an angle, where for instance birds tend to go back. If the pegs are 18 inches long and driven into the ground, cattle and sheep will be unable to knock them over, which removes the necessity of gathering and replacing the pegs after every shoot.

Facilities

Your beaters should have a comfortable shed, barn or room with a heater and proper tables and chairs. Toilet facilities and an area where wet clothes can be hung up are also desirable: remember you are competing with other shoots in the district. When a shoot cannot obtain enough beaters, the reasons are never hard to find and the main one is usually that they are not treated well enough or just simply treated badly.

Final checks

Go over the day in your mind from every aspect and every detail. Where will you take the beaters to blank in before the first drive? How far back will you need to go? How will the beaters' wagon be moved so that it will be available to take the beaters to the next drive? It is often best to nominate one person that you can trust to go back after the drive and recover the beaters' wagon, delivering it to the desired location or if this would be too great a distance he can take it there before the drive has started and go to a pre-arranged point to stop. Planning such as this must take place before the day itself, with alternative strategies worked out so that every eventuality can be covered.

Sharp birds

As has been pointed out previously, birds should be kept sharp, ie. have their food-supply curtailed, before a shoot, either by allowing hoppers to run down and having a hand-feeding system replace this, or in the case of a purely hand-fed shoot, the amount should be reduced leading up to the shoot.

On the morning of the shoot the drives which are to be shot should not be fed. Some keepers who are fortunate enough to have an underkeeper, use him to whistle in birds and lightly feed them just prior to the drive.

When the guns and beaters are in place, the underkeeper should discreetly move on to the next drive, being careful to ensure that the guns do not see him practising his deception as it is imperative on any well-run shoot that the guns see no sign that the birds are anything other than wild and free.

Weight of responsibility

As the first day approaches, most keepers become nervous, especially if he is new to his position or indeed it is his first head or single-handed position where he has full responsibility. Some experience sleepless nights, a situation which will do nothing to help his performance on the day, but this recedes with experience. Indeed, on commercial shoots, exhaustion soon arrives to cure any such problems. This may seem inexplicable to the uninitiated but the gamekeeper is one of the few people in life who displays the fruits of his labour and his skills for all to see: there is no hiding place for the keeper when things go wrong. Guns, beaters and pickers-up will all look to him to salvage his reputation as a disaster develops. It can be a very lonely place, with a distance almost visibly growing between yourself and people who you thought were your friends: failure is indeed an orphan and success indisputably has a thousand fathers. To avoid this scenario, the keeper should graft and plan so that the day itself is the easy part and he can then relax and enjoy it.

Equipment
Flags or sticks should be provided for the beaters, the sticks having been cut months previously and allowed to dry out. Make more than you need, as many are lost or broken during the season. Flags can be made from plastic feed bags stapled or fixed to sticks by felt nails.

Pay your beaters well: check that you are not the lowest payer in the district because although money is not the be-all and end-all of securing beaters, it helps. Many shoots give the beaters a can of beer which some drink at lunch but most take home to enjoy that night.

Count-down on the day
It is the morning of your first shoot. Rise early and check that everything is ready for use: beaters pay, beer, flags, sticks, dog leads, whistles, horns and radios.

Radios are important as they provide a link between you and your furthest beater, the pickers-up and the guns. Many employers do not wish to be encumbered with a radio on a shooting day, which is understandable as they want to enjoy a day out with their friends, without having an anxious keeper bending their ear at every critical point during the day. He pays you to carry the responsibility and worries of the day, and taking the strain is part of the keeper's job and you must learn to live with the pressure.

Arrive at the meeting point as early as possible, feeding drives early or the previous evening that are not due to be shot that day. If areas are to be blanked in before the first drive, send experienced and reliable men to do this, having briefed them beforehand as to their duties. New beaters and ones that you have not seen since the previous season should be greeted by a handshake and thanks for turning up, which makes them feel wanted and greatly improves morale.

Most employers like to introduce the guns to the gamekeeper before the start of the day. This usually means that the keeper must leave the beaters and move to the big house where the guns are assembling. A quick handshake and a few words are all that are required, as the purpose of this exercise is to allow the guns to recognise you throughout the day. Lose no time in returning to the beaters and getting the show on the road.

I prefer to pay my beaters at the beginning of the day, as it saves time later when things are liable to get hectic. Perhaps I have been lucky but no-one, as yet, has absconded on receiving the money. This is one of the critical times of the day. If you do not exercise your authority now, some beaters may drag their heels, holding everybody back when you should be getting into position for the first drive.

If you are starting at 9.30am you must ask your boss if this means moving off from the big house at 9.30am or being in position at the first drive at 9.30am. This varies from shoot to shoot and obviously timing is important. You must gauge how long it will take for the guns to get into position and also how long the beaters will take to get to the other end. If birds are on their toes for some reason (human disturbance, foxes, dogs or poaching) it is important that beaters are not in position for a long period before the guns. This is especially the case where cover is scarce and the modern strains of pheasant are present. The ideal situation is where guns and beaters arrive almost simultaneously into position. This also ensures that shooting commences almost immediately the guns are in position, a desirable situation. The alternative, where there is a long wait before any action, is to be avoided at all costs.

Starting the drive

Check, using your radio, that the guns are in position, then start the drive. This is the time of anxiety, especially on a new shoot, but such feelings will quickly disappear as the shooting starts, a good show of birds making the keeper relax and enjoy the drive.

Watch your beaters carefully. Some become almost entranced by large numbers of birds and the number of shots fired, losing concentration and taking no notice of the rest of the beaters. Correct them when they go wrong: gentle nagging is better than a full blast, which some sensitive souls find humiliating. Time and experience will teach you how to get the best out of your men.

The birds may not be going exactly the way you want them to go, perhaps funnelling over 2–3 guns. In these circumstances hold one end of the line and bring the other on. This can be difficult when you are new to a team of beaters but if you persevere explaining to them what you want them to do, and why, you will eventually produce an efficient team of beaters that can provide top class shooting.

If you have plenty of birds, experiment with the way you drive the birds, holding one side of the line then the other to see what difference it makes. Stops can also be moved. This can sometimes produce startling results with birds flying higher to avoid them. Always try to drive pheasants across the wind; this will provide the most difficult birds, producing curl and drift, although skill is required on the part of the keeper to get the birds over the guns.

When addressing the beaters it is a good idea to refer to them as 'gentlemen', as no one can object to that. As a general rule of thumb, guns should be addressed as 'Sir' unless your boss requests you to use some other term. For instance if the gun really is a 'Sir', he may like to be addressed as 'Sir Michael' or if he is a Duke, 'Your Grace' would be appropriate. Members or ex-members of the armed forces can be difficult as it can be a massive faux pas to under-rank them, especially where (this has unfortunately happened to me) two members of different rank are present on the same day and you mix them up. Due to this, whenever I am in any doubt I address such guns with the highest rank I can think of, assuming that over-ranking will cause less offence.

As the drive unfolds, check by radio with the head picker-up as to how successfully the guns are performing. You have probably been given a target for the day, say 300 birds from six drives, so obviously fifty birds would be the cut-off point if all the drives are expected to yield the same number of birds. When the head picker-up estimates that 40 birds are down, he should be primed to notify you of this. You must now gauge how many will be shot if you take the wood out steadily. If this will add too many to the bag, then you should either push the beaters through quickly or pull them out to the flanks, allowing the bulk of the birds to run back. Some keepers put their dog in but this may appear to be unprofessional – or the dog may do a better job than anticipated.

Timing

Be careful at the end of the each drive that the beaters do not become embroiled in the pick-up if you are short of time. This is because enthusiastic dog men can get far away and be difficult to recover, meaning that either you will be late for the next drive, or you will leave a beater behind. Ground rules should be laid down at the start of the day as to where and when beaters can assist with the pick-up, always checking with you before moving off to make sure that it is permitted. I am not, however, against beaters using their dogs to pick-up *per se*: it is a just reward for the work that they put in during a day to help to make it a success. The last drive before lunch and at night are good opportunities for the beaters to give their dogs a chance of a retrieve. Some pickers-up do not approve of this, wishing to keep clear water between the two groups and also perhaps not wishing to be embarrassed when a beater's dog succeeds where his paragon has failed. If you have a picker-up who does not approve of your policy in this matter, he has plenty of other alternative avenues to follow where he can work his dogs. You are in charge and the tail must never wag the dog.

Paid pickers-up?

As regards paying pickers-up, there has been some speculation in the shooting press that pickers-up should not be paid, it being claimed that the enjoyment they gain equals or exceeds the enjoyment the guns experience, therefore they should provide their services free of charge. This is balderdash and the keeper should have no truck with such a move, as he would lose all control and be unable to ask the pickers-up to do unpleasant tasks. The amount they are paid should be the same as the beaters receive. They would not swap and a shoot could carry on without pickers-up, but it cannot survive without beaters.

Lunch

After each drive your boss may wish to speak to you – or he may not. Ascertain his wishes beforehand as this will avoid misunderstandings. Lunch will arrive and it is best to leave the beaters to their own devices. They can relax when you are not there and discuss your performance freely without fear of offending you! Be sure to have the beaters assembled for the first drive after lunch in plenty of time to allow you to be in position. There are usually two afternoon drives and they will be, hopefully, the best drives of the day, the last drive especially good so that the guns leave in high spirits.

Sweep on the bag

As the beaters and pickers-up leave, thank them personally, not forgetting to remind them of the next day and how they will be needed. Some may help to hang birds in the game larder, transferring them from the game cart. These volunteers are usually your die hards who will be interested to see how many were in the bag. Some shoots run a sweep on the bag. This means that you will have to mark down beaters' names and expected bag on a card, as well as collecting money. This can be too much trouble for a busy keeper but if it can be done it causes much interest in the day and raises morale.

Final stage

Once you have the bag counted, mark all details on a card and take it to your boss. He may announce the total to the guns or you may be expected to do this. The guns will thank you for their day and it is all over till the next time, bar contacting the game dealer. You should enter the details of the day in the estate game book and make a note of any problems or areas of improvement which could be made for the next shoot in your diary. Improvements may take the form of moving guns further back or in a certain direction at some drives or changing the order of the drives. In an ideal world, a day of six drives would consist of drives of exactly equal quality and quantity but this is seldom realised.

The most important drives are the first, the last before lunch, and the last at night. These should be the best drives and release pens should reflect this but sometimes things do not proceed as predicted and changes must be made.

Your employer may wish to meet you a few days after the first shoot to discuss any improvements which he would like to see, or he may be totally satisfied with your performance and the way the day went. If this is the case you can relax, at least as much as any keeper can relax and enjoy the rest of the season. The work and planning which you instigated months previously have reached fruition.

End-of-season shoots

As the season comes nearer to its end, birds will naturally become scarcer. This is especially true on a commercial shoot where the number of days is far greater than on a private shoot.

On such a private shoot boasting two beats, the keeper may only have to provide 10–16 days shooting, while a keeper on the same size of ground would be expected to provide 30 days for commercial shooting, not to mention perhaps 15–20 rough shooting days. How does a keeper manage to do this seemingly impossible task?

The first requirement is to have plenty of birds. Husbandry has to be excellent otherwise disease will take its toll; and plenty of labour is needed to feed and dog the birds back. The rough shooting days are utilised as a dogging-in operation (in which the birds which have wandered from the pens are rounded up by dogs) with the only difference that the guns shoot birds and pay for the privilege. The workload on the keeper of such shoots is enormous: he will literally never have a spare minute where he is not feeding, dogging-in or running a shooting day.

What then does any keeper do when birds become scarce for whatever reason? The first thing he can do is to stop feeding unproductive drives, even catching up birds and moving them to more attractive woods. This will obviously reduce his options as regards the number of drives available but you will find that favourite woods will produce more birds, even if shot on consecutive days, than the less favoured ones.

Increase the tempo of the days so that you can increase the number of drives to eight or nine, the slightly longer days of January being helpful in this respect. While it is desirable to leave a fortnight between shooting a particular wood, if needs must, this can be reduced. I personally have shot the same wood on consecutive days, although in different ways. Hard weather greatly helps in these circumstances which I stress should be the exceptional: the aforesaid planning should have ensured sufficient birds and drives for the anticipated season.

The end of the season

The season will eventually come to an end and the keeper will view this with mixed emotions. If the season has been a tremendous success he will not want it to end, while at the same time he will look forward to the short period after the shooting season ends when the pressure is off.

If the season has been poor or moderate he probably cannot wait for it to end so that he can start work to make amends and improve things for next season, assuming of course that he is still in a job!

The Keeper's Day

The final act of any season for the keeper is to organise the keeper's day. This is where all beaters and pickers-up get the chance to shoot at the cocks which are left at the end of January. The first thing to do is to ascertain which helpers can come on the day or days that you have earmarked for the Keeper's Day. Check that they have public liability insurance as an accident may leave the estate liable for compensation and earn you the sack if the culprit is not insured. Once you have the numbers, work out how you are going to utilise them. 24 beaters can be split into 3 teams of 8. One team beats with the assistance of beaters who do not shoot. These beaters must be paid, usually from a whip-round by the shooting beaters. The standing guns can be double banked, the poorer guns in front. Numbers should be drawn at the beginning of the day, to avoid arguments about preference being given to a particular gun.

The keeper should keep strict discipline on such days, as inexperienced guns can sometimes become excited and take unsafe shots. At the same time, the keeper must not dampen the spirit of the day; indeed he should do all in his power to make it an enjoyable occasion for everyone. This is another example of the nature of the keeper's calling: he must possess a wide variety of qualities which an onlooker would be quite unaware. The Keeper's Day is a way of saying 'thank you' to the people who have helped you in the preceding season. Some employers have short memories when it comes to this day and do not realise its significance, and if the beaters perceive it as a grudged gift, it can lead to difficulties in recruiting in subsequent seasons. If this is the case, the keeper must do all in his power to hide the fact from the beaters, especially to his die-hards. Pigeon shooting, rabbiting, fox lamping and perhaps fishing should be used as a lure to ensure that their services are secured for the coming seasons.

The simplest way for a keeper to alienate his beaters is to invite men to shoot on a Keeper's Day who have not helped on the shoot that season. This happens more than one would think, insult being added to injury when these interlopers stand all day while the beaters beat carrying their guns. This is a very short-sighted policy and usually results in the keeper getting his just desserts, often an inability to recruit beaters and then, usually, dismissal. Do not go down this road!

CHAPTER NINE

Poaching

The punch, when it came, was unannounced and devastating. It was to have great and grave consequences for both of us and I will leave it to the reader to decide who benefited and who was damaged forever.

I had entered the pub on the way home from work one warm April day, the first of the year. I felt in need of some refreshment. As I approached the bar I noticed four men at the far end of the bar, the only customers apart from me. I recognised one of them, Callum Elliot, the keeper's son, who was a builder and I assumed that the other three were also employed in that capacity.

I ordered a pint and started to watch the television above the bar which was showing sport of some kind, which I cannot remember. I felt a touch on my shoulder, then the next thing I knew I was on the ground, my nose broken and Callum Elliot was pulling me up by my lapels, snarling in my face. 'That'll teach you not to poach my faither's pheasants.'

My next recollection, in what was fast turning out to resemble a very bad dream, was being ejected in classic saloon bar fashion by the burly bar-man, who added insult to injury by telling me that I was barred. Despite the pain of my nose and the humiliation suffered, my indelible memory of the incident was noting the laughing faces of the firemen as I travelled airborne through the door.

The doctor at the out-patients department was charming, telling me that the best he could do was to stuff my nose with cotton wool, but he didn't hold much hope, I wasn't exactly a matinee idol. His parting shot as I left was rather patronisingly to tell me not to get into any more fights till it had healed. All this was offered with a look on his face which suggested he had been assailed by a rather bad odour, leaving me even more dispirited than I had been on entering the hospital.

The reader must appreciate that I was innocent of all charges, which made me angry and vengeful, but before I extracted due recompense I decided to give my attacker the chance to explain himself and to justify his actions. My family were well thought of in the area and I thought it better that Callum's father, Bill Elliot, the keeper on the Blackhill Estate, should have a chance to apologise and make redress before a vendetta commenced. So it was that I drew into the yard of the keeper's house on the darkly named Hangman's Hill. A kennel of labradors barked loudly as I left my van and walked up to the house, the front door opening before I reached it and a middle-aged, tough looking man with sandy coloured, wiry hair and a cruiser-weight's build stepped out. I proceeded to argue my case, pleading my innocence and asking for some explanation for his son's actions, hoping that some regret or apology would be forthcoming. Unfortunately I was disappointed. Bill looked me straight in the eye, raising his fist to point a finger in my face which caused me to retreat to remove my nose from further harm's way. 'We know who you are now son, you've been at it and you've been caught.' He moved back to the house, entering the doorway, turning to me. A smug smile appeared on his face and, while looking directly at my injured nose, sniggered, 'You'll no be likely to dae any mair poaching now anyway lad.' The door closed and I heard laughter. Only then did I realise that Callum had been inside listening to the exchange and was now congratulating his father on a job well done.

I had lost rounds 1 and 2 but there was still a long way to go before the final bell would be rung. My first task was to find out the motive for their actions and to this end I asked my uncle, whose farm marched with the Blackhill Estate, for his theories on the matter. He stated that the Blackhill shoot was quite a good shoot, leased by a syndicate of dentists from Edinburgh. They released about a thousand birds and had six days' shooting starting at over a hundred birds and reducing to approximately fifty at the end. All had gone well the first two years of the lease but the third season had been disappointing, the rumour being that Bill Elliot had sold some birds to friends and had supplied a shoot he and Callum ran on the other side of the town with both poults and feed from the Blackhill syndicate. The end result was that the Elliots needed a scapegoat and, because I travelled to and from my uncle's farm past Hangman's Hill, often carrying rabbits on my bicycle, I had been marked down as a poacher who, when circumstances demanded, could become their 'Patsy'. I subsequently learned that Bill had blamed me to the syndicate for the lack of birds adding that his son Callum had sorted me out and that there would be no more trouble from that quarter.

When I heard this I decided that, if I was to be branded a poacher, then so be it, I would be a real poacher, like the ones my grandfather had described to me, a poacher who could strip a shoot so that little was left for the guns who had paid for their sport. I did not take this decision lightly as my grandfather had no time for poachers and had spent his entire working life combating them, so for me to follow this path left me with pangs of guilt. These however, disappeared every time my nose twinged with pain to remind me of the reason for my descent into infamy.

The first requirements for a poaching expedition are reconnaissance and intelligence. Reconnaissance will reveal the location of release pens and access roads and paths to and from them. The areas near the pens where the greatest concentrations of roosting birds are likely to be found are also worth discovering. Intelligence means learning all you can about the keeper. Is he lazy? Is he fit or out of condition? Is he brave or a coward? Does he frequent public houses on a regular basis? Is he clever or stupid? Does he night-watch? Does he own a night-dog? Can you see his vehicle at his house when he is at home? Does he sometimes walk round his beat leaving his vehicle at home?

Other necessary information needed is the attitude towards the keeper of the farmers, farm workers, foresters and estate workers who live on the estate. If they are friendly to the keeper, any strange lights or noises at night will be reported to him, as well as strange vehicles driving slowly round country roads at dawn, dusk or the dead of night. If, however, the keeper is unpopular, the chances of your detection are greatly reduced, as he will have to catch you himself and you do not have to especially worry about another inhabitant of the estate raising the alarm – they will worry little that someone is poaching his birds.

It was fairly easy to gain knowledge of the Blackhill shoot as my uncle was friendly with the main tenant farmer who divulged much information. He gave it willingly, as he had fallen foul of Bill Elliot on a number of occasions. There were five release pens, all accessed by a hard road and all within walking distance at the centre of the shoot. I also learned that Bill took his holidays before his pheasants chicks hatched and again after they went to wood, taking his caravan to tour the British Isles. This was a great advantage to me as Bill parked the caravan in full view of the public road and it was therefore apparent when he was away from home.

From the beginning of May I passed Bill's house at every opportunity until one day the caravan was gone. I returned after dark and the house was in darkness so I decided that the next day I would arrange a day off work and undertake a reconnaissance mission of the Blackhill shoot. I left home at 4.30am and drove to my uncle's farm negotiating a rough hedge-lined track which took me close to the march (the boundary between two estates) but also allowed me to conceal the van. I had but a short walk to the public road which formed the march between the two properties. Crossing the road I was at large on the Blackhill following a forest track, which by my calculations would eventually lead me to one of Bill's release pens.

It was now first light and I observed as much detail as I could. In particular I wanted to know how close to the houses or farms I had to pass and whether or not dogs were present, if so what breed of dog and if they were running loose or confined.

I arrived at the first pen, a sturdy new construction, 50 yards square made from new materials – the syndicate obviously were not short of cash. I noted that the surrounding trees were mature larch and hardwoods and the ground cover was sporadic laurels and rhododendrons. I found all five pens, some larger than others, all linked by the same road which avoided all habitation and was ideal for travelling at night and avoiding detection. I returned to the van without being seen, making a determined effort to memorise the route, remembering that a wrong turning in the dark could be disastrous.

A second excursion to the estate was undertaken in August when Bill took his second holiday, his son Callum looking after the birds in his father's absence. My early morning sojourn allowed me to view the eight-week-old poults in the pens and note which contained the most birds. This would be important if I was to take the maximum number on my first visit. The birds were whistled in to feed which meant that they were always on the hungry side, the theory being that they were less likely to stray as they were always waiting for the next feed. This may be correct but it also made them tamer and more easily approached and it was interesting to see that the birds, far from being alarmed at my presence, were willing to gather round me anticipating their breakfast. I returned home, careful not to leave any footprints or other sign of my presence on the Blackhill. Such a sign would have alerted an observant keeper and made him watchful in order to prevent any raids on his birds. This would have been detrimental to my plans: a complacent and relaxed keeper is always more easily poached than a man who has been forewarned and forearmed.

My next task was to acquire a suitable weapon for my task. This was solved for me because the manager at my work-place had been issued with a 9mm garden gun to shoot feral pigeons in the grain warehouse where I worked. The advent of shotgun certificates and safe storage require-ments meant that he was no longer willing to retain the weapon and he offered it to me as he knew that I had a shotgun certificate. Knowing that the ammunition was expensive for this gun I was reluctant to take it, but my hand was forced when he produced a large cardboard box containing 500 shells less the contents of one opened half-empty carton. This weapon is a useful tool at short range and makes little noise. The fact that it fires shot means that you do not have to be quite so accurate as with a rifle, which is useful on windy nights.

I taped a small torch with a pencil beam to the barrel which served two purposes: firstly it illuminated the target; and secondly it worked like a sight, as placing the centre of the beam on the pheasant's head resulted in a kill every time. My next piece of equipment was a large red Raleigh bicycle with enclosed chain, which was heavy but very strong. This I painted green and brown with matt paint in a camouflaged style, fitting red rear lights low on the front forks facing forwards. I reckoned that by hanging braces of birds on the handlebars, crossbar and the front and back panniers I could transport thirteen brace of birds at a time, my aim being to bag over a hundred pheasants in one night. I was careful to let no-one see the bike as I would possibly have to abandon it should I be discovered and I wanted no connection to such a distinctive vehicle.

My plan was to take the bicycle in my van and hide it in a disused hay shed which lay next to the aforementioned lane, then take the van to the end of the lane which was a short distance from the march. I would walk back to the barn, collect the bike, then cycle to the Blackhill, take the birds in four trips to the march with my uncle's farm, hide them over the hedge then, when my task was complete, cycle back to the hay shed, walk to the van and commence to carry the birds in a rucksack over the field from their hiding place, eventually taking them to the barn in the van where they could be hung to cool.

The weakness in my plan would be the cycle ride to and from the Blackhill where anyone seeing me would wonder what I was up to, especially if they noticed the gun-sleeve strapped to the cross-bar. Also taking the bike into the shoot right up to the pens was likely to make more noise than necessary and if Bill Elliot was night-watching, the game would be up straightaway.

The reader probably wonders why I didn't just go on foot so avoiding this risk. The answer is that the bicycle was essential to carry the number of birds I wished to bag, the pens being some distance from the public road, in the time that I considered I had available where detection was unlikely.

I had decided that the time to go would be as late as possible before the first shoot. This was to allow the leaf to fall from the trees and yet to have the maximum number of still-tame birds available to poach. My intelligence-gathering had revealed that Bill took his wife to a hotel every Saturday night, leaving home at 7.30pm, later visiting a friend's house until midnight, usually arriving home between 12.15–12.30am. This was a regular routine and I checked the hotel car park for three weeks before my poaching trip, to confirm that Bill was there.

On the night of my proposed trip I parked opposite the hotel car park at 7.30pm and after 15 minutes sure enough Bill and his wife arrived. I waited till they had entered the hotel bar, then slowly drove off heading for my uncle's farm. I drove to the end of the lane, collected the bike, gun and ammunition and set off for the Blackhill. There was a three-quarters moon and a 'tuggy' wind which I considered to be near perfect for my task. The only problem was that my 'rear light' lighting system did not illuminate very far in front, meaning that my speed had to be curtailed considerably.

The journey was also stressful because I had to strain my eyes and ears for any sight or sound of a vehicle or pedestrian travelling the same road. My plan if this happened was to switch off the lights and drag the bike into the hedge at the side of the road until my fellow travellers had passed, hoping that my camouflage clothing would allow me to continue unnoticed. If I was compromised, I had decided to return home and leave my expedition for another night as there was just too much risk that someone would tip off the keeper or the police, with whom incidentally I had been led to believe, Bill was extremely friendly, giving them spare birds at Christmas and inviting the local sergeant to his end-of-season cock day.

It was a relief therefore to reach the access road to the Blackhill estate. But relief turned to alarm when I found that instead of an inviting, unbarred entrance to the shoot, I was confronted by a new five barred gate and shiny new padlock. The reason for my alarm was not the obstacle itself, which could be negotiated, albeit with some effort (the old Raleigh was built to last in tubular steel, not light modern alloy) but because it suggested to me that precautions were being taken which had not been hitherto considered and I asked myself what other steps had been taken to deter or apprehend trespassers and poachers. I was now discovering the psychology of the miscreant: all sounds, sights and new obstacles encountered in the execution of his nefarious practices are assumed to be a direct threat. A cool head is a prerequisite for success.

I carefully carried the bike along the edge of the track to ensure no tell-tale tracks were left to betray my entering the estate. Lifting the machine over the gate I carried it up the edge of the track for fifty yards and only then mounted up, heading for the first pen. Reaching my destination I carefully hid the bike, covering the lights with old socks so that they would not reflect any torch shone in their direction. I then set to work.

The first tree holding birds was a large beech absolutely laden with them. The garden gun dropped them efficiently and soon I had a dozen well-fed pheasants. I was surprised how well they sat without flying off which was partially explained later by someone informing me that Bill was in the habit of checking his birds on the rearing field at odd times through the night using a torch. Whether or not it was this, the weather conditions, or the fact that they had never been disturbed, it was ridiculously easy to attain my target of thirteen brace. I carried the birds to the bicycle, loaded up, then set off for the march where I took the birds in relays through the hedge to my uncle's land. I repeated the journey another three times until I had 104 birds laid out in the field.

I headed back to the hay shed, hid the bike, walked to the van and moved the birds using a rucksack, bringing them to the hayshed in the back of the van. The next task was to tie them in braces and hang them up in the barn, by which time I was exhausted and I crawled into a sleeping bag till morning.

Dawn broke and I left the sleeping bag to inspect my booty. In the daylight the pheasants were a magnificent sight and I suddenly felt contrasting emotions of guilt, fear and most strongly, satisfaction that I had done what I had set out to do undetected, without leaving a clue as to my identity. I loaded the birds into my van and made my way to a butcher who normally purchased my rabbits and pigeons. I had warned him beforehand that I may be bringing in some pheasants but his eagerness to do business was curtailed when I opened the back doors of the van, which I had driven in true poacher fashion to the rear of his establishment. 'I didnae realise you were having a massacre son, I cannae shift all these birds, ye'll bankrupt me, whit a pity, whit a shame son, and I'm sorry son, I can only gie ye £25 son, whit a pity.' I took the money which was about half of what they were worth.

My reason for settling so easily was that poaching was taken more seriously in those days and pheasants were far scarcer, therefore someone trying to hawk 104 birds round various butchers and game-dealers would have aroused suspicion and my identity would have become common knowledge, which I did not want. This would have given Bill Elliot an advantage over me, and I was not finished with him yet. I knew that my butcher would be discreet as he had as much to lose as I had, and at the end of the day, profit was not my prime motivation for pursuing a career in poaching. My motive was revenge.

Bill had his first shoot the next weekend, shooting 85 birds when he would have been expecting over a hundred. It was commented on that he flushed the birds steadily to reach that total where normally he flushed birds in large numbers to make it difficult for the guns to shoot too many. The gossip was that the syndicate were not overly impressed by the number of birds that they saw, but were reserving judgement until the season unfolded further. My uncle informed me that his friend the tenant farmer on the Blackhill had been told by Bill that he would be shooting the wood behind his farm on the next day. This was unusual as this drive was normally kept back until after Christmas, when the other woods were getting light of birds.

This showed that Bill was concerned that he did not have enough birds and he was hoping that the reserve wood would buy him time until birds that had strayed returned to the home covers.

I was, however, certain that Bill knew that he had been poached, as he was no fool. His reason for keeping quiet was that he had 'cried wolf' the previous season, and to admit that he had been poached again would make him look inefficient or lazy, possibly both.

I decided to target the reserve wood before the next shoot. My tactics would be different, as cycling to the Blackhill would be too dangerous now that Bill was alerted to the activity of poachers. Bill would be desperate now as he would know that to lose any more birds could cost him his job and to protect his occupation Bill could possibly be a dangerous man. I did not relish being caught by Bill and his son Callum (I had no doubt that he would assist his father in trying to catch me) and intended taking every precaution to make sure that this did not happen. An added twist to the situation was that a keeper only three miles away from the Blackhill on the Brownpark estate had been badly beaten by poachers, leaving him unfit to work for several weeks. This had resulted in an understandable reaction from several local keepers: they now refused to enter woods at night, but instead took pot-shots at 'foxes' into the woods using a .22 rifle with a silencer fitted. The sound of a .22 hollow point bullet rushing past you in the dark is extremely disconcerting and this method of preventing poaching proved quite effective.

I, however, had a secret weapon to assist me, old Sweep. Sweep was the family pet and gundog who had a deep suspicion of strangers, betraying their presence by coming close and growling quietly. My father purchased Sweep from a shepherd who had got him as a pup from the keeper on the estate where he worked. His mother was a labrador-german pointer cross, his father a bull terrier-lurcher cross that the keeper had used to take foxes. He was a labrador-sized dog with a strange dark brindle coat and a powerful head and body. He had an exceptional nose and was a good worker, pointing and retrieving.

My father brought Sweep home from the pub in the boot of his car. 'I've brought you a present,' he said, opening the boot lid a couple of inches. A set of flashing white teeth announced the presence of the dog who was unsure of his new surroundings, but was determined to let everyone know that he would be no pushover. 'It's alright, he's attached to a length of clothes line, grab the end of it, take him a long walk, then feed him when you come home. He'll be your friend for life.' He opened the boot fully and Sweep jumped out. I dived, albeit tentatively, for the line and miraculously Sweep came to heel and walked with me quietly for a couple of miles, during which time he pointed a rather irate tom cat, eventually putting it to flight by sheer force of character. As instructed, I fed him on our return, Sweep spending the night at the foot of my bed, and within 24 hours he acted as if he had lived with us all his life.

Sweep always escorted me on rabbiting trips, running the two miles to my uncle's farm behind my bicycle. This, combined with good feeding, developed him into a fit and muscular animal, and none of the farm collies who used to try and bite my heels as I passed their farms, dared to challenge him.

One day, however, he was challenged. I had taken him for exercise in the local park and was just putting him through some obedience routines, one of which entailed making Sweep stay, while I walked a hundred yards away. To my dismay I saw from the corner of my eye that the Graham brothers were entering the park, accompanied by their large red and white boxer dog. The brothers always took great delight in allowing their dog to attack smaller, weaker dogs, enjoying in particular the squeals of pain from the unfortunate canine victim and the shrieks of anguish from the human (often female) owners. The Graham boys wasted no time when they saw Sweep, loosing Bengo, for that was the boxer's name, who homed in on Sweep with that peculiarly ridiculous running action. I whistled to Sweep, hoping that if he came quickly he could reach me before the boxer made good his attack. Unfortunately Sweep merely ambled forward, as if oblivious to the large dog rapidly closing in on him and he was still thirty yards away when the boxer made his final lunge. I winced and watched through half closed eyes waiting for the bone jarring impact and the tearing of flesh.

To my surprise, this did not happen. Like a middleweight prize fighter, Sweep changed feet, stopping suddenly at the last moment, then as Bengo careered past him, he seized the boxer by the side of the neck. Bengo roared in pain and anger, furiously trying to remove Sweep from his grip. Sweep grimly hung on, a strange faraway look in his eyes and, after what seemed a lifetime, the boxer ceased to fight, trying instead to extricate himself from his predicament.

Sweep sensed that his opponent was weakening and took his chance to take an improved hold on Bengo's throat. This caused the poor animal to choke, then Sweep went onto the offensive, driving with his hind legs until the boxer collapsed rolling onto his back, desperate to signal total surrender. Up to this point I had watched events unfold with awe and wonder, but suddenly the sound of the boxer in his last throes of life forced me to rush forward. I commanded Sweep, more in hope than expectation, to 'Leave it!'

To my utter amazement, Sweep looked up to me, then casually dropped the boxer, returning to sit at my heel. Poor old Bengo lay on the ground wheezing with blood oozing from the wounds in his throat, but at least he was still alive. However, another problem was fast approaching, the Graham brothers. 'What have you done to my dog you b★★★★★?' the elder brother exploded. The two brothers helped their dog to his feet, and although groggy, it was apparent he would be okay.

When they realised that Bengo would survive they turned their attention to me, stepping forward threateningly which caused Sweep to growl and show his teeth. The Graham brothers retreated quickly, which emboldened me and I reminded them that Bengo had dished it out but had met his match. The downside of this incident was that Sweep gained something of a reputation as a fighting dog and, while many owners crossed the road to avoid him, some macho owners deliberately set up situations to test the mettle of their dogs, a tiresome and pointless exercise, but I suppose 'it takes all kinds'.

My reconnaissance of the Blackhill shoot had been flawed as I had not realised that there was a release pen in the reserve wood. The reserve wood was positioned above Hillcroft farm with the main access road passing through the farm, entering the wood at the lower end with a Landrover track following the course of the stream sourced from a pond that covered the top quarter of the wood. The wood itself was a classic game cover, spruce trees protecting the outer skin of the wood while larch and hardwoods allowed light to enter the heart of the covert. The release pen was situated near the centre of the wood with a water supply piped in from the pond, the Landrover track giving good access, passing right past the main door.

The easiest approach to the reserve wood was to follow my previous route then take the farm road through Hillcroft farm. I was reluctant to do this as the Elliots would almost certainly be watching this route and also I did not want to compromise the tenant farmer in any way with my poaching activities, as this could have put him in a bad light with his landlord. I resolved to take a circuitous route from the north end of my uncle's farm, crossing a neighbouring property, then travelling south to the reserve wood. I would enter at the top end, then walk along the track which followed the edge of the loch, travelling downhill through the wood, shooting as I moved through the covert. One of my reasons for doing this was that it would be far easier to carry a bag of pheasants downhill, but my main motive was that the wind would blow from the south-west and therefore I would be moving into it at all times. Sweep's nose was so acute and his sensitivity to strangers so developed that I was sure it would be safe to proceed, should he show no indication of any human being in the vicinity.

My night of choice came. Again it was a Saturday, and I drove past the hotel and Bill's silver Saab was parked outside. I drove to my usual spot and set off with all the equipment I needed, now with the important addition of Sweep who bustled about for the first half mile, investigating the various scents of game which were held by the night air. There was a half moon, enough to see, but not enough for a poacher to be revealed when crossing bare ground and eventually I reached the top of the reserve wood.

Entering the wood I followed the track which skirted the edge of the loch. Alder and willow trees grew in the marshy edge and pheasants used them to roost above the water, but this was no impediment to me as Sweep was able to retrieve them as they fell to my little gun. I shot a dozen birds next to the loch, then entered the wood proper, the track falling away as the covert reflected the slope of the ground. I was thinking to myself how ridiculously easy this poaching lark was when Sweep suddenly leant against my knee. I felt, rather than heard the low growl which emanated from his throat. My initial reaction was to freeze but I forced myself to act as I did not know for certain how far away the threat was and what form the threat took. The hair on the back of my neck started to stiffen and rise up as I knew I was in trouble and if I did not make the right decision then I would be in even bigger trouble.

There was a large rhododendron bush to my right about twenty yards away. I quickly moved behind it then crawled to its centre, keeping the main branches at the centre between me and the track. I dragged Sweep with me, putting a woollen helmet over his head so that any light would not reflect his eyes (I had remembered that my grand-father had told me of the number of poachers caught after the advent of electric torches, especially long-netters after rabbits who hid in hedges hoping to go undetected but were betrayed by the reflection of their dog's eyes). I pulled leaves and branches over us and lay as flat as possible for what seemed an age. Indeed I was almost starting to think that Sweep had been mistaken, when I heard voices. Sweep's body started to tense and I whispered to him to be quiet, then the beam from a powerful torch could be seen licking through the undergrowth, illuminating the dark recesses of the wood. Two figures slowly came into view, Bill and Callum Elliot, Callum carrying a pick-axe handle and Bill disconcertingly carrying a double barrelled shotgun, the shiny barrels reflecting the moonlight from time to time.

The hair on my neck was now on end and a trickle of sweat, slowly at first but then quite freely, ran down to the small of my back as I realised that I had been set up. (I found out later that Bill had parked his car at the hotel, then walked right through and out another exit to be picked up by Callum). I had underestimated Bill and knew that if the Elliots caught me, I was in for a severe beating. I resolved there and them that, if discovered, I would set Sweep on Callum and try to disarm Bill, the best case scenario being that Bill and Callum would be knocked out and out of the game, the worst case would be Sweep being shot and me suffering broken ribs and probably worse.

The Elliots stood barely twenty yards away shining the torch 360-degrees, on more than one occasion the beam passing right over me. I heard Callum telling his father that he was sure that he had seen a light, then the torch shone in our direction and lingered. I made ready to attack, but to my great relief the torch moved to another area of the wood and then, after a few minutes, the Elliots moved on up the track.

I continued to lie still, hardly daring to breathe, thanking my lucky stars that Bill had not brought his labradors with him, as I had noted during my visit to his house that they were vocal and aggressive to strangers and this, added to the fact that most dogs are more protective after dark, would have meant that my detection would have been inevitable.

I checked my watch: it was 12.30am and I decided to stay put for at least two hours as my grandfather had described to me the tactic many keepers used when they suspected that poachers were present in a wood and as I had underestimated Bill once, I did not want to put his knowledge to the test and do so again. The tactic my grandfather employed was to enter the wood and make an obvious attempt to find the poacher while the underkeepers hid in the wood or at the exits. A great show was made of leaving the wood, hopefully leading to the poacher thinking that the keeper had gone home. The poacher, if everything went to plan, would either continue poaching, confident that he would go undetected and therefore be easily caught (a hunter who stays still always has an advantage over his quarry when it is on the move) or he would head for home and be apprehended en route.

I had lain in the wood for two hours and could thole it no longer. I dragged myself to my feet and tried to get the blood to move through my limbs again. I set off downhill following the track through the wood. I was sure that by travelling into the wind I would be able to escape undetected. I reached the gate at the bottom end of the wood without mishap, then used the cover of a thick hedge which led to the public road, still over a mile from my van. Reaching the road I was just about to jump the fence and take the easy route to my vehicle by walking on the tarmac of the public highway, when I saw headlights a quarter of a mile away. I cowered into the hedge, again covering Sweep's head and waited for the vehicle to pass.

It approached slowly which I found surprising as most cars on country roads in the early hours of the morning travel at high speed, unless they are up to no good. The car came into view, a police car. It slowly passed, then disappeared into the distance. Bill had called in his favours. Callum was assisting his father to patrol the coverts and the police were travelling the roads in the early hours, making life difficult for any poacher. I crossed the road then headed cross-country to my van, crawling into my sleeping bag, exhausted physically and mentally. Looking at my watch it was 3.45am. I dared not move the van in case the lights were seen and investigated so I spent the night in the lane, returning home at 9am the following morning.

Reflecting on my experiences later that day, I realised that Bill was a devious sod. This view was reinforced later when I found that he had told everyone that he would be shooting the reserve wood and that it was full of birds. This was intended to entice his poacher into a certain area which could be easily watched. It was a simple matter then to pick the most likely night for poaching, when conditions were suitable, and if it had not been for old Sweep I would have been well and truly stitched up.

It must be appreciated that, because of his workload, a keeper cannot be expected to night-watch every night so therefore he must pick and choose the nights to sit up, a good maxim being to pick the most likely and the most unlikely nights.

Had Bill possessed a night-dog I would have been a dead duck, a fact I was not slow to act upon when I later became a gamekeeper myself. A keeper who was known to keep a night-dog was quite often avoided by poachers who could find less dangerous venues to ply their nefarious trade. It is worth remembering also that it is not only the protection that a night-dog offers that makes his presence desirable, but the fact that detection of anyone trying to avoid capture is certain. The fact that Bill was armed was worrying, as it suggested to me that he really did not know who was poaching him and he was afraid of what he did not know. It is true that a brave man is not to be feared as much as a frightened man who may do anything when he is put under pressure. I decided therefore that to continue night poaching would be foolhardy, resolved instead to change tactics and poach during daylight hours.

Bill's season meanwhile, continued, he having to pull out all the stops to average fifty birds per day for the first three days. This left three days, the first of which was 28th December and because of the Christmas period, the syndicate expected to have a better day than usual. My aim was to poach the reserve wood prior to this date, but to do this I would have to know for certain that the Blackhill would be unguarded on a particular day. Luck was on my side when I heard on the grapevine that Bill and Callum, as well as all the other Blackhill beaters, always attended the big Boxing Day shoot at Cowhall, the neighbouring estate. A narrow twisting road connected the two estates and at 8.30am on Boxing Day I hid in the hedge next to the road, after having cycled from my home. I had come prepared as usual, except for this foray I had acquired a BSA Airsporter under-lever air rifle which was strapped to the cross-bar of the bicycle. At 9am the Elliots appeared in a Landrover filled with dogs and beaters, speeding past as if they were late for the start. This was the best chance I would have and as soon as they were out of sight, I jogged back to my bike and headed for the Blackhill. On arrival I hid the cycle in a hedge then walked cross-country using the same hedge for cover that I had followed to leave the reserve wood on my previous expedition. On entering the wood I chose to walk along the path that had been cut for the beaters, moving parallel to the main track. When I judged that I was level with the feed ride which Bill used to feed his birds, I cut across the wood arriving just right, in the middle of the feeding area.

What I found was interesting. It was a bitterly cold day and the birds were hanging around as if they were waiting to be fed, there being no visible evidence of any grain on the ride. I aimed at the nearest bird and shot him in the base of the neck, and was able to shoot three more before the rest of the birds became alarmed and slunk into the cover at the sides of the track. On looking round I noticed a metal bin at the other side of the ride which, when inspected, proved to be full of wheat with a convenient bucket which I used to distribute a small quantity of feed in front of my hiding place. After a few minutes the birds started to re-assemble, especially after the first birds started to feed. Whether Bill had deliberately starved his birds to draw them in to the feeds for the next shoot or whether he had just been too late rising that morning to feed them, I do not know. However, the fact was that their hunger, allied to the cold weather made them considerably less wary than they would have been under normal circumstances.

Taking the peripheral pheasants first, I was able to bag a further seven birds before they again retired to cover. The feed had been eaten, so I replenished it, then on a hunch decided to whistle, hoping that Bill, like many keepers at that time, called his birds to feed. The result was dramatic as birds appeared from all quarters and when I returned to my hide even more materialised. This shoot yielded twelve pheasants which was the highest bag in one sequence. From then on the number diminished until only one or two fell at each feed. Eventually, by 1.30pm I had fifty birds beside me in my hide and this was enough, as I had to move them in relays, first to the bottom corner of the wood, then to the hedge bottom next to the public road. Retrieving my bike I sped home to my van then returned in it, throwing the slain into the back, all the time dreading the sound of a vehicle approaching. To my relief I was able to load up unobserved, then I drove home by a roundabout route.

As I was gaining in confidence I haggled with the butcher over the price of the birds, eventually a deal being done. At least the Airsporter was paid for. My main concern was Bill's shoot on the 28th, and to my joy it was a disaster, yielding only 38 birds. At last I felt that justice had been done and I poached no more. Bill's reputation never recovered, the syndicate folded and Bill had to eke out a living doing a number of part-time jobs. He did not starve, however, and always seemed comfortably off, so I have no conscience on that score.

So there you have it reader, I have got form, a fact which does not fill me with pride but hopefully you will understand my position and accept that there were extenuating circumstances. The reader who is an aspiring keeper should also note the challenges I had in my vendetta and how Bill made it easier for me. Use this information to make life even more difficult for any poacher who dares to take the game in your charge. There is also a moral to the story in that a keeper has enough natural enemies, without creating more that he does not need.

The modern keeper is not as plagued by night poaching for pheasant as his predecessors were. The simple reason for this is that the price per bird at the game dealers is now a fraction of what it once was in real terms. Indeed in the early 1980s, pheasants were £4–5 a brace: now they are 50p a brace. If the previously high price of pheasants is added to the high unemployment at that time, it is no wonder that poaching was a problem then, but it must be admitted that in most areas it is not a great problem now.

This is not to say that pheasant poaching does not take place, as I am sure it does, but because far more birds are reared nowadays, any poaching goes unnoticed or a blind eye is turned because most keepers are so hard-pushed that they would find it difficult to maintain a regime of night-watching.

My own view is that there will always be men who will poach for the thrill and excitement that they gain from this activity, perhaps they have a contempt for authority or the perceived upper class and gain some satisfaction from taking game without detection or punishment. It is also true that restaurants or the general public have to pay considerably more for game than the estate receives for it and there is obviously a margin for a resourceful poacher to exploit.

How to catch a poacher

The keeper should exploit and cultivate any wet areas in his woods by forcing any intruders, both two and four legged, to pass over them, so leaving evidence of their presence. Woods should be deliberately left rough, with thorns and brambles uncut in many areas, especially where birds are likely to roost. Where there are easily accessed roosting birds, then the keeper should hide and wait there as it is certain that a poacher will strike there first, especially if he has visited the estate previously. Where night poaching is still prevalent, the keeper should consider installing an alarm system which can work from either infra-red beam or pressure plates. When these are activated, a signal is sent to the keeper who has a pager which indicates where the intruder is present. The weakness of this system is that deer can set them off and some systems are ineffective in hilly areas or dense woodland. A good idea is to purchase a few static cameras which take photographs when an infra-red beam is broken. Poachers and predators will be recorded on film and the keeper can examine at his leisure the threats to his game and make plans to counteract them.

Night dogs

If you discover that you are the victim of night-poaching the first step to remedy the situation is the acquisition of a night dog (a gamekeeper's security dog). I will deal in detail in subsequent chapters with the breeds which are suitable for this purpose and the methods employed to train such an animal.

The next step is to be out and about at night when you are most likely to be poached. Each area of the country has favourite nights for poaching and there are many theories for the most suitable nights and the safest periods after dark to avoid detection. One thing is certain: if you never go out, the poacher has a free run, and can pick and choose the time and place for his sortie onto your manor and is likely to return again and again.

A quick drive round the estate in the Landrover then back home to bed is an inadequate method of preventing poaching, although this can be a useful bluff if the keeper then switches all house lights off, before setting out on foot to patrol his coverts.

A further trick to add to this tactic is to fit a lamp in a window of your house to a timer which activates the light at various times of the night. This is obviously more effective if your house enjoys a prominent position on the estate (which many keeper's dwellings do) and can make any trespasser on your ground uncertain as to whether or not you are about to venture forth to patrol with your night dog. Some poachers employ a look-out whose job is to observe the keeper's house and notify his colleagues, should he see any activity which would suggest that the keeper has risen from his slumbers.

There are favourite nights to go poaching, Saturday night after the pubs have closed being one. There are a number of reasons for this. Firstly the poachers may have drunk too much of their pay and are looking to recoup some of their losses; secondly the police are almost certainly tied up dealing with town centre disturbances, and thirdly the poacher who is in employment (and the majority are) has Sunday to recuperate before he starts work again on Monday. Friday is second favourite for similar reasons and Thursday probably third favourite due to the poacher needing funds before the weekend.

Sunday night is first favourite amongst poachers who follow this trade in a professional way, especially if they are unemployed or work a shift system. This is because in the small hours of a Monday morning, the rural roads are at their quietest with the chances of a police patrol interrupting proceedings unlikely. These poachers know that the keeper will night-watch Friday and Saturday then need to rest on Sunday as Monday will be a day for catching up on replenishing feed-bins etc which is hard work and needs a rested body.

The truth is that the only sure way to prevent night-poaching is to watch every night. This is feasible where sufficient keepers are employed, ie. a minimum of three, each sitting up one night then taking two nights off.

Modern communications such as mobile phones mean that help can be summoned, which is a great boon compared to the old days, so that today even a single-handed keeper is able to contact the police while at the same time observing and following poachers. In the past, he would have had to tackle them himself or return home to phone, risking that his quarry could have fled, leaving an embarrassed keeper to explain himself to a pair of sceptical coppers.

By using the methods already described, the keeper should know where and when he is being poached. Now you must discover how they arrive at your estate. Again the stealth cam cameras can answer many of the questions. If the estate is criss-crossed by public roads, then access can be from any direction and clever poachers will change their point of attack to keep the keeper guessing. However, where access is limited, the keeper can park his vehicle off road where he can observe any vehicle entering the estate. This may be enough to deter all but the most daring of poachers as there will be easier fish to fry in the area and most poachers look for an easy life.

Where access is unlimited and a reasonable amount of traffic moves on the road all through the night, such as in the vicinity of a town or village, the keeper must second-guess his opponents and hope to catch them in the act. The normal technique employed by poachers is for a driver to convey the poacher or poachers to the targeted area then wait to be summoned by mobile phone when their foray has been completed. The keeper can steer a poacher using torches hanging from a long string in the woods to deter intruders from other areas. Compact discs and old reflectors from extinct vehicles placed near lay-bys that the poachers would use as drop-off points can also be effective as would be scare-crows clad in fluorescent jackets.

The keeper meanwhile should pick a sheltered, comfortable spot where he can observe the most likely area to be poached. He should have come prepared accompanied by his night- dog or dogs, his clothing should be suitable for the occasion with steel toe-capped boots, shin-pads for shins and forearms (a downwards blow from a baseball bat or baton can break a wrist or arm, as the natural reaction is to put up your forearm to protect yourself). Gloves which give a certain degree of protection from knives can be purchased and should be used, especially if the poachers in the area have a reputation for violence, with a cricketer's box and reinforced waist-coat to protect ribs giving added insurance. This may seem an over-reaction, but the keeper must be fit for work, as there is no-one to deputise for him and, if he suffers broken ribs from a poacher's boots, he will be unfit for work for weeks and may miss the entire shooting season. For this reason, head protection and shot-repellent glasses should also be worn, as it is not unknown for a poacher to react by shooting at the keeper when he is surprised in the dead of night.

The poachers' arrival

You have come equipped and have been waiting for a couple of hours then, just as you are about to go home, a car slowly drives up and two figures alight. One carries a torch, the other an air rifle slung over his shoulder, both men carry large rucksacks and head towards you into the cover. They shoot a number of pheasants and come within range. You wait for the marksman to fire his weapon, then shine your torch on them, telling them that the game is up and to stand still. At this stage anything can happen. The best case scenario is that they see the dogs and decide discretion is the better part of valour and come quietly. The next-best scenario is that they decide to run for it, whereupon you have the choice of giving your dogs some exercise or letting your quarry go scot-free hoping that they never come back. Both alternatives have some plus points.

Sending in the dogs

If you send in your dogs, they may savage their victims, in which case it is advisable to take them back to the road, then retire a safe distance and wait for the poacher's pick-up car to take them to hospital. On no account should police be called in these circumstances, as you would be almost certainly charged with assault. Few poachers will go to the police on their own accord, but their solicitor might well advise them to make a counter charge of assault, should they be charged with poaching. This scenario will reduce poaching immediately as word will spread about the ferocity of your dogs and your cunning in intercepting the poachers.

Back-off

This scenario, of having given them a scare but allowing them to walk off, may be less spectacular but may have just as much effect, as few poachers are prepared to risk the possibility that you may loose the dogs the second time and you are also in no danger of prosecution or creating a vendetta situation.

Poachers fight back

The worst case scenario is that the poacher or poachers are so incensed that someone should have the temerity to curtail their activities, that they attack head on. This is the reason for allowing them to empty their weapon before you challenge them, as an empty gun can only be used as a club. If you are confronted by such an attack, do not hold back, as these individuals are desperate men. Your dogs, if they are worth their salt, should nail your assailants, but still there is no time to waste: knock one of the men to the ground, then hand-cuff him in any way you can, tying him to a tree. Now turn your attention to the second man, calling the first dog to help. Assuming he is more easy to subdue, then return to the first man and make sure he is fully secured. In these circumstances the police should be called, as an assault has taken place and your dogs have only acted in your defence, therefore it will be far more difficult for your poachers to make a complaint of assault against you.

Again, irrespective of the outcome of any court case, such an incident will reduce poaching immediately and you will have gained a reputation amongst the poaching fraternity that will set you in good stead for the rest of your career.

Rabbit and hare poaching

Thankfully, due to the low cost of birds, such confrontations are, nowadays, quite rare, but there are other avenues for those of a poaching inclination to pursue their calling. Rabbit and hare poaching have always been popular amongst the 'fraternity' and as the prices of these animals have held relatively well, this activity is still common today. The methods employed are many and varied, from snaring, ferreting, long-netting, lurchers, shooting at night with air-rifle, .22 two rim-fire or shotgun using artificial light, to the chap with a gundog which has the knack of pegging bunnies in their 'seats'.

Snaring is an old method of catching lagomorphs, probably dating back to the time ancient man discovered natural material such as animal sinew or plant material that was strong enough to restrain a rabbit or hare long enough for the hunter to despatch it. Six strands of brass wire twisted to form a rope then fed through a brass eyelet such as would be utilised to thread the laces through boots, became the standard device in the nineteenth century. The wire noose was attached to a cord which could be fixed to a peg or the trunk of a hedgerow bush next to the run that passed through it, and this was the preferred choice of the poacher as many snares could be secreted about his person.

This type of poacher tends to walk country lanes and the edge of woodland, inspecting likely spots for well-used runs through hedges and fences. The experienced and dexterous man can set a snare in seconds then he immediately walks upright, his head facing straight ahead but his eyes darting from side to side to see if he has been spotted by the keeper. A pigeon feather or freshly-cut twig above the snare allows the poacher to check his snares quickly without having to pause and search and if he finds one has been successful he may carry on walking to check that he is not being observed, before removing his prize from the snare. Rabbits and hares may be the main quarry for this type of poacher but if there is any population of pheasants on the ground he will catch many and will regret it not one bit.

This type of poaching is most common near villages where the population takes daily constitutionals into the country on the roads which traverse an estate and the keeper should walk the hedges and fences regularly to gauge the extent of any activity being practised. If he disturbs the poacher or he thinks that the poacher has seen him observing him, then he should lift the snares, as the likelihood is that the poacher will not return. The numbers caught using these methods will not be large if the keeper is vigilant, but if pheasants are caught in snares, the flapping and distress suffered by the birds will be transmitted to the surviving birds and they will become shy and wary, even relocating to another wood.

Poachers with ferrets

Ferreting is enjoyed by every section of society and as rabbits become scarce these sportsmen can become tempted by the forbidden fruit on your beat. Fine frosty weather from September to February are the best times for ferreting, with weekends and holidays a favourite. The vulnerable areas should be watched at these times and, as in all keepering, prevention is better than cure. Likely burrows can be covered with barbed wire or blackthorn cuttings, making the use of nets difficult and also slowing down the poacher, hopefully making him try for easier pickings elsewhere.

A keeper I know had been suspicious of three young lads for some time, as he had seen them coming out of the nearby village to watch rabbits returning to their home wood from the neighbouring fields. Then one day, to his surprise, they arrived at his house asking him if he would sell them a ferret. Thinking fast the keeper agreed, charging them the exorbitant price (for that time) of £5, which the youngsters only just managed to raise by pooling their saved pocket money. The keeper knew that they intended to poach his rabbits, but had to laugh at their brass neck in hoping to use his ferret.

The next day was a fine bright day in early February. The keeper had been charged by his employer to severely reduce the rabbit population on the estate and had been given the incentive of being allowed to sell the carcases for his own benefit. He had covered all the estate and was only left with a bramble-covered bank in the wood near the village, the task of clearing which he knew would be unpleasant. The keeper had a hunch that his young poachers would head for this bank, so he moved quietly through the trees to a vantage point where his suspicions were confirmed. Fired by the enthusiasm of youth, the lads were clearing the bank using garden shears. The keeper estimated that this would take them to lunch-time then they would start ferreting, so he left them to it. At 2pm he returned to find them almost three-quarters through, so he waited another hour for them to finish, whereupon they gathered up the bag which amounted to more than fifty, hanging them on a number of poles that they had cut from the wood.

The keeper decided that now was the time to intervene. Shouting to give them plenty of warning, he approached and, just as he had hoped, they made a run for it, leaving everything behind. The keeper inspected the rabbits. All had been cleaned, albeit roughly, and would fetch a pretty price at the game-dealers. Then something caught his eye: it was his erstwhile ferret staring at him from the mouth of a hole. He squeaked using his lips and the friendly creature gambolled towards him. The keeper duly put him inside his jacket then set off for home, smiling to himself all the way.

Long-netting

Long-netting used to be a favoured method of poaching rabbits, as a large number can be caught in a short time for little effort. A long-net can be any length, from 25–100 yards long by 3ft high. The net is actually two nets, the net nearest to the rabbits having smaller mesh than the adjacent net so that a rabbit charging through the first net is caught in a pouch formed when the first net is pushed through the second. Wooden stakes are placed at intervals to support the net with a cord at the top and bottom helping to keep the whole thing in place. Windy nights are best for setting a long net, the object being to intercept the rabbits between their feeding grounds and their burrows. Two men usually set the net up, then wait at each end to dispatch the animals after they are caught and reset the net if it is knocked over when a rabbit hits the net, the thump of the impact travelling along the cord, alerting the poacher to a catch being made.

A further pair of men, often with a dog, drive the rabbits to the nets. In days gone by when many poachers were experts in this field and rabbits were numerous, good bags could be had using this method and twenty pair of rabbits could be sold for an average wage, so it was little wonder that it was widely practised.

The generally accepted method to deter long-netters was to strew the vulnerable fields with bushes of blackthorn or similar; even barbed wire was utilised. I have found that scrap rabbit net cut into pieces then rolled into a ball with a number of rough edges protruding is the most effective, the added bonus being that the 'balls' can be used year after year. The object of these impediments is to snag and tangle the net when it is being set, causing the poacher to waste much time untangling his net. Indeed in some cases, he will abandon it when it becomes badly torn.

Lurchers

The use of lurchers seems to have grown in recent years, many being utilised to catch rabbits and hares caught in the beam of a powerful lamp. The fields next to centres of population are perpetually illuminated during the dark nights of the winter months. These people are a nuisance, although normally not so violent as the daylight coursers who pursue hares, often following in four-wheeled drive vehicles. These hare poachers are almost certain to assault any keeper who tries to halt their activities and I would urge caution to any keeper who is forced to deal with them. Again, prevention is better than cure so if your land is attractive to this type of poaching you should take steps to change this, the first simple step being to severely reduce the population of rabbits and hares on your beat. The second is to make access to fields difficult, blocking gates and ploughing trenches. The third step is to stretch electric fencing, preferably off the mains, over the favourite fields, in effect creating a number of small fields where there was one large one. Horses, pigs and even wild boar can make lamping less attractive, but the main deterrent is the vigilance of the keeper who must patrol on favoured nights and at week-ends, always remembering to take a mobile phone with him in case the police need to be summoned quickly. If these measures are ineffective, the only option left is to virtually exterminate the rabbit and hare population, so that lamping and coursing are no longer worthwhile. This is a drastic step which many keepers would be reluctant to take. However, if your workload is already heavy, and you are receiving little assistance from the forces of law and order, then there may be no alternative.

Deer poaching

Deer poaching takes many forms, the most basic being the individual who takes a small shoot at a bargain price, then uses it as a base for poaching the surrounding area. When challenged, the poacher explains, often quite plausibly, that he has wounded a deer on his own shoot which has unfortunately travelled on to your ground and, being a sportsman, felt duty-bound to pursue the unfortunate animal to put its suffering to an end humanely. If the police are called in such circumstances they may be reluctant to prosecute, as a trial would be unlikely to find the defendant guilty. The keeper, when faced with this scenario, must return to the old maxim that prevention is better than cure and undertake some or all of the following measures.

Reconnaissance and intelligence, as usual, are essential to find out if there is a pattern to your neighbour's poaching expeditions. If there is a pattern, be on the boundary to deter him every time he visits or failing this, use the stealthcam cameras which, if they show him entering your land, may yield evidence which at least can be shown to the police who then may want to ask some questions when your friend's firearm certificate comes up for renewal.

Another tactic is to build highseats overlooking the boundary. These seats, which can be anything from 10–20ft high, are used to observe and cull deer and foxes, but the important point in this instance is that the seat itself is enclosed so that any intruder cannot be sure that someone is not observing or even filming his activities. As can be imagined, this has an inhibiting effect on your poacher's incursions, hopefully ending them completely.

The most serious type of deer poaching involves lamping from a vehicle, then shooting with a centre-fire rifle. This is often well organised, with a three vehicle team being utilised. The first car travels through the area to be poached, looking for any activity or individuals who might compromise them. If the coast is clear, the first car contacts the second by mobile phone or, in yesteryear, CB radios. The second car contains a driver, a man to operate the light and a rifle man. If a vehicle appears travelling in the opposite direction, the first car alerts the second and the mission may be aborted. A third car may be used to wait at any suitable junction to warn of any approach from the rear. When a deer is shot it is gralloched by the occupants of the third vehicle then hidden at the side of the road and the area marked using a coke can, cigarette packet or similar, the deer being collected the next day by a different vehicle usually containing a man and his wife and family, ostensibly out for a family drive in the country. The beauty of this poaching system is that it is difficult to connect the men with the light and rifle to the deer that has been shot, especially if the man collecting the deer is not known to be connected to the rifle man who invariably has shooting rights on a piece of land, which, if stopped by the police in a roadside check, he claims to be returning from. The techniques employed here have echoes of paramilitary and counter-terrorists tactics used in Northern Ireland and it is believed that a member of the Territorial Army learned these methods during his service and developed them to help ply his other trade of poaching.

The keeper must be cautious when dealing with these individuals, as they have a lot to lose if captured: their firearms certificate or, if they do not have one, their liberty with a five year prison sentence for illegal possession of a Section One firearm. Many readers may be surprised that someone can get hold of a deer rifle without a certificate, but the trade in illegal firearms is not restricted to hand-guns, with wrong-doers seemingly able to buy them at will.

Confronting deer poachers

What does a keeper do when confronted in a remote area by a car or van load of deer poachers? The first thing he must do is to contact the police, then hope that they turn out. The modern bobbie is not, usually, a country man and can be out of his depth when called to deal with poaching. This can manifest itself in a 'reluctance' to appear, unless 'mob-handed', an understandable stance to take as they could not care less if your deer or pheasants are poached. Some policemen are, however, keen as mustard on catching poachers and you must pray that one such is on duty when you call. Remember to be calm, giving your name and address and an accurate description of the vehicle, registration number, how many and description of occupants as well as the exact location.

Again the keeper's vigilance is paramount in preventing this activity. A good look-out position where the roads crossing the estate can be surveyed without being seen yourself, will need to be utilised allowing the keeper to alert the police without warning the poachers that they have been observed.

Dummy deer

Dummy deer which have 'cats eyes' or compact discs placed in the eye holes can be effective but they must be moved every day, any holes or even the disappearance of the dummy, indicating poaching activity. These dummies can be made by dipping the carcase of a deer in a tub of formaldehyde, firstly using lengths of wire to mould the animal into a standing position before rigor mortis sets in. An alternative method involves injecting formaldehyde at various points to preserve a previously set up carcase. The eyes will have to be removed and replaced with 'cats eyes' or similar. It is preferable that the dummy falls over when shot, so a bag of sand should be placed in the chest cavity to arrest the bullet, rather than it travelling straight through. The dummy should be placed far enough away from the road to make its artificiality more difficult to recognise and in rough cover, making it inaccessible, causing much delay and frustration to the poacher.

Lurchers and deers

The use of lurchers on deer is quite common, usually while lamping. The deerhound cross often with alsatian or bull cross added, can kill roe deer quite easily and can take the larger species as well although the damage to the carcase can be quite considerable. These poachers normally travel the roads spying for deer using a lamp. If deer are observed they may course them from the side of the road or pursue them on foot. Level ground is ideal for this sport as the lurcher travels at such a speed and is so intent on his quarry that a ditch, electric fence wire, single strand of barb wire, farm machinery in the corner of the field, even a sheer drop can be fatal to the dog. Remember the deer lives on the ground and becomes accustomed to any obstacles while the lurcher, however, has only one thing on his mind and has no knowledge of the topography of the land.

When the keeper is on patrol or lamping for foxes, he may observe deer feeding away from woods in the fields and he can be sure that he will not be alone in observing this phenomenon and the local poachers will also be aware. A shot over the deers' back may make them wary and less likely to naively stand and be approached by a lamper with a dog.

Once the keeper has ascertained the areas vulnerable to this type of poaching he should inspect them closely. Tracks leading from the woods, perhaps through a hedge or over a low part of a fence or wall, are obvious avenues used by the deer. These routes are likely to be used by the deer to escape from a dog and often as the deer hesitates before negotiating an obstacle the lurcher will make his kill. To counteract this, make the entrances to the wood more easily accessible, hopefully allowing the deer to escape into the wood. Most lurchers, however, will pursue the deer into the wood and may even use their nose to locate them. A line of old pallets which become green and slippery placed closely either side of the deer pad will cause the dog or dogs to slip and slide losing their footing, giving the deer a few extra seconds to make good their escape.

Enjoy the challenge

My final word on poaching is to enjoy it. The battle of wits with your enemy is one that can become quite entertaining. Sometimes you will be beaten but if you use all or some of the methods described, you will be successful in the majority of instances. Always treat anyone you apprehend as you would expect to be treated yourself, remembering that if there were no poachers, there would be far fewer gamekeepers.

And what of old Sweep my poaching accomplice from earlier in the chapter? He continued to hate the human race apart from his immediate family who he trusted, and gained a rather bad reputation which my father did nothing to dispel. This was due to an incident one evening when my mother answered the door to a travelling salesman who tried the 'foot in the door' technique which alarmed her. Sweep, hearing a note of fear in her voice, sped to the rescue and sank his teeth in the man's thigh, ripping his trousers in the process. A commotion ensued with my father telling the man to go. He in turn stated that he was going to the police, which he did, two uniformed officers arriving within the hour. The neighbours, of course, had a field day, although the result was not my family being led away in hand-cuffs, as would possibly be the case today, after the passing of the *Dangerous Dogs Act*, but with my father paying for the cost of a new pair of trousers, which he did grudgingly, telling the salesman that he had been lucky not to be a boy soprano!

As with all such incidents, the story spread fast and lost nothing in the telling, with Sweep being portrayed as savage and out of control, having chewed the man's leg almost in half. My father told the police officers that he viewed the attack very seriously and would take the dog in hand, which I took to mean that he would punish poor old Sweep. However, the 'punishment' came the following evening, when he returned home from work with a large marrow-bone which Sweep guarded jealously for the next week. Sweep continued to show extreme antipathy to anyone wearing Wellington boots, workmen's overalls, and any dark uniforms such as postmen or policemen, but the worst enemy in his eyes was the coal-man, who he hated with all his being. His saving grace was that, providing a member of the family was present, he would be tolerant of any stranger, so long as they did not threaten his loved ones, in which case he became a terror and would have died in their defence.

As with all dogs however, Sweep grew old, his eyes became blue, his muzzle grey and his joints stiff. I put off the day I dreaded for weeks, until one morning Sweep could hardly get to his feet and was obviously in some pain. I decided it was time for his last hunt so took him to the van with my gun and spade. When Sweep saw the gun he started to whine, his tail wagging feebly, his ageing body still eager to accompany his master in the field once more.

These hunting days had been more and more infrequent in latter years, as Sweep grew old. I had replaced him with a new dog, Sam, who Sweep hated deeply, and if he had been ten years younger would have killed. Such was his jealousy. I drove slowly to my uncle's farm, Sweep's tail beating the sides of the van like a drum and all too soon I arrived. It was a quarter of a mile to the hay meadow below the dead ash tree where generations of the family's dogs had been buried. Where Sweep would once have bustled around, checking every patch of cover for partridge or rabbit, he now lagged behind, unable to keep up, whining in frustration at his body's lack of strength and I had to wait for him, fondling his ears then walking on and calling him to follow.

Eventually we reached the site of Sweep's last resting place and I started to dig, Sweep lying down wondering why no rabbits appeared after all that digging. At last I was finished. My throat had a lump which almost choked me and my heart felt like a lead weight. I picked up my gun and produced a partridge, Sweep's favourite game, from my pocket and held it below his nose. His tail wagged furiously as I pretended to throw the bird for him to retrieve but put it back in my pocket. Sweep stood alert, his failing eyes and nose searching for the fall of the partridge, when I shot him behind the ear, killing him instantly.

I cut some bracken and laid it in the bottom of Sweep's grave, then placed him gently in his lair. I then gathered stones from a nearby rock-pile and built them up round Sweep's body, carrying a large flat stone to cover and entomb him. Hot tears hissed on the cold wet stone, as I slowly realised that I would never have as good a dog again.

CHAPTER TEN

Dogs

A Celtic keeper was lucky enough to attain the position of gamekeeper to a Saxon lord who owned a large tract of Ireland. The parish Priest who was a keen red setter man, lost no time in asking the keeper, who was one of his flock, for a day at the grouse: no guns of course; just the dog work. The young keeper could not refuse, indeed he looked forward to seeing the Priest's red setters, which were famed the length and breadth of Ireland, in action.

The day came in September when it was suitable to go out. A stiff breeze blew but it was fair and warm and shirt sleeves were the order of the day. The pair walked from the keeper's house over the moor but grouse were scarce until they progressed over the summit of the gentle hill which was the highest point of the moor.

The setters slammed on point, crouching, one backing the other and mirroring its every move, the Priest gently cajoling his charges in Gaelic as they slowly homed in on their quarry. Eventually the Priest, after exercising control over the two dogs, commanded them to flush, which they did with force and style and joy, dropping immediately the grouse took to the air and watching them arrow away, before drifting round the shoulder of the hill.

The young keeper watched in awe and wonder at the skill of the Priest and the beauty and drive of the pair of setters, while at the same time he looked out over the small fields of this part of Ireland which lay beneath him like a patchwork quilt to the blue sea that shimmered beyond. Small boats crossed the bay beneath a cloudless sky and he felt lucky to be alive. The young keeper eventually spoke. 'Father,' he said, 'is it true that a dog cannot enter the Kingdom of Heaven?' The Priest thought deeply before answering 'Yes my son, a dog has no soul so he cannot enter the Kingdom of Heaven.' The young keeper frowned and thought before he replied, 'It can't be that good then, can it?' The Priest could only smile.

During the second World War British soldiers based in India, before heading east to face the Japanese, decided that they needed a mascot. A dog which was half starved and seemed to belong to no-one was lured aboard a ship by the use of food. Once on board the dog was wormed, de-loused, washed and fed until it was unrecognisable from the cur that was originally rescued. The dog was named 'Tommy' and treated like a Lord, his every wish granted, until he became quite spoiled and overweight.

Eventually the regiment was deployed, spending months in the jungle, 'Tommy' becoming invaluable as a sentry dog, averting several attacks by barking or showing his special handler that strangers were about. The time came to return to India with 'Tommy' lauded as a hero and a lucky charm. The ship anchored and the regiment marched back to into Tommy's home town, he taking pride of place at the head of the men as mascot. Suddenly a small group of semi-feral dogs ran by, and Tommy joined them, despite orders then pleas from his handler. Tommy never came back and although he was seen from time to time running with his small pack, he never showed any inclination to return to his role as mascot.

These two rather pointless stories have been placed at the start of this chapter to illustrate that a dog can be the finest asset a man can have, but he can also let you down just when you least expect it. Primitive man probably had the best dogs. This may seem a sweeping statement but if we guess how he acquired his first dogs, we can gauge how useful they were to him and how they developed their usefulness as they became interdependent, their relationship becoming secure as man became more developed and prosperous.

Primitive man probably saw dogs at first as a food source. Pups would be acquired after the parents had been killed, perhaps for food. Then perhaps pups would be reared on spare food until they were large enough to be themselves killed for food. Perhaps a young dog accompanied hunters and proved useful in finding a wounded deer or pig, helping to haul the stricken animal down and hold it until the hunters could despatch it. When strangers or wild animals approached their camp the dog would bark a warning, even attacking the threat, causing the tribe to value the animal and eventually breed more like the ones they had to ensure continuity. Some dogs, of course, would not conform to man's requirements: some would be too brave and foolhardy and would be killed by large carnivores, or worse they attacked the children of the tribe and would have to be culled. Some would have no nose or little guarding instinct and would inevitably end up in the cooking pot but, slowly, over the generations a dog would be produced which fulfilled the tribe's requirements.

In modern times certain breeds still meet tribal needs: the Anatolian Karabash, or Turkish mastiff, is used by herdsmen in Turkey and surrounding states to guard their flocks against thieves and wolves. These dogs act almost like sheep, blending in and accompanying the flocks, completely accepted by them. But they are formidable, capable of breaking a man's arm or leg with their bite, while completely subservient and controlled by even the youngest of the shepherd's family. The selection of the most suitable animals has produced, over generations, the perfect dog for this purpose.

The requirements of a keeper's dog

Contrast this with the situation with which a young keeper today is faced when trying to acquire a dog to fulfil his requirements as a keeper's dog. Such a dog should hunt cover and flush game, but not so vigorously that large numbers are in the air at once, returning to his handler or at least standing still at each flush. He should retrieve from land and water, taking directions where necessary. He should excel in the collection of wounded game, having a keen nose and the instinct to follow a line. A vigorous constitution is a prerequisite for a keeper's dog as he cannot afford to keep a dog which may not be available for service on a specific day. The keeper's dog should have a placid temperament, as a hyperactive dog can be hard to live with for a busy keeper who may not have the time at certain busy periods to devote to a highly-strung individual. He needs to have stamina as, especially on a commercial shoot, the hours and work will be long and hard, any shortcomings in this department being cruelly exposed.

Where does one find such a dog, which breed and sex is best and how do you train him to your requirements? Hopefully I will be able to answer these questions in the following chapter. The following is a list of breeds which should be suitable for the role of a keeper's dog. The list is in order of popularity, with my opinions on the state of each breed, its strengths and weaknesses. This is a great risk for me to take as there is no surer way of upsetting a man or woman than by criticising their dog, or indeed the breed.

The labrador

The labrador is one of the most popular and successful breeds on earth. Its versatility has led to it being used in many spheres apart from the one for which it was originally bred. Drug and explosive detection, guide dogs, guard dogs, army scout dogs, police dogs: the list is a long one but the most striking quality of the labrador is the number that are kept as pets, their adaptability being the main reason for this. Argument over, you may think: the labrador is the ideal keeper's dog. If this book had been written 20–30 years ago, this would have been agreed.

My reason for qualifying my assessment of the labrador is that very few people actually breed the type of labrador which keepers admire. The current trend for field trial devotees to breed lightly-made, highly-strung dogs which can be put on a sixpence at long distances has produced a surplus of dogs which are too high powered for the average handler. The collection of runners is not valued as it once was by field trial judges, or if it is, the guns are encouraged to back each other up so that runners are rare, this being a deliberate policy of the field trial elite who are afraid of adverse publicity and the subsequent attention of the animal rights industry.

This means that a field trial champion might not have a superior nose or possess great ability on runners, a fact of which many laymen are blissfully unaware. Some professional trainers have used placid show dogs on field trial bitches to pacify the pups so that they can be sold to the average joe public who merely wants a shooting dog which will also fulfil the function of a family pet, having no desire to invade Poland with his dog.

So where can a gamekeeper acquire a suitable labrador for the type of work he will encounter? The answer is to look for someone who has a bitch which has all the qualities that you require: placid, active, sound in mind and body, easily handled, takes directions, good in water and perhaps most importantly, good on runners. When you have identified this paragon, ask her owner if he intends breeding from her. If the answer is yes, book a bitch pup and pray that she takes after her mother. If you know the dog that he intends to use as a stud, look for characteristics that may be passed on to the pups: this may help you to select a pup that takes after her mother. My advice is to buy a bitch as they are easier, as a rule, to train and although they come into season twice a year, because at any shoot there are bitches in season, coming into season or just out of season, a labrador dog is often in season all season long.

The English springer spaniel

Almost all that I have written in praise of the labrador can be applied to the English springer, apart from the fact that he is probably a bit too boisterous to make an ideal family pet. Modern field trial strains have become smaller, lighter, faster and more highly strung. The lack of colour which has resulted in many springers being almost all white is probably due to the introduction of jack russell terrier blood in the 1980s. As well as the lack of colour, this has caused mouth and temperament problems which were rare in the years previous to this. Speed has become the prerequisite of the modern field trial springer, with many being too fast for beating or even rough shooting. The ability to take the line of a runner is no longer bred for: speed and style with a white dog is the aim of the springer devotee. Stamina has deteriorated also, as this is never tested at trials, a twenty minute run being considered a long hunt. All these factors mean that it is difficult to find a good solidly-built, coloured, placid, cover-bashing, runner-collecting spaniel that will hunt all day and the next and the one after that. The solution is to find that bitch which has all these qualities. Trust only what you see, not what you are told. There are good springers out there, the problem is finding them.

The golden retriever

The golden retriever has never been popular with gamekeepers, apart from a handful of devotees. However, I feel that this may change as they have all the qualities that a keeper could wish for. They are more sensitive than a labrador or springer and will not suffer heavy-handed treatment but a good one is a joy to own, being more likely to hunt close like a spaniel while at the same time content to wait and watch birds falling as would a peg labrador. Again, look for that bitch and check the pedigree, for a preponderance of working dogs, as the show strains are worse than useless.

The cocker spaniel

The cocker spaniel is one of the gundog breeds which has made great strides in the last thirty years, due chiefly to the efforts of a gamekeeper, Mr Jack Windle, owner of the Jordieland strain of cockers. When cockers were at their lowest ebb in the 1960s and 70s Jack resolutely kept his strain going, all the time trying to improve his 'wee dogs'. The cocker spaniel was indeed lucky to have this man as its main devotee because quite simply he was a genius with dogs. I doubt whether any man trained such a variety of dogs to such a high standard, his dogs always displaying dash and verve with style and outstanding game-finding ability. Jack listened to other people and took on board their criticisms, slowly eliminating the faults in the breed while at the same time accentuating the positives.

In the 1990s labrador and springer men suddenly recognised the qualities that cockers possessed and the cocker became popular again, a situation which has continued to the present day. Jack, sadly, is no longer with us but his legacy lives on in his dogs and it is hoped that the coming generations realise that the Jordieland prefix meant more than the title 'Field Trial Champion'.

Other gamekeepers have taken to this breed. They are feisty, easily housed and fed, as well as being game finders. They can be easily handled, one celebrated keeper in the south of Scotland takes a dozen out to pick-up with on shoots in his area. The same rule holds true: find one that you consider is excellent and book a pup.

The flat-coated retriever

The flat-coat was once described as the 'keeper's dog' but this was probably not meant to be complimentary. When the fashion swung to labradors, few keepers kept flat-coats, aspiring to own the faster, more eye-catching labrador. The motive for this was probably monetary, many looking upon a dog as an investment, either as a trained dog or a breeding enterprise.

This usually results in a popular breed attracting admirers who only stay loyal as long as the breed commands top dollar, either as a pup or trained animal. The result has been that working flat-coats are rare but they do exist, and a good flat-coat is, for a working keeper, the equal of any other retrieving dog.

The curly-coated retriever

These used to be the ultimate keeper's dog, hunting cover, retrieving from icy water, killing vermin and biting poachers. They have fallen from favour however, probably because they are one-man dogs and formidable with it, so that a prospective buyer of an adult dog would probably have to possess a degree of courage not that common in the average gun dog buyer. This meant that the aforementioned profiteering keepers and dog breeders viewed the curly as a bad investment, especially when the motorcar became more popular and the breed's notorious smell when wet became a major drawback. There are still working strains about and if you want a versatile dog and do a lot of duck shooting, the curly will not let you down but remember he will not suffer fools gladly.

The Chesapeake Bay retriever

My appraisal of the curly coat applies to the 'Chessie', only more so. He is the rottweiler of the gundog world and is not a dog for the beginner or the faint-hearted. He is, however, one of the most loyal dogs in the world and if you can afford to buy one, he is an excellent dog for a keeper, especially if he is restricted to only one dog. Care must be taken with males to ensure that they are introduced to other dogs when they are young, otherwise there may be 'territorial' disputes with other males when attending shoots.

The German short-haired pointer

This is a great dog ruined by British breeders. In its homeland and other neighbouring countries, the short-hair is used much as a keeper's dog ought to be used. In September he will be used to pick-up on duck shoots and to point and retrieve on walked-up partridge days, then, as cover shooting develops, he will hunt and retrieve much as a gundog would in Britain. After the game shooting season is over he will be employed driving out roe does or boar to standing guns, assisting in finding dead and wounded animals that are difficult to find.

Foxes will be accounted for on these shoots, many short-hairs being capable of despatching a fox single-handed. These dogs are expected to hunt rabbits and hares from cover, giving tongue like a hound alerting his owner to the game approaching.

When roe bucks come into season, the short-hair will accompany his master, often pointing and alerting him to a buck that is totally obscured by cover. If his master wounds an animal, be it buck, stag or boar, the short-hair is expected to find the animal, baying until his owner can approach and despatch it. This will take him through almost to September when the ducks come in again, so it can be seen that the continentals get far more from their short-hairs, indeed all their dogs, than does the average sportsman in Britain.

The German short-haired pointer makes an excellent watch or sentry dog, being capable of scenting a man 2–300 yards away. Remember, this was the breed used to cross with the rottweiler to produce the doberman pinscher. This may have convinced you to buy a short- hair but I cannot say 'go ahead' without reservation. Very few people value the breed as a versatile all-round worker. Most, if not all, specialise in one task only, even showing, which means that buying a genuine short-hair is difficult: there is just too much chaff about to find the wheat.

Imported lines may be the answer but they will be prohibitively expensive and even then, the Germans seldom sell their best dogs, unlike after the war when they were desperate. This period, for 20–30 years after the war, produced the best British short-hairs but unfortunately the breeders could not recognise the good dogs that existed then and took several dead-end routes, with the present state of the breed being apparent.

The breed is ideal for the grousekeeper, being useful for counting grouse and also locating stoats and foxes. A young grousekeeper should therefore make enquiries to ascertain if a keeper in his area has a good bitch which may be having pups.

The German wire-haired pointer

This breed is similar to the short-hair but obviously has a rougher coat and is slightly larger, as a rule. He is perhaps more inclined to deer work than bird work but nonetheless many keepers have adopted the breed as a genuine all-rounder. They tend to be slower than a short-hair and are useful for dogging-in, as the birds can be flushed or chased back in the right direction, the handler using the dog on point to position himself to the best advantage. A good wire-hair may be easier to find than a good short-hair and is definitely worth considering especially in the north where the coat is more suitable to the harder weather.

The weimaraner

The weimaraner is a scenting hound which points. His natural pace is slow and he could be used by a keeper beating and picking-up, especially if he has deer stalking duties as well. He is not fond of water, so is not a good choice if duck shooting is a major part of your shooting itinerary. He can be a formidable guard so could be a dual-purpose dog if that was an option. Working weimaraners are scarce so I would not advise anyone setting his heart on obtaining a weimaraner to fulfil the role of a keeper's dog.

The large musterlander

These are a good choice as they are a bird-orientated Hunt-Point-Retrieve dog (HPR) with a number of working breeders. Their coat is suitable for hard weather and water. They are one of the easier HPRs to train, the only drawback being the price. They tend to be expensive.

The setters and pointers, I have not included in this section, as they are not versatile enough to be suitable as keeper's dogs. Of course if the keeper is employed on a dogging moor and his boss wishes him to use English setters then the employer would be expected to finance the purchase of such, but such scenarios are rare nowadays and the pointing breeds have become something of a luxury item owned and worked by a minority of devotees.

However, a first cross setter or pointer, usually with a labrador, will produce a 'dropper', ie. a hybrid between a setter and a retriever. These dogs are often very useful and should be reasonably priced. Similarly a first cross using a labrador dog on a short-hair bitch can produce a top class keeper's dog.

The most popular cross at present is the sprocker, ie. a cross between a springer and a cocker. This appears to improve both breeds but perhaps it tells us that neither is perfect. There has always been underhand matings in the cocker breed, a springer being used on a cocker bitch and the papers fabricated, indeed one famous dog which won the cocker championship was undoubtedly a sprocker. This is not as outrageous as would at first seem, as in living memory spaniels were classified as cocker, springer, field or sussex according to their size and colour with two or three litter mates being registered as different breeds. Sprockers may be the answer to your prayer but cheap they are not: you may have to pay more than you would for a pure bred English springer.

The springador, a cross between a labrador and a springer, can be a useful dog usually looking like a small labrador with feathering and a white spot on the chest. Remember in all these cross breeds the progeny can only be as good as the forebears of the parents. The fact that the pups are cross-bred themselves will do little to enhance their working ability.

Training

We will assume that you have bought a labrador bitch pup. How then do you proceed to turn this small appealing creature into a useful working keeper's dog? The first thing that you need to do is spend time with the dog; failing this, ask your wife to take her indoors for short periods to accustom her to noises and unusual sights which will alarm her slightly at this age but may frighten her witless at 6–9 months old if she has not been introduced to them at an early age. Some breeders anticipate this and play transistor radios to the pups from birth to eight weeks, hopefully helping the pups to adjust to the sounds of the modern world. Exercise should be limited until the pup is six months old and weight monitored so that she does not become overweight. An overweight labrador pup which is allowed to run after an adult dog from the age of 4–9 months is an ideal candidate for hip dysplasia, the strain on the hip joint when the bone is soft being thought to cause this. This can occur even if the parents have been x-rayed for this condition and found to be normal.

Start early

Some authorities state that the training of a pup should not commence until she has reached six months of age or even older. This is misleading baloney perpetuated by professional trainers who are too busy to spend time with young pups. Many of these trainers are so case-hardened that they would terrify a young sensitive pup and so prefer an older, ebullient and tougher pup which will need to be curtailed, some would say broken, rather than trained using encouragement and conditioning.

To this end many trainers of the old school would allow a pup of 6–9 months to hunt for themselves, chasing anything they flush. This guaranteed game-finding and avoided pups which were reluctant to hunt but created a dog which had to be 're-programmed' removing the undesirable faults such as chasing. The fact that dogs were produced by this method which fulfilled the function of a gun-dog tells us how tractable some of these animals were. However, a veil should be drawn over the failures, the dogs which, once they had tasted the forbidden fruit of the self-hunt, could not be 'adjusted'.

This is not to say that the trainer should rush headlong into pushing his pup too far too soon but should condition her to act in a way which will make her more amenable to training in subsequent months. An example of this is at feeding time. The pup has been used to competing with her brothers and sisters for food from the day she was born. This is a strong instinct, the instinct of survival.

When you feed her, hold her bowl over her head and say 'sit'. This does not have to be a loud command, indeed the whole concept of a command is an erroneous one as you are merely conditioning the pup to act in a certain way once a certain noise is heard, be it the human voice or for instance a whistle. Nor does the voice need to be a high-pitched falsetto as claimed by some experts. You can only command someone if they understand the language that you speak, so if you 'command' a Chinese man who speaks no English to 'sit', he would do nothing but if you gave him money every time he sat down when he heard you say 'sit' he would be conditioned to do it but he would not have learned English. Gently push the pup's back end down as you say 'sit' while still holding the bowl above her head, then place the bowl on the ground, holding the pup for a few seconds before releasing her with a 'release' word which can be any word but remember not to use a word which will confuse the dog in subsequent lessons. Some people click their fingers as a signal to release the dog from the 'sit' or 'stay' position.

As this lesson progresses, the pup should sit on hearing you say 'sit', place the bowl down but immediately lift it above the pup's head if she moves and tries to eat the food before being released. An intelligent pup will soon realise that moving triggers a negative response, ie. the food disappearing, so you are able to condition her gently at an early age without placing undue pressure on her. After a short time, depending on the trainability of the pup, she will sit and wait for the second stimulus before eating. You have now taken the first step towards producing a gundog.

The next step is to make a small dummy from a pair of old socks, then hold her facing away from you, waving the dummy in front of her nose. When she appears to be interested, throw the dummy about five yards and still hold for a few seconds before releasing her. This exercise should take place in a confined area with little to distract the pup, a restricted space outside her kennel which she is accustomed to would be ideal. She should dash out and pick up the dummy if all goes according to plan and if so, get down on your hands and knees, calling her and, with luck, she should come back proudly carrying the dummy.

Do not remove the dummy from her mouth but gently encourage her to sit, while at the same time stroking her beneath the chin so that she holds the dummy high, all the time praising her so that she associates the experience with a pleasurable result. Say 'dead' and gently remove the dummy from the pup after about a minute or so, making sure that she has no opportunity of dropping it before this. Only one retrieve should be given and the exercise should not be overdone, perhaps every second day would be sufficient; much depends on the temperament of the pup and her breeding.

Travel and the puppy

Take the pup in your car or other vehicle for short trips, gradually increasing the distance and duration until she is totally comfortable travelling. A pup which is not a good traveller should be accompanied by another dog which is a good traveller, if available. This tutor animal can be used to teach the pup to jump into a vehicle on hearing a command such as 'get in'.

Livestock

This period (under six months) is also the best time to introduce the pup to livestock, as at this age she will be intimidated by even sheep and will probably be put off domestic livestock for life, totally ignoring and avoiding them ever after, which is the desired result. The pup should always be on a lead before being taken into a field containing cattle, who will probably come to investigate. Great care should be taken as some types of cattle can be aggressive, especially if they have calves, and as soon as the pup shows signs of being intimidated, she should be removed from the field, this usually being sufficient to ensure that the pup will be stock-proof for the rest of her life.

Sheep are more difficult as they are more inclined to bolt on seeing a man and a dog. The best place therefore to introduce the pup to them is when they are penned for some reason. Enlist the help of a friendly farmer (they do exist, I have been assured of this!) and take the pup to a pen containing a ewe with a lamb or lambs and lift her over the fence, still on the lead, and place her near the sheep. The ewe will adopt a defensive posture stamping her feet and even charging the pup. Again when you feel that the pup has had enough and wants out of this situation, remove her then take her to a field of rams or older lambs that are not pregnant or feeding lambs. The pup should be on a long lead and walked towards the sheep. If they bolt, tug the lead and admonish her by shouting 'bah' even if she shows no sign of chasing.

Leave things for a few days then repeat the exercise, closely observing the pup's reaction. She should show signs of a lack of confidence at the first sight of the cattle. These signs may include a lowering of the head and tail and a desire to come very close to her human companion, some pups growling from behind their owner's legs as a false show of bravado. If this is the case then it is job done as far as cattle are concerned but temptation from sheep is far greater and the exercise may have to be repeated several times before the handler is fully confident to allow his dog to run loose where they are present.

Introduction to gunfire

When the pup is six months of age she can have her first introduction to gunfire. For reasons which will become apparent later, this should be a completely isolated exercise and should not connect in the dog's mind with retrieving or game flushing. You will need an assistant armed with a .410 who will position himself 100 yards away. Take your tutor dog with you and walk the two dogs, allowing them to play, then signal to your assistant to fire a shot 100 yards away from you. Take note of the pup's reaction. With any luck she will be so enamoured of her playmate that the gunfire has no effect. If so, repeat the exercise the next day, reducing the distance to 75 yards, the next to 50 yards, which should be enough until the pup is nine months old. If there is a reaction at 100 yards, repeat at 100 yards the next two days until there is no reaction. If the pup is obviously distressed by the shot, either running to you or trying to get back to the kennel or vehicle, then you may have a problem and great care must be taken to accustom the pup to gunfire.

Exposure to gunfire at too young an age can induce gun nervousness. The type of gunfire is also a factor, the sharp crack of high velocity .22 and centre-fire ammunition are more alarming to a dog than a 12 bore shotgun. A good idea is to use a 2½ inch .410 cartridge to introduce the young dog of 6–7 months, gradually introducing the twelve bore as described.

Finding the dummy

At this age the trainer should start hiding the dummy without her seeing it thrown, at first making it easy for her to find. A new stimulus should be introduced such as 'seek' or 'hie-lost', which should signal to her that there is something to be found. It may take a little time for the penny to drop but she should eventually start to hunt an area when she hears the stimulus 'seek', for example.

You should now introduce the whistle as a replacement for calling her name or saying 'here', for example. This can be achieved by calling her then whistling alternately with plenty of praise when she returns to you until she will respond to the whistle alone. Similarly the stop whistle replaces the word 'sit', usually accompanied by a raised arm.

Parallel to this, direction signals should be taught. Sit your dog 10 yards in front of you, then throw one dummy to the left of the dog, about 15 yards away from her. A second dummy is thrown right, again 15 yards or so away from her. The dog will want to retrieve the dummy to the right, the last thrown dummy, so point to the dummy on the left saying 'fetch'. If she moves to the right call 'sit', even putting her back to her original position.

Some dogs are very quick to learn this trick, it is useful leading up to this lesson to point to the single dummy on a blind retrieve: an intelligent dog will realise that this indicates the dummy's location and act accordingly.

Now that the pup will hunt for a dummy on hearing 'seek', for example, she can be taught to quarter. Use hand signals to direct her where you want her to go, stopping her by using your stop whistle when she goes too far, then redirecting her back within range. Similarly if she goes too far ahead, call her closer before signalling her left or right. A tractable pup will soon realise the parameters she has been set and after a few lessons will quarter her ground after a fashion, it being a good idea to hide a dummy on her beat for her to find, bearing in mind that she should be hunted on ground that is free of game at this stage.

First test

The time has now come for you to test her to see how well she has absorbed the lessons so far. Make her sit using your chosen word then walk five paces away holding your hand up to signal her to stay. You should have chosen a site similar to a lane where the pup will be restricted if she wishes to run past you. Throw the dummy away from the pup so that if she runs after it you can stop her (hopefully) always keeping an eye on her so that you can nip any charge in the bud. If she is steady, call her to you and praise her then walk away from the dummy calling the pup, then when you are back to where the pup has been sitting, make her sit and praise her, before sending her for the dummy.

Repeat this exercise once or twice a day in different situations until you are confident that your pup is steady.

The next test requires a tennis ball with a white ribbon attached which you should hide from the pup. Take her for a walk off the lead in an area which she is accustomed to, then without warning throw the tennis ball in front of her in a tempting way, immediately admonishing her with 'leave it!' This should be delivered forcefully so that she is in no doubt that you must be obeyed. If all goes to plan she should sit and if she does so, keep her sitting by raising your hand, then collect the tennis ball, hiding it from the dog again. Repeat this using different temptations, for example a dummy with pheasant wings attached, until you are sure that you can hold her under any temptation that you can invent for her.

233

It may be useful at this stage to have a resumé of the stimuli and related skills that the pup has learned.

2–4 MONTHS
1. Sit until allowed to move. Stimulus 'sit', click of fingers to release

2. Retrieve to hand. Stimulus 'fetch' and 'dead' to release dummy
3. Travel in vehicle

4–6 MONTHS
4. Enter vehicle on hearing 'get in'
5. Steadiness to livestock
6. Fire .410 at distance to accustom to gunfire

6–9 MONTHS
7. Blind retrieve. Stimulus 'seek' or 'hie-lost'
8. Check steadiness to thrown dummy
9. 'Leave it!'
10. Directional signals
11. Quartering
12. Introduce 12-bore at distance

These tasks are not set in stone, they can overlap, but it is important that you do not proceed until your pup is perfectly adept in all these exercises or tests. If you are not confident in one aspect, concentrate on it until the pup is proficient. I have not included walking to heel as I feel that it can be taught later, which avoids a sensitive pup becoming reluctant to hunt away from her master due to being curtailed at too young an age.

Hunting in a straight line
It is not totally necessary to have the pup hunt away from you in a straight line but it can be useful on long water retrieves to be able to push her out using a trigger word such as 'go back'. The easiest way to do this is to walk the pup down a lane where she is restricted as to the direction she can run. As you proceed, throw a dummy, telling her to 'leave it'. The pup should have marked the dummy but you must make sure that

she does not run in but follows you as you walk on.

After 50 yards or so, make her sit, then walk on ten yards before giving her the signal 'get back'. If all goes well she should have remembered the dummy and will dash back to collect it. That will do for the first lesson. Subsequent lessons can be undertaken alongside fences or walls until the command 'get back' sends the bitch in a straight line away from you. The distances the dog travels back can be gradually increased until she will go back hundreds of yards if required. When the bitch is proficient in this exercise, plant an unseen dummy or dummies, then take her to the area and using the same command, attempt to get her to find the dummy. If you are lucky she will go straight back and find the dummy (it helps to send her into the wind). If not, return to the original exercise for a week before trying again.

Once this skill has been perfected on land, take the bitch to water and allow her to watch 3 or 4 dummies thrown into the water. If possible have a strong wind blowing away from you which will blow the dummies further away. Send the bitch to retrieve, which she will do unaided for the first two or three dummies but may have difficulty finding the last one or two which by now may have blown some distance away. Blow the stop whistle and the bitch will almost certainly look at you. When this happens give her the command 'go back' and then hopefully she will swim straight back to one of the dummies and effect a retrieve. This will do for one day. Always end on a success as little will be gained from having her exhaust herself looking for the last difficult dummy or dummies.

Walking to heel

Now is the time to teach her to walk to heel. A lead and a metal choke chain will be useful, although most gun-dog trainers do not use the choke chain. Make sure that the choke chain is fitted properly in the correct way so that it slackens immediately the tension on the lead is removed, then proceed to walk with the bitch. The lead should be held in both hands with the dog on the left side. If the dog pulls forward or to one or other side jerk the lead saying 'walk', immediately releasing any tension that is placed on the choke chain.

Dogs do not like the noise or the tightening of the chain and will soon realise that if they walk close to heel when they hear the word 'walk', then these unpleasant experiences do not happen. This is not, however, an excuse for you to virtually hang the dog in an effort to impose your will. Use your brain: you are more intelligent than the dog (admittedly I have seen several instances where this did not appear to be the case), and you must anticipate the consequences of any action you take. Harsh treatment may be forgiven by some tough nuts but the average dog will be ruined by it.

After a few lessons your pupil should be walking to heel without challenging the chain in any way. When this happens, unhook the lead and allow her to walk wearing just the choke chain. Hopefully she will walk to heel as before and if this is the case and you are confident in your ability to control her by voice alone, remove the choke chain after a few lessons. All should now be well but if she reneges, go back to the beginning and use the choke chain and lead.

Introducing game

Up to this point the pup should have been kept away from areas where game was present as far as was possible, but now you should take her to ground where pheasants or other game can be found. Choose ground such as bracken or rushes where you can observe the dog's movements as you will need to anticipate when she flushes birds. Avoid thick cover where a dog can chase unseen or, worse still, pursue a bird or rabbit for a distance without her owner being aware of it.

Once you have selected an area take the bitch there, at heel, and sit her in front of you. If she is the right type she will look to you for the signal to hunt, for example 'seek'. When she hears this, she should start to hunt and become interested in the game scent, possibly becoming quite excited.

Watch her closely. Most dogs indicate by a change of expression that game is very close, their tail action becoming faster or stiffening just before a flush. When this happens get ready, and when she rushes in to try and catch the bird, blow the stop whistle and hopefully she will stop and watch the bird or rabbit away. If this occurs, leave her to sit for perhaps a minute before calling her to heel, then praise her. If she chases, you must stop her, if possible, then take her back to the spot where the game flushed. Do not be severe on her or you may stop her hunting altogether. Allow her to cool down then call her to you, praise her then end the lesson for that day.

Correcting a chase

If your bitch has chased, it is not the end of the world but this must not be allowed to become habitual and must be nipped in the bud. Purchase a clothes line and cut it to a length of 20ft. Attach this to your choke chain and place it on your dog. Proceed as you did in the previous lesson but do not remove the chain or line, keeping an eye on the line so that, should she chase, you can grab the end of it, so terminating the bitch's pursuit. When she chases do not jerk the line but stop her as gently as possible, calling her back to the flush and praising her on the spot.

Look for another opportunity to repeat the exercise and, with luck, she will not chase on this occasion. Repeat the lesson on subsequent days, shortening the line until you only have 2ft trailing from the choke chain. If she is still steady for several days, remove the line altogether and continue with just the choke chain until you can remove even this with confidence.

A dog cannot be worked as a gundog wearing a choke chain, there is too much risk that she will be caught up in branches or wire, especially in water, with fatal results. A compromise can be achieved here by using a light collar which is held by a small piece of Velcro so that if the collar becomes entangled it will come apart and free the dog.

Some dogs are too intelligent to be fooled by lines and collars, in which case the handler will have to use different tactics. These dogs will often not leave the handler's side when a collar is fitted, refusing to hunt until it is removed. Take a light choke chain and tie the two rings together putting the chain in your pocket before taking the dog out for a training session. Put your lead and choke chain on the dog and walk her for a distance before removing both of them. Select an area where there is unlikely to be any game, signalling her to hunt. After a minute or two blow your stop whistle just before you throw the light chain at her backside, which will hopefully cause her to stop dead in her tracks. Hold your hand up and try to hold her in that position while at the same time approaching her to retrieve the light chain. Hold the chain in your hand and show her it shaking it, so that she recognises the sound. Walk back to the position you were in when you threw the light chain and signal her to hunt again. Watch her closely; she may keep an eye on you, and if so signal her to hunt where you want her to go.

After a period suddenly lift your arm as if to throw the chain and blow your stop whistle, hopefully with the desired results. If it works, great: repeat every night for a week before returning to a gamey area where you can find out just how well she has learned her lesson.

If this does not work, you must go back to the beginning and grind her into submission until she is steady.

All this can be avoided if you select a tractable dog at the beginning and follow the steps slowly and surely as I have described.

Dogging-in straying birds

Once you are convinced that your bitch is steady use her to 'dog-in' birds that are straying. This is only feasible, obviously, if the bitch's progress coincides with the period when birds are straying, ie. September onwards. Make her stop at every flush and return to you before allowing her to continue hunting, always keeping alert for her trying to catch one of the birds. If this happens, blow the stop whistle and call 'leave it', which may do the trick. However, if she does catch a bird and ignores the whistle then you must go forward quickly and remove the bird from her jaws, allowing it to fly or run away while you hold her to prevent her chasing. Tell her again to 'leave it' so that she associates the words with the action of letting the bird go.

At the same time as you are teaching the dog to hunt without chasing you must teach retrieving as a parallel lesson. This is because at no time must your bitch associate a bird flushing or shooting with the pleasurable experience of retrieving. The way that I achieve this is to use a species different to the one that the bitch is hunting eg. a crow or a feral pigeon. These birds have the added advantage of being unlikely to be crushed by a young dog. The reason for this is that most dogs do not like to lift crows or feral pigeons so that when they are asked to retrieve them, they do so gingerly and, usually therefore, gently. This is in contrast to the seizure of game by a brash young dog, who may bite his quarry through sheer excitement.

Continue training these two roles, hunting and retrieving, on parallel lines until the shooting season proper when your bitch should be accustomed to flushing birds before returning to your side, exactly what you require in a beating dog. In the run-up to the first shoot, walk her to heel amongst large numbers of game to attempt to replicate the conditions at the end of a drive where birds are thick on the ground and any hunting dog would be likely to flush large numbers of birds, an undesirable scenario.

First day's beating

It is a good idea to take your dog beating on a shoot other than your own for her first day. Make sure that you take a lead and your whistle and do not be afraid to slip her onto the lead at times during the shoot when she will be under great temptation. These danger times are: first thing when you arrive at the shoot and other dogs are milling about; during the drives themselves when other dogs may be running wild and chasing; and at the end of the drives when dogs are retrieving birds past your dog's nose.

The first days are critical. If you can negotiate these safely then your bitch is less likely to go wrong on later days but you must be vigilant and nip any sign of unsteadiness in the bud, using the lead without hesitation if you are unsure that you can hold her. This may cause some comment from the 'experts' who are found on every shoot but ignore them, it is better to be safe than sorry with a young dog.

On your own days, when you will have responsibilities handling beaters etc, it may be prudent to leave a young dog at home until you can fully trust her as it is a difficult task to control beaters and young inexperienced dogs at the same time. However, once you are fully fledged as a keeper, you will be expected to have a competent dog with you on these days, which is where the easily-handled, placid dog comes into his own.

Retrieving game

Retrieving game should not be rushed into until the first half of the season is over. At this time the dog should be allowed to retrieve cold game kept back from the previous day's shoot, these birds being hidden in cover to replicate the situation you will encounter after a drive when the pick-up commences. If the young dog is rough on some of these retrieves, do not make a fuss. She will either settle down with experience, or if not, he is hard-mouthed and there is little that you can do about it. Do not reject such a dog, he will still hunt and be steady and if he does crush the odd bird it is not the crime nowadays that it would have been in days past when game was valuable. I would rather have a dog with a mouth problem that collected runners, than a velvet mouthed dog that couldn't find its breakfast. I am talking here of the dog which pushes one side of the rib cage in, not an animal that crushes game so badly that the bird is nearly chopped in half.

239

Collection runners

The collection of runners is the prime function of the gundog. This talent is the one which, if your dog possesses it, sets it above its peers and makes it a valuable asset which is a joy to own. Some people start very young pups by dragging a piece of tripe over a lawn, then allowing the pup to follow the trail with the reward of food for the pup. Later a dead bird or rabbit can be used similarly. These methods can help a dog to follow a line but my own view is that a dog with this instinct will not need to be taught while a dog without the desired instinct will never learn to perform this task, even adequately, despite all the training in the world.

TERRIERS

Terriers are a useful tool for any keeper but to the grousekeeper, or any keeper with an extensive acreage to cover, they are essential. There are a number of breeds which are popular and I will list these with the advantages and disadvantages of each breed.

The border

The border terrier is easily kept. He is placid and tolerant of other dogs. He is one of most trainable of terriers and can usually be called out of an earth, even when in contact with his quarry. His coat is ideal for the north of the country, being both warm and water-proof. He can be versatile for both beating and deer tracking and has few health problems.

His disadvantages are that he is slow to start (ie. they need to be more mature), although that is offset by the fact that he does not get beaten up as often as other terriers and will therefore work to a greater age. He can be too large for the typical earth in some parts of the country and his colour can be too similar to a fox, especially when he is covered in sandy soil. He can be expensive to buy, with working strains becoming rarer as the breed increases in popularity as a pet.

The Jack Russell

The Jack Russell is readily available, reasonably priced, starts early and can be biddable if his handler takes the trouble to train him. His white colour is ideal, as he is easily seen in cover.

His disadvantages are that he can be impetuous and aggressive with other dogs so that kennelling more than one may result in kennel fights, especially if they are not worked regularly. This can be avoided by selecting strains from breeders who have deliberately taken steps to breed out this undesirable trait.

The Lakeland

The Lakeland is tough and agile with a vigorous constitution and he fears nothing on this earth. He can be headstrong and difficult to call off when his dander is up and may be too large for the smaller enlarged rabbit holes that are common in some parts of the country. His leggy agility makes him ideal for crags and rock holes; in other words, the type of country where he was bred originally, ie. the Lake District. The Lakeland can be argumentative with other dogs, so kennelling may be a problem and you would have to take care that kennel-mates are compatible.

The Patterdale

The Patterdale is an all-black derivation of the black and tan Lakeland. He is named after the district in Lakeland from where the breed is said to have originated. Some terrier experts are not sure of this and say that they are merely Lakeland crosses that have bred true. I am not qualified to comment on this but the Patterdale does enjoy popularity with keepers, especially in the north of the country. Many people criticise them for being too hard but I have seen one working which was the ideal keeper's terrier, easily called out, placid and totally reliable and biddable. Perhaps selective breeding by keepers has produced a suitable strain custom-made for the gamekeeper. The breed is quick to start and needs firm handling when young as parameters need to be set if he is to become an asset rather than a liability.

The Plummer

The Plummer terrier was purpose-bred by Brian Plummer, the famous author and dog expert, to produce a terrier which suited his requirements. He used many breeds including Jack Russell, beagle, pit bull terrier and fell terrier, resulting in a flashy, fast, sharp, red and white terrier which has an excellent nose and packs well (ie. hunts in a pack) if you require a terrier to hunt cover and woods to drive foxes to standing guns. He is quick to start and his colour is ideal, standing out in heavy cover. His temperament is lively but tractable. Perhaps the only drawback is that he can be a problem to kennel with other dogs as fights can be serious, probably due to his ancestry.

The teckel

The teckel is the wire-haired version of the dachshund and he is totally a working dog. He has a great nose and is often used in Germany to track wounded deer or boar. He will go to ground and can be biddable, especially the females. They can be trained as gun dogs so there is less chance of gun-shyness which can be a problem with some terriers. He is not as athletic as most terriers, a deliberate policy by German breeders who use the breed to move deer and other game animals to standing riflemen, the slow methodical tracking style of the teckel causing the quarry to move slowly, looking back to see where its pursuer is rather than moving in the blind panic induced by a fast breed which a deer would see as a more immediate threat. If the keeper has deer stalking responsibilities, the teckel would be an option, the only deterrent perhaps being the price as teckels are expensive compared to other terriers.

Cross-breeds

Many breeders of working terriers crossbreed to gain the benefits of hybrid vigour. The most popular in times past was the Border/Lakeland cross. This produced an excellent working terrier which was very popular with keepers. The reasons for the success of this cross are not clear, Border men saying that the Border blood put brains into the Lakeland, while the Lakeland men claimed that Lakeland blood put fire in the belly of the Border. Whatever the truth, this cross worked, to such an extent that some strains are now breeding true. Many crosses involve the Border terrier with another terrier, perhaps the breeder wanted Border blood to calm the temperament of his strain or perhaps the owner of a Border bitch wanted to gain early starting and a different coat colour. Remember that breeders of working terriers are not wholly driven by financial gain and many are trying to improve the working abilities of their dogs.

Training a terrier

The keeper should construct a number of false earths on his beat. Stone, breeze blocks, brick or pipe can be used with a sleeping chamber covered by a paving slab. Drill the slab with two holes and feed steel snare wire through the two holes and a length of alkathene pipe. This makes a comfortable handle which facilitates the lifting of the slab to recover your terrier if this should be necessary. Once the earths have been in place for a time, rabbits or even foxes will take up residence and a young terrier may decide to investigate and if this happens all well and good.

If difficulty is experienced in entering a terrier, introduce him to a freshly killed fox and try to induce him to 'rag' it. If he does so and becomes keen, take the carcase away from him and take both the fox and terrier to the false earth. Push the dead fox into one of the entrances as far as you can then remove the fox lifting the lid of the chamber and placing the fox in situ. Tie a length of wire or baler twine to the fox then replace the lid and release your terrier who should enter the pipe and seek out 'his' fox. When he encounters the fox, pull the wire or string which will make him keener to 'rag' it so allow him to do so for a time, then go to the entrance and call him out. Praise him and even give him a tit-bit then allow him to re-enter if he wishes before calling him out again. Then secure him and remove the fox from the earth. With the right sort of terrier this will only have to be done once for him to be keen to enter and he will never look back.

Many keepers do not attempt to train their terriers which I think is a mistake. A biddable dog is always more pleasant to own than a wilful dog which is a law to itself. Obedience training can take similar lines to the training of a gundog with special attention to domestic livestock, as an untrained terrier loves nothing more than to chase and kill. Dogging-in can be undertaken by terriers, as can deer work, meaning that the small dog has a more all-round role than seasonal work if he is restricted to foxing alone. Add to this stoat, mink, rabbiting as well as the hunting of woods and cover for outlying foxes in early spring or late summer, especially in and about release pens that are about to be filled with vulnerable poults, and you can see that the terrier has an important role to play in a keeper's life and should be treated accordingly.

GUARD DOGS AND SCOUT DOGS

Gamekeepers have used dogs to detect and apprehend poachers and other felons since time immemorial, long before police forces utilised a dog's unique talents to deter and catch the wrong-doer. Indeed the first police officer in Germany to use police dogs was a sergeant who was an ex-keeper. It is, however, with some misgivings that I have decided to include a section on guard dogs in this chapter.

The badly trained and/or handled guard dog is more dangerous than a gun and the keeper must accept the responsibilities that he acquires when he owns or trains one. Recent adverse publicity has put the ownership of dogs for personal protection in a bad light and a keeper with an uncontrollable, savage animal may end up in court facing a jail sentence, so it is imperative that he is careful in the training and handling of his potential canine guardian.

Certain breeds are suitable for the duties of keeper's protection/ scout dogs and I will list them and try to point out their advantages and disadvantages.

The German shepherd

This is the most recognisable guard dog in the world. Every police force uses them and for good reason as they are easily handled and trained, yet are aggressive, powerful and fast. They are very discriminating in that they seem to recognise when they are needed to be aggressive or when they should be accepting of a stranger. The drawbacks are that they are becoming harder to find as fewer are bred as working dogs and more for the pet market and for showing.

Adult dogs can be acquired, often cheaply, from homes which they have outgrown and probably dominated their owners. Such dogs are best acquired at under 18 months of age but be careful, many owners buy German shepherds and indeed the other guarding breeds for guarding purposes and think that it is a good idea to tease the dog and teach it to snap at a dummy sleeve or similar. If they do not inform you of this (such people do not think it important to warn a prospective purchaser of this early 'training') you or one of your family may unwittingly trigger the dog to attack with disastrous consequences.

It is advisable, therefore, to take care when selecting an adult dog and if you are in doubt as to its reliability, make some excuse and look elsewhere. The advantage of the adult is that you can see the finished dog: if he is formidable it is there for you to see, whereas with a pup you may be unfortunate enough to buy a dog which becomes a poor specimen of the breed. Most people, however, believe in the old adage 'buy a pup and any problems are your own fault while an adult has them already', and I would agree. Unless you need a dog urgently then an adult is the only choice. When buying a pup look for a breeder who produces large, fearless working dogs, check the parents, pay your money and take your choice and chance.

Sable-coloured German shepherds seem to have a high percentage of good workers. Avoid long-coats as they are too difficult to keep clean when working in woods and muddy conditions and most importantly, only buy where the parents and grand-parents have been tested for hip dysplasia.

The rottweiler

The rottweiler is a very powerful animal, capable of inflicting severe damage to anyone foolish enough to tackle him. He has become very popular in recent years but this has brought with it problems as some of the breed can be volatile, attacking without warning with devastating results. Selection is therefore critical and care must be taken when buying a rottweiler. The same rules applying as in the case of the German Shepherd.

One advantage of the rottweiler is that both sexes are effective as working dogs, whereas many German shepherd bitches, for example, are too small.

Another advantage of the rottweiler is that he will not be deterred by pain as some other breeds would be, indeed pain makes him if anything more determined, a useful attribute if the keeper encounters a group of violent poachers who would like nothing better than softening the ribs of anyone who stands in their way. In such situations a pair or trio of dogs are desirable and should deter even the most determined and deranged wrong-doer.

The rottweiler at his best is tractable and obedient, placid and protective, many people describing them as the ultimate guard dog who needs little or no training to be a protection dog, it being natural to him.

The disadvantages are that he can be dominant and needs an experienced handler and is not so inclined to search a wood looking for his quarry as would a German shepherd for example. At the end of the day he is a great deterrent to any poacher and as such is almost certain to fulfil his function.

The doberman

Much of what has been said of the rottweiler can also be said of the doberman but he is faster, sharper and more highly strung. I cannot recommend him to the keeper, however, as working dogs are scarce and many seem to feel the cold and wet, making them unsuitable for service outdoors in the British winter, especially at night. He can be extremely keen on deer (as can the German shepherd) probably because German pointer blood was one of the different breeds used to produce him by crossing to the rottweiler (greyhound is also rumoured to have been used which probably exacerbated this undesirable trait). This obviously makes him useless as a keeper's dog as he would probably be half a mile away chasing a deer while poachers were knocking seven bells out of his master.

The bullmastiff

The bullmastiff was custom-bred by keepers as a poacher catching dog (his other name is the keeper's night-dog). The cross was between the mastiff and the bull-dog – not the bull-dog we know today but a breed more akin to the Staffordshire terrier. This produced a dog after a few generations three-quarters mastiff and quarter bulldog, which was powerful, active and aggressive. They were apparently taught to down their victims by jumping on top of them pinning them down then growling at every move of the unfortunate man. Many were used as yard dogs, protecting premises at night after the owners went home and there is a documented case of a bull-mastiff holding a thief for several hours until his owner opened up the next morning. There are no working strains, as far as I know, at the present time but the breed is still very formidable, capable of inflicting severe damage on anyone unfortunate or stupid enough to get on the wrong side of him.

Brindle would be the preferred choice for a working dog, being the perfect camouflage. The breed is very quiet and placid but is not for the novice handler, bitches probably being a better bet than males. This was the case in yesteryear when keepers found that male dogs could take too much interest in the female dogs which accompanied poachers.

The Belgian shepherd

The Belgian shepherd is smaller and lighter than the German shepherd but is more agile and faster. The Malinois type, which is fawn with a black mask, has many adherents who breed for work. The coat is ideal for outdoor work and the breed is easily trained and tractable. The keeper who wants to keep several dogs would find these excellent as their size is small enough to pack three or four in the back of a Landrover or small pick-up. They are excellent as scout type dogs, being predatory by nature and keen to find their quarry.

The border collie

The border collie can make a first class guard, some strains being quite large, the only proviso is to check for gun-shyness as this is very common in the breed. The other disadvantage is the breed's obvious interest in sheep. This can be a serious disadvantage in sheep country and is one of the reasons why the keeper is best advised to buy a pup from one of these breeds, because to stop an adult collie, German shepherd, doberman or Belgian shepherd from chasing sheep once he has started can be very difficult. Such a fault, even when cured, will make the handler distrust the dog, fearing that if he is released he will revert to his bad habit.

Dual-purpose dogs

There are some breeds which are dual purpose, being able to be used as gun-dogs and guard/scout dogs. These are Chesapeake Bay, curly-coated and labrador retrievers. Some people may be surprised at the inclusion of the labrador but he had been used as a police dog for many years until quite recently. He can be tough.

I remember as a boy the local dairy kept a large alsatian which used to attack passing dogs on a Saturday when the gates were left open for some reason. A man who we had never seen before was walking towards the gates accompanied by a large labrador. We warned him that the alsatian was loose and that it would attack his dog. He smiled and bent down to remove his dog's lead and collar. We chose a safe spot where we could see the 'action' and awaited developments.

The alsatian charged, a slavering inferno on four legs enraged at this trespasser on his patch, hit the labrador like a steam train and the two dogs became embroiled in a seething mass of fur and teeth when suddenly the alsatian screamed and raced for the sanctuary of its kennel, the labrador's owner stopping it from pursuit with one word (something I have never forgotten). The alsatian sat in his kennel looking fearfully back at the labrador. We noticed something strange about him, a dog we had held in awe and fear for years: he had only one ear. The labrador had bitten the other one off!

A ghillie from the north of Scotland moved to a position in the Western Isles where he discovered that the locals were doing a fair bit of poaching. He was offered a labrador dog of suspect temperament which proved effective in curtailing these activities. One evening, while walking alongside the river which he watched, he met a man with a male English bull terrier. Before long a battle royal developed. The ghillie was fearful that his dog would be severely injured but no, the labrador trounced his opponent and to this day he does not know if the man and his dog were sent by the local poachers to disable his labrador. In any event his reputation was enhanced, conspiracy or not. Police forces, the RAF and the army all used labradors as security dogs, only switching to German shepherds because their appearance was more intimidating than the labrador.

Other dog breeds

The other breeds are the German short-haired pointer, the German wire-haired pointer and the wiemaraner. These breeds are used as guard dogs as well as hunting dog by German keepers or Foresters, the nearer to the original German lines the better. The advantages of these dual-purpose dogs is that they are used all through the year, especially if poaching is not a permanent problem, in which case the dog can be utilised in another capacity. Once the keeper is known to have a guard dog, the number of poachers who are prepared to try their luck will be severely reduced, most going elsewhere for a quieter life. This obviously means that your dog will become almost redundant, a desirable scenario but some role should be found for the dog to keep it fit in mind and body.

This is where the dual-purpose dog comes into his own. I have found that it is quite possible to combine both roles, most dogs realising that different situations demand different reactions: witness police dogs that can be petted by children minutes before engaging in man-work.

Salmon poachers

Let us look at the various scenarios where a dog may ensure that the keeper does not have to enlist the aid of a stick to continue walking after a confrontation with poachers.

If the keeper has a river to watch, he will have to patrol the riverbanks at night during vulnerable times when fish are running. This is a dangerous situation for the keeper as fish poachers can be desperate men, especially now that fines and imprisonment are severe, and they are capable of extreme violence to evade capture. The fact that they often operate mob-handed makes the acquisition of a dog even more desirable.

These gangs almost always engage a look-out to forewarn the salmon poachers that someone is approaching, at which point they merely withdraw into cover until the threat is past. Many keepers, to counteract this, try to second-guess the poachers and lie in wait at the most likely or vulnerable spots on the riverbank which can be successful. But a better method is to wait at one likely spot while sending out smaller groups or even single men with dogs and radios/phones to summon help to less likely areas. In this scenario, always work into the wind, watching your dog to see if he indicates the presence of intruders, then, once you have confirmed that they are operating, summon assistance, all the time observing to see if they try to escape and if so, the route they take.

Off-season dummy runs should be undertaken to give the dog experience and also to learn to 'read' the dog's actions. The rottweiler or bull-mastiff is the best dog for this type of poacher as salmon poachers will stop at nothing to escape with their haul of fish and are almost certain to seriously outnumber the keeper. Remember not to send the dog into the water to apprehend these felons, despite the temptation, as the dog loses all the advantages he possesses over a man once he enters the water.

Dogs and hare poachers

Hare poaching using lurchers or greyhounds is common and the participants are capable of violence when attempts are made to curtail their activities. Because of the presence of dogs used by the poachers, bitches will be less likely to be distracted from the job in hand, which is desirable as these lads seem to relish confrontation and will often seek out the keeper rather than avoid him. Again, rottweiler or bull-mastiff bitches would be the preferred choice, probably in pairs. When travelling the roads in your vehicle, remember to allow the dogs access to the front of your Landrover if you are using one. This is because poachers have been known to box a keeper in with a vehicle in front and behind so that the dogs could not be released from the rear door which could not be opened.

Day poaching

Day poaching is becoming more popular as a sport, these lads using air-rifles to pot any game which crosses their path. They often walk long distances to their intended target wearing face masks and real tree camouflage clothing and can be a real problem to catch. A dog which can search for an intruder is a real asset but it must be under control, holding its victim at bay by barking, and only biting to protect its master. The German shepherd, Belgian shepherd (malinios), labrador or the German hunter-pointer-retriever breeds are the most suitable for this task as they are more easily trained to stand-off rather than bite.

Night-poaching

Night-poaching is not as common as it once was but it still goes on and a dog is the most effective deterrent to this activity. The dog will have to be stock-proof and broken to deer, as well as completely ignoring other game, if it is to be fully efficient in its role. Two dogs are best, one staying at heel as a defence dog, the other a hunter whose only desire is to close with his quarry, possessing a drive more developed by training than is normally found in an ordinary dog.

How do you train such a dog? Some people do not but merely acquire a dog of doubtful temperament and patrol the woods with this animal on a long lead, never letting it loose. This can be effective enough so long as no-one calls your bluff and the very fact that you have a dog will reduce poaching by itself but most people prefer to own a dog which is not a paper tiger.

Building confidence in your dog

We will assume that you have acquired a suitable dog by whatever means and it is now 9–18 months old. The dog should have been trained in obedience along similar lines to the ones set out in the gundog section. The dog should not have been cowed, however, as such a dog will never make a guard dog as – it must possess a degree of self-confidence to be effective. You will need to enlist the assistance of a 'criminal' who should not be known to the dog. Arrange for him to approach the dog's kennel at dusk and observe the dog's reaction from a distance. Hopefully the dog will be hostile, barking, growling and showing his teeth and whenever he does this the 'criminal' should retreat and go home, allowing the dog to think that he has scored a victory. This should be repeated three or four times with the same result, ie. the dog emerging victorious.

Now fit a collar and a long lead to the dog, one which is strong and comfortable to hold and take the dog to a pre-arranged place where your 'criminal' is hiding. This should be in a wood in a situation where you would possibly encounter a real poacher and your 'criminal' should have an escape route so that he can retreat from the dog. Walk into the wood and hold the lead firmly as you do not know at this stage what your dog's reaction will be. The 'criminal' should step out and approach threateningly. Your dog should react correspondingly, barking, snarling etc even lunging at the 'criminal'. Again when this happens the 'criminal' should make good his 'escape' and go home. This exercise should be repeated in different situations until the dog is very keen on encountering his adversary.

If possible introduce different 'criminals' and put the dog in situations where totally innocent people are encountered who should be made aware that they must be totally indifferent to the dog, no matter what happens. During all this training the handler should keep the dog on a tight lead and quash any aggression by the dog towards the tame 'criminal' with as much force as is necessary. It is the simplest thing in the world to train a dog to bite someone, but to produce a dog which can be used in a professional manner, the animal must possess a level of discrimination that will make it safe in all but the most exceptional of circumstances. It is to be remembered that you are likely to encounter far more friends than foes while travelling your beat, therefore you must allow your dog to encounter both if he is to stand any chance of becoming selective and safe.

A stage further

You should now build a cage for your 'criminal' which can be made from scrap Rylock and should be big enough for a man to stand up in. Place the cage in a easily accessible part of the wood where your 'criminal' can gain access to it quickly. Repeat the previous exercise as before but when the 'criminal' retreats he should run to the cage which should be outside the view of the dog. When you are sure that the 'criminal' is safely caged, release the dog who will probably run to the last place that he saw the 'criminal', and encourage him by saying 'Where is he?' and if he is the right sort he will use his nose to find his enemy and on doing so he should bark and the 'criminal' should encourage him to do so.

As you approach the dog, praise him, allowing him to bark while you stand alongside until you put him back on the lead. Allow the 'criminal' to exit the cage and then escort him back to your vehicle, placing him inside before taking him to a pre-arranged destination.

During the escort keep the dog on a short lead and do not encourage him to the extent that he wants to attack. The dog should adopt a neutral yet alert attitude in this situation learning that if a cornered poacher is submissive he should not be attacked. The cage should be made portable so that it can be placed in different woods and the exercises repeated until the dog is proficient.

The next step is for the 'criminal' to hide in the cage in the wood and for the dog to find him and bark and bay without needing the stimulation of the chase first to get him going. Encourage him by asking 'Where is he?' and he should start to look for his old adversary and when he finds him he should bay as before. Again repeat this until the dog is proficient, always capturing the 'criminal' as before so that the dog always thinks that he has won and the situation mirrors what will happen in a real situation.

Muzzled practice

The next step is to try the dog while he is wearing a box muzzle. These can be purchased from specialist firms and are of strong construction, made from leather and attached to the dog's collar so that he cannot remove it. The purpose of this development is to teach the dog to avoid blows from an assailant's stick or boot in as natural a situation as possible. The muzzle should be placed on the dog for short periods at first until he ceases to see it as a disagreeable experience. Once he is comfortable with the muzzle, arrange for the 'criminal' to hide in a wood and proceed as before, the only difference being that the dog should have a short line attached to his collar and the criminal should take the precaution of having vulnerable parts of his body such as the forearms and genitals protected by some form of padding just in case the dog succeeds in removing the muzzle.

When the dog finds the 'criminal', the man should keep the dog off using the stick, while at the same time aiming kicks at the dog's ribs. The dog should dodge these attacks while at the same time attacking the 'criminal'. Some very powerful dogs will, despite the man's defensive actions, knock the 'criminal' to the ground and if this happens the handler must haul him off using the short line giving the command 'Stop!' This is not a bad sign, it just means that he is a whole-hearted dog but you must go back a stage and reinforce the obedience lessons before progressing.

On the command 'Stop', the dog should lie down, ceasing its attack. The dog can only really be tested on its adherence to this single command while it is in the process of attack, as the level of excitement it experiences during this experience cannot be replicated in any other situation.

Remember to also allow the dog to encounter good guys when he is wearing the muzzle, checking any aggression firmly and ensuring that the people encountered act in a neutral manner. It is not permissible to work the dog in real situations wearing the muzzle as a poacher would immediately take advantage of this and kill the dog, taking great pleasure in the act. Also the finished (fully trained) dog should not attack one particular part of the body and hang on, where he will be vulnerable to a knife or heavy stick since many poachers, if not all, are armed. The dog should only bite to defend his handler and should select the most convenient place to sink his teeth, avoiding the genitals and the area above and including the neck.

Unmuzzled

The dog should be tested using different 'criminals' in the cage and using the muzzle alternately, until you are certain that you can hold him no matter how excited he becomes, at the same time ensuring that he is still reliable with the general public.

If you are confident that he is safe and under control the next step is to try him unmuzzled against a criminal who must be wearing suitable protective clothing. This is expensive to buy but may be available second hand over the internet or you could possibly hire it from a professional dog trainer. Modern protective suits are far less conspicuous than the early models, which were bulky and unnatural but many 'criminals' were only confident working with a dog and handler that was an unknown quantity wearing a full suit.

It is possible to make the padded sleeves etc yourself but remember that some dogs have a very powerful bite inflicting pain on the 'criminal' so always err on the side of caution, paying particular attention to the groin area and the upper body including the face and head. When you have protected your 'criminal' sufficiently, set up the normal situation with the difference that the dog is not muzzled. If all goes to plan, the dog will find the man and corner him baying, allowing you to approach and take control, telling him to 'Stop' whereupon the dog will lie down.

You should then approach the man who will attack you, causing you to call out. The dog on hearing you should attack the 'criminal' and the dog should be allowed to win the battle at which point you should command him to 'Stop', the dog ceasing its attack and lying down.

Once the dog is reliable in this exercise he is ready for active service, always remembering to allow him to encounter innocent members of the public on a regular basis, especially underkeepers who might accompany you when you venture forth to catch poachers. Underkeepers and close associates should never be used as 'criminals' as this would be too confusing to the dog and may lead to a situation where the dog attacked them rather than the poachers.

Attack or self-defence?

Many of you may wonder why the dog is not taught to chase a poacher and pull him down. My reason for this is part legal and part training. If I send a dog in to attack someone, it could be construed in a court of law as an assault even though the methods I have described produce a dog which only attacks when his handler is attacked. Also, because the dog has never been trained to chase, it is easier to control because the very basic instinct of the dog to chase has not been encouraged. The time to worry is when the poacher is running towards you, not when he is running away.

Another query may be raised at the lack of sleeve work, concentrating on the right arm. This may be desirable for a police dog in an urban setting but the average poacher, on encountering a dog, will lure it into grabbing a coat or some thick fabric wrapped round his arm, then stab the dog while it is engrossed in the sleeve.

Some may also wonder why the dog is not commanded to attack when the handler is attacked but this should be an automatic reaction not requiring a command, especially as the handler could be felled by a stick and rendered unconscious, unable to give any command.

The protection dog will be a great asset to any keeper and should be treated accordingly. His kennel should be spacious and should give him a good outlook so that he has something to interest him during times that he is not working. Ideally, it should be situated near to the keeper's house but at the same time be away from people who may torment the dog, safe in the knowledge that he cannot escape. He will be a big dog so he must be fed enough and good quality food to keep him in peak condition. The acquisition of such a dog will change the attitude of the keeper: he will almost look forward to the visits of poachers so that he can try the dog out, although once he has gained a reputation, these poaching visits are likely to be few and far between.

CHAPTER ELEVEN

Guns, Grouse and Deer

The reader may think it strange that this book makes first mention of firearms in its final chapter. This is quite deliberate on my part, as many young keepers join the profession every year thinking that they are entering a land of non-stop shooting opportunities: pigeon, rabbit, deer, fox, even ducks and game, affording him a sporting itinerary that he could only have dreamed of in 'civvy' street. He quite rapidly becomes disillusioned, for keepering can be a long, grinding job of checking traps and feeding and watering birds and if you are not interested and dedicated you will soon be found out.

Every year the Situations Vacant column of *Shooting Times* contains advertisements from September to December for a vacancy to be filled out-of-season due to someone finding that the job was not as glamorous as they had expected. There can be sport available but much of this will be reserved for older keepers and a young keeper will have to earn the right to participate fully. This may not sit well with the present generation, as they have grown up in a 'have now' environment and the philosophy of working and saving for something is alien to many of them.

The reader may think that I am being a tad miserable and discouraging to prospective young keepers, but I refute this. I am doing many young people a service by telling them as it is and I reiterate: unless you are interested only in providing game for other people to shoot as your prime motive for becoming a keeper, you will never be successful. Many people enter the profession hoping to go shooting every day or to train dogs for field trials but they are seldom successful and prevent other dedicated potential keepers from attaining a position.

Another reason for leaving firearms to this late stage in the book is that there is a wealth of literature describing shooting techniques and a bewildering array of different weapons available to the young keeper. For this reason I will try to advise on only the best options and hopefully prevent the reader making the same mistakes as I did at the same age.

Shotguns

Where shotguns are concerned, the keeper should posses one gun and use it for everything. This is because all guns are slightly different and to chop and change can be fatal if, for instance, a fox gives a very difficult shot and then is gone. My choice would be a Benneli multi-shot semi-automatic on firearms certificate, giving the keeper up to eight chances, a comforting option when waiting for a fox to bolt or a hoodie swooping from her nest.

Some keepers keep a 'good' gun which they use when invited to shoot elsewhere at Keeper's Days etc. Many find that they do not shoot as well with this gun as they do with their everyday 'working' gun, which is quite understandable as they are bound to become more proficient with a gun that they are using every day. The Benneli is quite expensive to buy new but there are many good second-hand ones available, the advantage of them being that they process virtually all cartridges available. Recoil is reduced due to much of it being absorbed in ejecting the spent shell and reloading a new one. This can be desirable as many shooters who have used heavy ammunition from an early age suffer neck and shoulder problems in later years. It is preferable to purchase a multi-choke which allows the shooter to change from tight choke (long range) to improved cylinder (short range) with several options in between.

If the keeper is short on finance and cannot afford to purchase a Benneli, he should buy an inexpensive side-by-side. These can be obtained from most large gun shops for little money, the popularity of over-and-unders causing the less fashionable side-by-sides to be available at bargain prices. Remember to haggle and use cash. Once he has the side-by-side, the young keeper should start to save for a Benneli, this being good for the young keeper, it giving him a target to aim for.

Rifles

The first rifle that the young keeper should purchase is a .22 rim-fire. If the rabbit population is not too great, a bolt action fitted with a sound moderator should fit the bill. The Czech BRNO is widely available and is very accurate and reliable, my only criticism being that the trigger pull is heavy. This has been avoided in the newer models which have an adjustable trigger mechanism allowing the shooter to find the trigger pull which most suits his style of shooting.

If rabbits are very plentiful the keeper will have to spend many nights on a quad bike shooting large numbers of rabbits. Under these circumstances a semi-automatic .22 is a real asset, allowing the marksman to take several shots without having to lift his head from the stock as he would have to if he was using a bolt-action. A sound moderator and sub-sonic ammunition are essential for this type of pest control, and it is preferable to purchase a rifle which has already been screw-cut so that it can accommodate the moderator. If the rifle is not already screw-cut it will have to be done by a competent gunsmith with an obvious increase in cost.

Telescopic sights

Telescopic sights are essential for the professional and the best quality you can afford is advisable. Cheap scopes which are primarily designed for air rifles can be adequate but if the keeper steps up a level to a good quality scope, it is well worth the extra expense. Many modern scopes have systems incorporating bullet drop compensators which can allow the marksman to shoot at long range by using the reticules on the scope as a range finder. These scopes have various horizontal reticules and, with practice, the shooter will know which reticule coincides with a certain range, ie. 50 yards, 75 yards, 100 yards up to 125 yards. A rough range finder can be used by fitting a target, say a rabbit, between the reticules which are different widths apart. Practice will tell the shooter how far away the rabbit is by which gap he fits into eg. 75 yards, whereupon he knows to use the 75 yard reticule to aim at the target.

Before zeroing a rifle, it should be checked and the sound moderator should be fitted and fully tightened as it will be used when you are shooting for real. The mounts, the plates attached to the action to which the scope rings are fitted, should be checked to make sure that they are tight and have not become loose, some people using a little 'lock- fast' glue on the threads to ensure that they do not slacken off with use.

The rings should be steel and good quality; it makes a difference if they are so, and the scope should not be tightened in them until the eye relief, ie. the comfortable distance between the eye and the lens of the scope, is adjusted. Most good quality rings use allen keys to tighten them, usually supplied with the rings.

Once the rifle is checked, an adequate supply of ammunition should be available, obviously the same ammunition that you will be using on live quarry. A large board 4ft square with a circle 1 inch in diameter marked in the centre should be nailed to a post and the shooter then retires 25 yards away. It goes without saying that the target should have a back drop, safe and secure such as a bank or hillside, with no possibility of any stray bullets causing injury or harm to anything or any person. Fire one shot and you should be able to see through the scope where the bullet has struck. It is likely to be some way off target unless you have used a bore sighter, a device which aligns the barrel with the scope. These are fairly expensive but it is possible that you could borrow one from the gunshop where you purchased the rifle and ammunition. We will assume that your shot is, say 5 inches high and 4 inches to the right of the target. Your telescopic sight will have two turrets, one on top and one on the right hand side, covered by screw on caps. Take these caps off and you will see a dial underneath, which usually says ¼ inch click at 100 yards, for instance, and an arrow indicating which way the turret should be turned. In the middle of the arrow on the turret on top of the scope should be the word 'up'; on the one on the side an 'R' will indicate right (check that this is indeed the case as I remember zero-ing a rifle for my employer which came from a famous London gunmaker, the scope having been fitted with the side adjustments on top and the other on the side which caused much confusion until it was turned to its proper position).

You are 5 inches high, therefore turn the turret down, ie. the opposite direction to that indicated for 'up' on the scope; try 10 clicks. You are 4 inches to the right, so turn the turret 8 clicks in the opposite direction to that on the turret indicating 'right'.

Try another shot: you can now see how far your adjustments have moved your shot and act accordingly. For instance if your 10 clicks on the 'up' turret brought your shot down halfway to the point of aim, it obviously would need the same again to be dead on target. Similarly the lateral adjustment can be gauged from how far your adjustments moved your second shot left.

The rifle should now be on target and it is now the time to move to the distance that you would normally shoot your quarry, say 50 yards. Fine-tune the adjustment until you are hitting a 50 pence-size target with every shot at this range. The scope may have had to be adjusted from its original zero to be spot on at 50 yards.

When you are confident at this range, try 75 yards and check where on the scope's reticule you would have to hold, then try 100 yards, 125 etc. Some shooters record the different aiming points on paper and tape them to the side of the stock or keep them on a small card, so allowing the marksman to hold on the correct point every time.

Range finders

Once you have started to use this system of range adjustment you may wish to purchase a range finder. These tell the shooter the exact range of an object from 0–800 yards. They resemble a monocular or small camera and the target is viewed through a lens and a button pressed, whereupon the range is displayed. These can obviously be used for centre-fire rifles also and are a definite asset for a keeper who has a beat with a lot of open ground and who spends much time ambushing foxes and crows.

Centre-fire rifle

Virtually every keeper possesses a centre-fire rifle for fox control, usually lamping at night. There are numerous good quality rifles available and all of them will do the job. For lamping, a .222 is quite adequate as the ranges will not be long and the bullet drop from all small calibre centre-fires is similar up to 200 yards, give or take an inch.

Sound moderators can be fitted although they are expensive, it being a moot point whether they help to shoot more foxes. Perhaps the main advantage is the reduction in disturbance to people in the neighbour-hood where you shoot.

If the keeper has deer control responsibilities I would advise the purchase of a .243 to be used for both fox and deer. The only proviso is that if the keeper needs to shoot large red or sika stags he may feel that he needs a heavier calibre. My own view is that if the shooter looks into the various bullet weights and loads, he will be able to get a bullet in .243 to shoot stags and another to shoot flat to 250 yards for foxes.

This can be made easier if the keeper loads his own bullets, and can fine-tune loads and bullets to suit his rifle, a far greater consistency and guaranteed supply being other reasons for home-loading. The obvious advantage is that the keeper will only use one rifle, the scope and trigger pull being the same and also there will be a great saving in cost as he will only have to buy one rifle. In these circumstances the .243 fits the bill perfectly although there are advocates of the .308. Home loads in a .243 can go from 60 grains to 105 grains, American firms producing heads for 'varmints', ie. from fox coyote etc to deer, up to elk.

The zeroing of a centre-fire is undertaken in the same way as for the .22 rim-fire but obviously the ranges are greater. Sandbags or a bench are a great asset when trying to shoot straight, with most shooters zeroing at 150 yards. Again check where the rifle shoots at 50 yards, 100, 200 and 250 yards so that you know what to do when confronted with such a shot.

Wind should also be considered and a check should be made as to how far a bullet is moved at 200 yards by a cross-wind. This requires a meter to gauge the strength of the wind and a record as to how much the bullet will be blown off course, which can sometimes be a surprising amount, especially at long range.

Choice of scope

The choice of scope should be made with its light-gathering qualities as the main consideration. This can only be judged by taking several scopes out at dusk and assessing which still allows the viewer to identify a pre-selected point, say 75 yards away, for the longest time. The results are usually that the most expensive are the best but there can be bargains out there, and sometimes a good quality second hand scope may be a better buy than a new cheap scope. My own preference is for a Swarovski, with Bushnell making good light-gathering scopes at the more reasonable end of the market.

The light-gathering scope comes into its own when lamping, as the marksman can clearly see his quarry at a far longer range and can therefore pick his point of aim. Too many night time shooters merely see the eyes of a fox and a rough outline and guess where they are shooting. This may be satisfactory for a 'sporting' foxer but it produces too many lamp-shy foxes and accidents to be a satisfactory practice for a professional.

The rings on a centre-fire scope must be of top quality and I have found Warne rings to be entirely satisfactory. These rings are slightly more awkward to fit as the joints are on a vertical plane rather than the more normal horizontal. The advantage is that they can be aligned to a mark on the top of the scope so that they are easily fitted allowing the scope and barrel to be on the same vertical axis, greatly facilitating the accurate zeroing of the rifle. If this is not done and the scope is not perfectly vertical any adjustment will move the shot slightly to the side as well as up and down.

The trigger and stock

Many rifles come with a less than satisfactory trigger, it being too heavy and harsh for really accurate shooting. This can be improved by having a special trigger fitted. These can easily be adjusted and can transform a mediocre rifle into a good one.

Pay special attention to the stock, these usually being wooden and liable to warping, or debris becoming present between the barrel and the stock. This is because most barrels are free floating, ie. they do not touch the stock from the action forward. Any contact between stock and barrel can throw a bullet several inches off and is obviously disastrous to accurate shooting. There are several gunsmiths up and down the country who will bed the action and rub the inside of the stock down to improve your rifle but obviously this costs money.

Much can be done by the shooter himself by taking the stock and metalwork apart and rubbing down the channel which houses the barrel using a piece of dowelling and sandpaper until it is glass-smooth. Some people bed the entire channel with plastic padding, the flexible body filler usually used for car body repairs and this works surprisingly well. A professional job entails drilling out the screw holes which house the bolts that fix the action to the stock and bedding them in. It is beyond the scope of this book to describe this in detail but there is no doubt that a gunsmith can improve your rifle, at a cost, there being some measures that you can take to improve things yourself.

Many rifles come with artificial stocks which are good, especially where the keeper is working in damp conditions with great variation in temperatures, the scenario in which wooden stocks can cause problems. Some go the whole hog and use plastic stocks and stainless steel actions and barrel, obviously designed to cope with the worst of conditions.

Special fox rifle

Some keepers, despite my advice, will want to keep a special rifle for foxes and will probably opt for a .22/250, .223, or .220 swift. All of these are excellent for the job and in many areas may be mandatory as some police forces do not allow shooters to shoot foxes with a designated deer rifle and require them to purchase a .22 centre-fire. There is some indication that this ridiculous situation is about to be relaxed. I have never quite understood the logic of it, because if it was to be taken to its logical conclusion, a keeper would have to take two rifles with him everywhere or dash home to change rifles if a fox appeared when he was deer stalking, for instance.

Up to 200 yards there is little to choose between a .222, .223, .22/250 or a .220 swift or indeed for that matter a .243 but at longer ranges the .22/250, .220 swift and .243 (60 grain bullet) come into their own, being capable, if you can shoot at long range, of taking foxes at over 300 yards.

These ranges are when even the .220 swift starts to drop quite markedly and a range finder and target turrets are essential. Target turrets can be adjusted without removing caps and are clearly marked 1–10, usually with individual clicks between each. It is possible to buy plastic covers, which are fitted over the original turret markings, on which you can designate the zero for 100 yards through to 400 yards or beyond.

This is a highly specialised skill and requires much practice to become proficient but it is useful for grousekeepers on large open beats where they can sit at first light or dusk and take foxes that would be difficult to get by other means.

The great range that the shooter is taking these shots in daylight does not scare a fox as much as you would think and a second shot is often possible if the first misses. This is therefore quite different from the long range shooting of foxes at night, where a miss will result in an educated fox who may never be accounted for by a lamp and rifle.

GROUSE

The grousekeeper is a true keeper in that he produces a purely wild bird. Therein lies the problem: a wild bird requires habitat that is suitable, even perfect, for him and he requires complete protection from predators. At the present time it is very difficult to fulfil these requirements.

In the last two decades the management of the British uplands has become a political battle over land use, with gamekeepers obviously on the side of the status quo, while the new socialist activists present in large numbers in bird protection societies, government quangos etc are determined to change things to their way, a way which is untested and unproven.

Pressure groups have exerted their will on weak governments who have been afraid to stand up to them for fear of retribution at the ballot box. The new breed of politician does not do anything without consulting some advisor who tells him whether his action will be a net gain or loss in votes. Any organisation with more than a handful of members and a political zealot in charge can wield amazing power over the men and women we have elected to rule us. Many socialists, disenchanted with new labour, have transferred their energies to causes where they can carry the flag against their oppressors and make their life miserable, finding this more satisfying than the long slog of knocking on doors in inner city areas trying to drum up support for politicians.

This situation is at its starkest in Scotland where land ownership is a dirty word amongst a high percentage of politicians. Scotland has always lived in Never Never Land, being supported by the rest of the United Kingdom and blaming it for its woes while its industries have slowly declined. New Labour fretted over Scotland and it feared that forty safe seats could be lost if Scotland gained independence. This was the reason for the creation of the Scottish Parliament: to shoot the 'nationalist fox' as it was graphically described. In effect they created a pretentious palace for pygmy politicians which has had the opposite result from that intended, with Scotland being nearer to independence than ever before. Many of the elected members of this Parliament are irresponsible and will vote for anything that their party advocates or any hare brained private members bill without considering the consequences of their action.

This is a serious situation for the countryside, especially the uplands, as Scotland is one of the most divided nations on earth with the vast majority of the population living in an urban environment and having no knowledge of the workings of the countryside.

People in the rest of Britain may think that this does not affect them but this is not so: many of the policies that are tried in Scotland are only a dummy run, Scotland being used as a guinea pig before laws are implemented in England, for example. Any mistakes inflicted on the countryside and rural populations can be corrected later, the Scottish people, especially those who live and work in the countryside, being renowned for not making a fuss even under the severest provocation.

The grousekeeper

The grousekeeper therefore is under pressure from everyone. His boss wants him to produce grouse but not to break the law. The police and raptor study activists pay great attention to everything that he does, often hiding and putting him under surveillance using SAS-type tactics. It is little wonder that the grousekeeper has become a little paranoid, always looking over his shoulder.

Under surveillance

Searches are common. Prominent successful moors usually are targeted. Why this is I do not know: perhaps the assumption that grouse cannot be produced without breaking the law leads the police and bird watchers to closely monitor such estates. There is no doubt that in some areas Police Wildlife Liaison Officers (PWLOs) and raptor study activists work closely together, collating information and co-ordinating surveillance of suspects.

Let us examine how this works. When a PWLO is appointed in an area he will be expected to make contact with various agencies who have a role in wildlife protection, indeed he will undoubtedly be approached by such people very shortly after he takes up his post. These agencies will include bird protection charities, animal protection charities, badger groups, as well as those protecting otters, hedgehogs, squirrels etc. The PWLO is also expected to circulate in the rural community, beating and meeting keepers, not to collate information as in the case of the previous groups but rather to glean information from the 'grapevine' which might be useful in starting or assisting investigations.

This is in stark contrast to yesteryear when the keeper was a useful ally to the erstwhile village bobby, now sadly a relic of the past, who could rely on the keeper to supply information on any suspicious vehicles moving along country roads at dead of night. The chances of criminals travelling unobserved in well-keepered areas day or night was quite remote, most keepers noting make and number of any strange vehicle as well as a description of the occupants and the time that they were seen.

Nowadays police officers are not taught at training college specifically as regards poaching legislation but rather are expected to have more than a basic knowledge of the *Wildlife and Countryside Act*. This has meant that keepers have been suddenly moved from being allies of the forces of law and order, to potential criminals in the eyes of many police officers, especially those from an urban background. Modern legislation is more likely to gain a conviction than the outmoded poaching laws, but one wonders how much rural communities who suffer at the hands of today's criminals, have missed the co-operation that used to be common between the keeper and the forces of law and order.

Once the PWLO has made his contacts he can wait for tip-offs that offences are taking place. These will not be long coming in, as many of these people spend an inordinate amount of their spare time trying to prevent wildlife crime and/or catching offenders. Many PWLO are very keen also, spending much of their time off walking moors and visiting estates to look for evidence of wildlife crime. After a few reports are received, a pattern may develop, eg. remains of dead birds of prey found on an estate and the PWLO may consider that there is enough evidence to justify a search.

He will approach his superior officer who will assess the evidence and decide whether to go ahead or not. If he decides that there is enough evidence, he must meet a Justice of the Peace or similar who will consider the evidence and, if he agrees, will sign the search warrant.

The law is quite complicated as regards searches: only certain offences justify the search of a dwelling house for instance and the search of outbuildings require a search warrant – but the search of land to gain evidence apparently does not. Department of Environment officials have powers of search also, although these seem to be restricted to inspections and do not allow arrest or seizure of evidence.

If the superior officer decides that there is insufficient evidence to justify a search then he may ask the PWLO to get more, which is when surveillance may take place. On grouse moors this will mean that the keeper's house and surrounding area will be watched, often by 'volunteers'. These are usually raptor study group activists who will note the keeper's movements, the registration mark of his vehicles both work and private, and the details of any visitors, their car numbers etc. Indeed there was a rumour recently that ex-SAS veterans had been employed to watch keepers. This may have been a psychological ploy to intimidate keepers but there is no doubt that these observers are experts in conceal-ment, accessing their hide-outs before dawn and only leaving after dark. Nest sites, usually hen harrier, peregrine or short-eared owl are also watched, cameras recording any activity by keepers who approach them. The legality of this is open to debate but what can a keeper do to protect his privacy, which is surely every man's right? In Northern Ireland the SAS were sometimes compromised by farm dogs when they were hidden in observation hides, often in hedges near farmhouses. Once terrorist sympathisers realised this, they used to walk their farm collies up the hedges overlooking their farms on a regular basis, making it more difficult to maintain a covert presence.

The keeper, if he wishes, can use the previous chapter to train a dog for this purpose, making it difficult for anyone to secretly watch his house and family. A dog which tracks can be useful in these circumstances as it can be used to follow a person who enters your ground and you can then find out what his intentions are. If you find a person or persons hidden in camouflage clothing, you are perfectly entitled to call the police and have them checked out: any other citizen of this country would do the same in similar circumstances and would be perfectly entitled to do so.

How to handle the search of a keeper's house

When a keeper's house is searched it is a harrowing experience, especially for his wife and family. The normal time for a search is first thing in the morning so that there is an element of surprise. At least the early morning search is likely to mean that the keeper himself is present: some later morning searches have found the keeper's spouse alone and having to deal with up to a dozen police officers dressed in 'swat' gear, the search taking several hours. These searches are thorough: no stone is left unturned, including the keeper's wife's clothes and the children's toys. The reason for this is that when a search is asked for and authorised, the police officers involved have stuck their necks out a little and, if nothing is found, questions may be asked, especially if a complaint is subsequently made.

Therefore any result, be it firearms in an unlocked cabinet, ammunition in a jacket pocket, drugs, untaxed vehicles, illegal traps or stolen goods will go a long way to justifying the search and making a complaint difficult.

If you are confronted by a police officer who has a search warrant you should ask him to wait until you can summon assistance, either the estate manager, employer or solicitor. Special care should be taken to ensure that only persons mentioned in the search warrant are allowed to enter premises, and it is preferable that all officers are observed while they conduct the search. Do not adopt an aggressive stance: this will only be counter-productive.

The 'expert witness'

If an expert witness is involved in the search, he in particular should be watched and notes taken of his behaviour. These expert witnesses can be employees of bird or animal protection charities and as such do not really have the power to search your house but may be called upon to advise police officers on whether or not evidence found is important or relevant. There is evidence that some of these people have exceeded their authority in the past, even, it is rumoured, directing police officers and taking charge of the search, so it is important that you gain legal advice and support.

After the search

If the search proves fruitless you have two options: you can carry on as before and pretend it did not happen or if you feel that it was unjustified or even illegal, after consulting your solicitor you should write to the Chief Constable and make a formal complaint. A covering letter containing a copy of your correspondence to the Chief Constable should be sent to your M.P. This, at least, will ensure that any future dealings with the law will be done professionally and you will be offered the respect that every citizen deserves.

Best job in the world

The preceding chapters may have deterred many readers from embarking on a career in grousekeeping. This has not been my intention but I feel that I would not be doing anyone any favours by painting a rose-tinted picture of the job without informing prospective grousekeepers to the drawbacks. That said, the grousekeeper still has the best job in the keepering world. He is a true gamekeeper, as I have stated at the beginning of this section, because he is producing a truly wild bird. He does not have to carry tons of food about all winter and he has more opportunities to beat and pick-up on partridge and pheasant shoots. When his own shooting days are over, he can relax and enjoy the rest of the season on other keeper's shoots.

Now, more than ever before, grousekeeping is looked upon as a young man's job, many employers considering that a man over 40 is incapable of doing the job effectively. Head grousekeepers can be in their early twenties but they must remember that they will reach 40 all too quickly and must have an alternative means of employment to fall back on when they are regarded as being 'over the hill'.

Success at producing grouse

How do you produce grouse, why are some keepers more successful than others? There is no magic wand and while some gardeners are green-fingered, some keepers appear to be 'grouse'-fingered. These men, however, on closer examination are seen to be merely dedicated keepers who are expert vermin killers. They spend long hours on their moor and do not travel elsewhere to enjoy themselves. Like all keepering, you only get back what you put in and these men generally end up on the best moors which have been well managed for years. The sum of excellent keepering and excellent habitat produces the end result: plenty of grouse. It is likely, however, that any young keeper reading this book will only arrive on a grouse moor that is run down and part of a larger shoot concentrating on pheasants or perhaps partridges.

This scenario was common in Scotland in the post-war years, where grouse were taken for granted and it was assumed that they would always be there. Keepers became tied up rearing pheasants and they neglected the moor. Two or three bad breeding seasons coupled with an increase in predators and perhaps uncontrolled burning and the moor became unviable, a situation which is very difficult to rectify.

Another factor was the increase in forestry in Scotland in the post-war years. Not only did this allow an increase in the fox population, it also fragmented grouse populations, leading to some moors becoming isolated. This meant that when a moor's breeding stock of grouse became dangerously low there was no chance of surplus birds from neighbouring moors augmenting the existing population.

In England the situation has been far more favourable. Grouse have always been valued and correspondingly their keepers have been valued also. Stocking rates of sheep have been closely monitored so that over-grazing has been limited. The average grousekeeper in England looks after a far smaller acreage than in Scotland where it was not uncommon for one man to try to manage 10–20,000 acres. English keepers have moved to Scotland and gained excellent results, often due simply to increasing the keepering force so that each keeper was able to cope with the vermin situation more easily. The maxim here has been to increase the number of keepers to counteract the fall in grouse numbers, while the general Scottish attitude had been to reduce the workforce to cut costs.

IMPROVING A RUN-DOWN GROUSE MOOR

Grouse-count

The keeper who finds himself on a run-down moor must first find out how many birds are on the moor. This can be done in early spring either using pointers or setters or walking in line. A note of all pairs should be taken, as well as evidence of predation. This may take the form of kills, fresh fox droppings or even sightings of the various predators that kill grouse. Whatever the results of this grouse count, you must do all in your power as quickly as possible to protect the birds that are left. It can be difficult to say with exact certainty what predator killed a grouse but clues are:

- Wing feathers chopped off, almost certainly a fox, also a half buried carcase with the wing showing.
- Bird with head missing and many plucked feathers usually indicates a peregrine or a harrier, the neck being cleaned of flesh and feather.
- Stoats will bite the neck of their prey often eating into the rib-cage to consume the vital organs.
- The tail of a rabbit which has been severed from the rest of its body shows the kill of a fox.

All such signs will give you an idea of the scale of the problem that you face.

Predators may be the main reason for a lack of grouse on the moor but it is likely that there will be other factors. Are there cattle over-wintering on the moor? If so this is a major cause of deterioration of heather. Heather will be trampled in and pulled out by the roots, drains will be destroyed leading to wet areas developing where heather will find it difficult to survive.

The stocking density of sheep will also have a bearing on the amount and type of heather cover. Too many sheep will over-graze the heather, allowing grasses to take over so smothering the heather. Taller heather, which grouse use as escape cover and for nesting will be reduced leading to a reduction in the suitable territories available. Every moor has a perfect number of sheep that it can carry and this carrying capacity is dependent on the rate that the heather grows and the quality of the land.

Heather burning will also determine the state of the heather on the moor. Large fires will clear much of the long heather which is essential for grouse and the large swathes of short regenerating heather will leave grouse and their young vulnerable to predation. Strips burnt 30 yards wide are desirable to provide suitable conditions for grouse to thrive, the aim being to provide many different ages of heather in small areas producing the maximum number of territories the moor can sustain.

If you, as the keeper, find that you have no control over sheep stocking, cattle grazing and burning, then you have an impossible task. Many moors are let with tenant farmers having no clauses in their leases stating how many sheep can be carried on the moor and barring them from heather burning. This always causes conflict and the keeper will require the wisdom of Solomon and the negotiating skills of Henry Kissinger to produce grouse in such a situation. Even where the farming is in hand, an unsympathetic farm manager can be as detrimental as any tenant farmer.

The situation is often exacerbated by the estate charging high rents for a tenanted moor. This obviously leads to the farmer stocking more heavily to recoup his rent. New EEC rules on subsidies may help as they have been previously determined by the number of stock on a farm unit, whereas now there is a single farm payment. Whether this will lead to more moderate stocking levels remains to be seen but we must always be optimistic.

Relations with tenant farmers

Where a keeper has a good working relationship with a tenant farmer he must do everything that he can to ensure that this relationship is not soured. Respect and consideration will go a long way to retain the good terms that you enjoy already. Lamping unannounced in the early hours of the morning near his house, shooting parties arriving without warning and a plague of rabbits which the keeper does nothing to rectify, can all make the tenant farmer less amenable to any requests for co-operation that the keeper may make. Going beyond this, a shoot dinner at the end of the season where beaters and tenants can be invited, Keeper's Day invites and any other perks all should be made available to a co-operative farmer.

...and with shepherds and others

Where a farm manager and/or shepherd comes into the equation different tactics must be employed. A good shepherd is essential to the running of a successful grouse moor. He should be interested in grouse and invited to beat on shooting days as well as to shoot on Keeper's Days and vermin forays. In return the keepering staff should assist at busy times such as shearing where labour is always needed. The shepherd should move his sheep over the moor every day so that no area becomes over-grazed and all cattle and most of the sheep should be removed from the heather areas in August.

Ticks

Regular dipping of sheep which have been 'hefted' over the hill will greatly help to reduce the tick population, the main source of louping ill, a tick-borne virus which can greatly reduce the grouse population. It was once thought that removing all hosts – sheep, deer and hares – from the moor would greatly reduce the population of ticks but it is now thought that the ticks are then even more likely to concentrate on the resident grouse population, so infecting them with louping ill. Not all ticks carry the virus. The only way of finding this out is to blood-test sheep on the moor for antibodies. Sheep are susceptible to the virus also so it is in the shepherd's interest to embark on a policy of regular dipping for ticks, this being more effective where the sheep are moved over the hill, 'mopping up' the ticks on a regular basis.

Other grouse parasites

The Strongyle worm is another serious parasite affecting grouse. This worm is present in the grouse's gut and virtually all birds have them. It would appear that in times of stress, during the breeding season or when food is in short supply, the worms increase until they greatly impact on the bird's health, often killing them. This usually manifests itself in spring time so it is a good idea to test birds shot in the autumn for worm burden and, if this shows a high challenge, to embark on a regime of worm control.

This can be done by direct dosing, where the birds are caught and dosed with an anthelmintic drug, usually in very early spring, although many keepers do not approve of the practice. The other method is to provide medicated grit. This is quartz grit, dosed with a drug which kills the worms, which grouse use in their gizzards to help to digest their chief food source, heather. Grit should be made available to grouse all over the moor so that every pair has their own supply and the medicated grit should be placed where the grouse have become accustomed to finding it.

Heather burning

The control of heather burning should be in the hands of the keeper. He will require sufficient manpower and equipment to do this job efficiently and safely. The shepherd should always be asked to assist if available and he should be asked, if only out of politeness, if there are any particular areas which he would like to be burnt. The amount of heather to be burnt depends on how fast it grows, a factor which may be known from previous years' burning. It is then a simple calculation to decide how much should be burnt every year. Each burn should be measured and a note taken of the acreage burnt. This allows the keeper to know how much he has burned and if he is falling behind schedule, in which case he may need to employ more men, especially if the weather does not look too promising. You cannot legally burn after 15th April. The important thing when burning is to anticipate where the fire is going and back-burn strips to prevent the fire reaching forestry or the bottom of a hillside thick with long heather. When a fire reaches such a hillside it will immediately accelerate as the flames are reaching up into the cover on the hillside and will suddenly become far more difficult to control.

The strength of the wind and the dryness of the heather all should be taken into consideration before attempting to burn a dangerous area: if in doubt, leave for another day when conditions may be more favourable. Back-burning is safer because you are burning into the wind but it is not desirable to adopt this type of burning over the whole moor as it burns deeper into the peat and regeneration is slower. However, it may be the only safe method in some situations.

Bracken

Bracken is a major problem on a moor. It encroaches every year, especially if fires are burnt into it from areas of heather. When this happens the bracken is allowed to spread into the burnt area, suppressing the heather unless measures are taken to eliminate it. There are many ways of controlling bracken: helicopters can spray it, tractors pulling flails can chop it up, hand-held sprayers can be used to spray it with 'Asulox' and quad bikes equipped with 'wipes' can be used to run round small areas to reduce them in size.

Dead bracken is a major breeding ground for ticks, another reason for eliminating it if at all possible, although this may be very difficult unless adequate resources are dedicated to this task.

Shepherd's incentive

All of these extra duties may mean that a shepherd is busier on a grouse moor than he would be on another location and for this reason I would advocate that he receives a bonus related to the annual grouse bag. He usually receives a lambing bonus on the number of lambs that he produces, so I think it is not unreasonable for him to receive a reward for a successful shooting season where his work went in some way to helping to produce this result.

Roads

Roads are a great asset on a moor, allowing access to areas for burning or taking beaters out to drives which would be difficult or time-consuming to attempt on foot. They also greatly facilitate lamping, which on a grouse moor must be undertaken on a regular basis as grouse do not go up to roost and are always vulnerable to fox predation. Any measures which help to control the fox are desirable as he is by far the major predator of grouse. Roads also make it easier for guns to reach the butts and keepers to take materials for the repair or building of butts.

Grouse butts

Most butts are established and permanent on moors because the flight line of driven grouse never changes. However, the keeper may be starting from scratch, in which case I recommend four wooden pallets formed into a square with round stobs inserted through them and driven into the ground, the door having only one stob so that it can be swung open. The floor should be laid with treated 4 x 4 square battens and covered by one inch weld mesh lightly stapled down. The pallets can be treated with wood preserver of different colours, eg. brown and green in camouflage pattern to make them unobtrusive. These butts can be easily disassembled if they prove to be unsuccessful and moved to a new location. Even if they are successful, the keeper may wish to replace them with bespoke butts of stone or heather turfs and move the pallets to another experimental drive.

It can be seen from this that the keeper's aim should be first to protect the grouse that are already present and then to improve the habitat, ie. the quality and quantity of heather cover on the moor, making improvements which will make this more practicable. Grants are now available to re-seed areas to allow them to return to heather and these options

should be considered as obviously the more ground covered in heather, the better for grouse.

Predicting how much shooting is available

July will come round all too quickly and the time has come to decide if there are enough grouse to make shooting a viable option. The cycle of the moor should be known from shooting records, the peaks and troughs of grouse populations on cyclic moors following a remarkably predictable pattern over the years. If the moor has been run down there may have been little shooting, or shooting may have taken place where stocks were insufficient. This situation is fraught with difficulties for the keeper. He must ask for resources but his employer may be reluctant to provide them if he thinks he is supporting a lost cause. On the other hand if he allows shooting to take place before there is a shootable surplus, he is eating into his breeding stock, an undesirable option.

It is therefore necessary to count the grouse in the second half of July. At one time it was considered bad practice for anyone to go on the moor in July but in recent years it has become acceptable to use pointers and setters to cover pre-selected areas of a moor to allow the keeper to predict how much shooting can take place. This is most successful where the practice has taken place over a number of years and a comparison can be made but at least by doing this the keeper will be able to ascertain the number and size of the coveys. This is one task where a German pointer, short or wire haired, can be useful, these being more versatile for a keeper than a traditional pointer or setter. If this is not an option then there are many pointer and setter handlers who may be willing to help with a count. They may, however, be in demand at this time of the year so it would probably be reasonable for a keeper to keep a versatile HPR.

Once you have decided to shoot it is important to decide the point when shooting will end. Many moors do this by stopping when bags reach a certain level per day, say 75 brace, certainly for most moors to continue shooting days of less than 50 brace would mean that they were shooting their stock. At one time it was thought that, in peak years, it was impossible to overshoot grouse. This was always optimistic but nowadays, with the increased pressure from birds of prey and foxes it does not take into account the numbers that will be lost during the winter from natural causes and predation.

If you decide that shooting is not viable, be very sure of your case. One keeper, who must have been something of a pessimist, told his boss not to shoot and this greatly surprised his employer as he thought that signs were promising and therefore decided to over-rule his keeper. The moor shot well and the keeper was delighted, until he received his marching orders at the end of the season!

Advice from neighbouring grousekeepers

The young keeper who finds himself in a potentially good job on a run-down moor should contact a neighbouring, experienced grousekeeper and ask his advice, picking his brains and observing how he does things. Most hill keepers are forthcoming in helping young keepers, they being more generous in character, perhaps, than their low-ground counterparts. This does not mean that the young man should ape his older colleague: he should always adapt and improve any knowledge he gleans, for only by doing this will he become a truly outstanding keeper.

DEER

Deer, like grouse, have become a political football in the last few decades. In Scotland they are blamed for the lack of native trees in the highlands, for it is claimed that the population is too great to allow natural regeneration of Scots pine. It is true that the population of red deer has increased but the acreage of forestry has increased greatly also. Bad forest design meant that deer populations were allowed to increase because there were no open areas to allow stalkers to cull them. This, added to the fact that many forests were planted with no access roads made the culling and extraction of carcases difficult or even impossible. These problems may not have been foreseen by land managers but they should at least accept some responsibility for them.

The whole of Britain has seen an increase in deer of all species meaning that deer stalking is now more widely available than at any time. Grants have been made available to the humblest of land-owners to plant small woodlands which has created habitat that has not been available to deer for centuries. Set-aside has also created more potential territories for deer, and the end result is that deer populations are thriving, creating both opportunities and problems for keepers.

In Scotland any keeper who has a large area of woodland to protect will be expected to control the deer population and record the number, age and sex of the animals culled. These records will be supplied to the Deer Commission for Scotland every year so that an overall record of the total deer cull in Scotland can be estimated. Grants are paid to land-owners who establish new woodland and these are paid in stages and are subject to certain conditions being fulfilled. If these conditions are not fulfilled, eg. if deer have eaten more than 5% of trees planted, any grants paid may have to be refunded, which puts much pressure on the gamekeeper to keep on top of deer numbers.

Many keepers do not take part in deer control on their estate; it is let to a stalking tenant. This is especially the case in lowland Britain. This can work well but it depends on a good working relationship between stalker and keeper. These recreational stalkers often defray costs by taking paying guests out after roe or fallow bucks, even red and fallow stags, the tenant retaining the venison also, for his own. This means that in real terms the rent gained from stalking is quite small and most estates could yield a larger income by keeping their stalking and letting it by the day, retaining the venison income. It really depends on how busy the keeper is. If he has a large rearing programme, it would be difficult for him to find time to take out stalkers but if there is labour available in the way of underkeepers, they might be happy to take out a client after a buck as a change from rearing pheasants.

Revenue

Let us look at the revenue available. For roe deer an outing will generally be between £50–100 with a charge for a trophy buck of £30–100. The venison is kept so it can be seen that an estate shooting 40 bucks could expect an income of, say (we will assume two outings per buck) £100 plus £50 plus £25, these being the outings, the trophy fee and the venison giving us a total of £175 x 40 = £7,000. Forty does would be shot yielding outings of £50 per doe plus £25 venison = £75 x 40 = £3,000. This gives us an income of £10,000 which would be quite possible on an estate of 2–3,000 acres of woodland. Extra income can be made from siting a residential caravan or letting a holiday home for the times that the stalkers are visiting, many of them preferring to 'rough' it rather than stay in a hotel or bed and breakfast. These charges are conservative and more could be expected if the estate is attractive. Remember that most stalking done in commercial forestry takes place in the most austere of surroundings.

It is important to remember that many tenants may not be totally forthcoming about the number of deer that they actually shoot, for fear that the rent will be increased so this must be taken into consideration if you are comparing the income from letting the stalking to a tenant or taking over the letting by the day yourself.

Experienced stalking gillies

Accompanying a stalker can be a difficult task for the professional keeper, especially if the stalker is inexperienced or a poor shot. It is expected that a stalker will shoot at a target to prove that he is competent and also that his rifle is zeroed and accurate. This may not be conclusive evidence that the stalker is able to shoot straight at live quarry. The type of person who loves to hunt is also liable to get excited when about to take a shot, especially if the buck or stag is an exceptionally good one, sometimes leading to the affliction called 'buck fever'.

The day of the stalk

Let us go back to the beginning. Your boss has decided to invite paying guests to stalk on your estate. If you have been culling the deer previously you will have a good idea where they are to be found but it is advisable to take time to check the whole estate and see where likely bucks are showing, so that you are not working in the dark, so to speak, when your clients arrive. Once the stalker arrives you should make contact with him, introducing yourself and explaining the itinerary for the week ahead (we will assume that he has booked in for a week's stalking).

You should be upbeat and optimistic while at the same time assessing your client: Is he experienced? Is he fit enough to walk far? Is he serious and quiet or extrovert and vociferous? It is up to you to deal with any problems that he may have in his accommodation or travel arrangements and you must arrange a time and a place to rendezvous with him for the coming outing.

Many estates work on a system of clients being taken stalking on foot in the mornings and being placed in high seats in the evening. If labour is available, an underkeeper can accompany the stalker in the evening, so giving the keeper a break, and this is advisable if several weeks' stalking is booked.

Arrange to meet the stalker before dawn and remember to take a knife, roe sack and stick with you. Suitable clothing is essential, either tweed suit or camouflage clothing; and a face mask and gloves are desirable. Boots which are comfortable and quiet are a big advantage if you are not to warn every deer in the district that you are coming. You should have checked the wind before you left home as this will determine the best stalks to try that morning. The aim is to walk into the wind along a route which allows you to travel quietly and observe deer before they see you. This can be easier said than done as it is only with experience that you will recognise and pick out the partly hidden shape of a deer, whether you spot its head partially obscured by a birch sapling or the outline of its back above a ditch when its head is down feeding. Reconnaissance trips along prospective routes should have been undertaken, removing obstacles and cutting little paths to facilitate your goal: shooting deer.

Until you have experienced it, you will be surprised at how tiring woodland stalking is. The concentration required to ensure that you see a deer before your stalking guest does is the reason for this, hence my advice to take a break where possible. Carry your client's rifle for him and keep a close watch to ensure that you are not tiring him out. He may not be used to hilly country and it serves no purpose to walk him into the ground to prove how fit you are.

The kill

Eventually you will see a buck, hopefully before he sees you, and you must think fast, looking for the best spot for your stalker to take his shot. If he is 100–150 yards away it is easier, as there is less chance of him hearing or seeing you. We will assume that the wind is okay, so you must crawl to the nearest high point so that there will be no obstacle between you and the buck. This should provide a good rest for your client, which is desirable. If the cover is high it may not be possible to shoot from a prone position, in which case sticks can be used, either from a sitting or standing position.

The stalker should be asked if he is confident of taking the shot and, if not, you must attempt to get closer, only moving when the buck is feeding, freezing when he looks around alert, using any cover available to conceal your presence. If you rumble into a buck, ie. he sees you first, the only thing you can do is freeze and not look directly at the buck. If you have full camouflage and a face mask and have not harassed the deer previously, there is a chance that he will continue feeding, often looking up suddenly to see if you have moved. You must stay immobile until he moves on, perhaps behind a tree or into a ditch, then move quickly and silently to a point where you can observe and wait for him to reappear.

The gralloch

If this is successful you will have a dead deer on your hands and he must be gralloched, ie. eviscerated immediately. The first thing to do is move the beast so that he lies with his head to the left on his right side. Insert your knife into the depression between the left shoulder and the breast bone as far as it will go. This will enter the chest cavity and allow any blood held there to escape. Depending on the knife it may also penetrate the heart. This is desirable as a bled ruminant has superior meat to one that has not had the blood drained from its body.

From this initial cut make an incision in the skin on the front of the neck up almost to the head. This should expose the wind pipe which is white, resembling a miniature corrugated pipe used in washing machines. Pull this free from the neck and detach the feed pipe which is attached to the back of the wind pipe. Cut the feed pipe and make a hole near the end, turning the pipe through this hole several times to seal it. Some more sophisticated stalkers use small cable ties for this purpose.

Now cut the wind pipe, removing the exposed length before moving to the other end. Put your feet on the hind legs to hold the carcase steady and remove the penis and testicles, using the cut so formed to make an incision up to the rib cage, being careful not to penetrate the stomach bag which would contaminate the meat. The stomach bag will now almost fall out of it's own accord; remove it and the intestines before twisting the bladder several times so that when it is cut off urine does not contaminate the meat, again small cable ties can be used.

At this stage you can cut the diaphragm which separates the abdominal cavity from the chest cavity. This should be done with a circular cut near the ribs, exposing the vital organs, heart, lungs etc. Insert your right hand and feel towards the front of the chest cavity and locate the feed pipe: pulling it should remove the entire contents of the rib cage. A small saw is useful to cut the bone which covers the end of the intestine. Once the bone has been cut through twice at the base of each hind leg, the intestine can be cleanly cut out.

The heart, lungs, liver etc should be placed in a separate bag from the carcase and the stomach before they are taken home for disposal. The lungs, liver, and lymph nodes should be checked for disease before the carcase is sold and the keeper will have to sign a declaration to the game dealer that he has done so.

The carcase must be hung in the game larder as soon as possible. The deer should be cut at the hock of the hind legs allowing hooks to be inserted and the deer hung up. The legs should be cut at the joint nearest the foot just below the hock. This is quite difficult if you are not handling large numbers of deer but once you have the knack it becomes much easier. The joint left should be quite flat if you have selected the right joint, not the typical knuckle joint if you have chosen the wrong one.

The sternum will have to be cut using a fine-toothed saw. First cut the skin away to expose the sternum (the bone at the bottom of the rib cage which connects both sets of ribs together) and then saw from the stomach cavity towards the neck.

The head can be removed, bearing in mind that if the stalker wants the full head mounted by a taxidermist you will have to cut and remove the skin well down the neck, leaving far more than you think you need. If the stalker wishes a normal skull mount he may want you to do this. First remove the head from the body, then cut level with the jaw round the back of the neck and remove the lower jaw. Skin as best you can the skull removing the nose and eyes as well as the ears. Boil the head in a suitable pot for 15–30 minutes depending on the age (an older buck will be longer). A quantity of washing powder may help to remove any fat or meat that has been left on the skull. Remember to keep the antlers out of the water or the colour may be damaged. Remove the skull from the water and scrape remaining meat from the bone including the nasal passages. The actual cut is best used in conjunction with a custom-made vice which holds the skull and guides the saw so that no mistake can be made. These are not too expensive and are available from game suppliers. Once you have done this the skull must be bleached. This is done by painting the bone with 30% hydrogen peroxide: again make sure that you do not allow the antlers to be touched in any way.

Most estates do not measure heads as such, probably because it is such a complicated procedure, and merely charge per point, usually £10, making a six pointer worth £60.

Evening stalking

Many estates use high seats for the evening outings and these must obviously be safe and comfortable as well as being in the right place. Moveable seats can be home-made using horse rails 14ft long and threaded rod for strength. These are intended to be leant against a tree but in some situations there may be no suitable tree in which case a pole can be dug in and used as a prop. A three feet deep hole should be dug just large enough for the pole which should be packed in with stones after it is inserted in the hole. Guy wires can be used to steady the seat and pole, remembering that they must be secure enough for a marksman to take an accurate shot.

Permanent seats should only be built where there is a guaranteed long-term view. These seats can be made using telegraph poles or scaffolding and should be covered and comfortable giving good viewing over a large area whatever the wind direction. Windows should be made from glass and be easily and quietly opened. If this is not done and the seat is not enclosed, owls or other birds may take up residence with the ensuing mess having to be cleaned up every year.

High seats can extend your letting season as many continentals enjoy calling roe bucks at the rut. It is difficult in most lowland woodland at this time of year (July/August) to see the deer because of the height of the undergrowth. This can be facilitated by the use of a tractor and jungle buster to keep cover low by regular cutting and the use of high seats, as obviously the stalker is looking down from a height. The calls used mimic a fawn, hoping that this will bring a doe and in turn a buck, or a doe in season, the aim being to bring an amorous buck out into the open. The keeper should experiment himself, as the stalker may not be an expert in this art. He will find it an interesting and exciting experience.

The methods I have described are intended for a keeper who has a population of roe deer in a lowland environment. The stalking of red deer on an upland estate is beyond the scope of this book as it is not within the remit of a general gamekeeper, but a skilled job in its own right, although there will be some highland estates where the grouse-keeper accompanies guests to the hill to stalk stags.

However, a keeper employed on a lowland estate which has red, fallow or sika, can adapt the stalking on offer to suit his needs, remembering that there are few weeks of the year when stalking cannot be let if females are to be taken also.

Culling

The culling of females must not be neglected if the population is to remain healthy: females which are old, with only one or no young accompanying them, should be the priority. But in vulnerable areas, for instance where new hardwood plantations are being established, the keeper will have to be severe on the deer population. In these circumstances, always shoot the adult female: her calves will not go far and can usually easily be shot also. Even if one runs away, if you wait for a few minutes she will normally return to look for her mother. The true keeper or sportsman takes little pleasure from this task, it is a job that has to be done and the only satisfaction that the keeper can glean from this exercise is knowing that he has done it in a humane and professional way.

The keeper may be asked to take exceptional measures to cull the deer on his beat. This usually occurs where there are vulnerable areas planted and difficulties are experienced in achieving the necessary cull. Red and sika deer can become very cunning and secretive where there is great shooting pressure brought on them. They become largely nocturnal with the sika in particular becoming very difficult to come to terms with. When this happens, many forestry firms apply for night shooting licences as a last resort. These licences are meant to be issued where all other measures have failed but some people have complained that it is too easy to obtain such permission.

Lamping deer

Let us look at an area where lamping deer has been particularly effective. In Galloway the red deer population was at one time regarded as having some of the best examples in Scotland with heads rivalling those in the south of England. There were many complaints of deer damage from foresters and private land owners, there being little tradition of deer stalking in the south west of Scotland as practiced in the highlands. A policy of shooting at night was implemented by forest rangers and the following tactics were employed. A large vehicle normally used to transport forest workers would be adapted so that up to five marksmen could shoot from the inside of the vehicle to either side. A driver and a man to operate the lamp would make up the team.

When deer were spotted, the rangers would automatically know that the left rifle took the left deer, the second the second deer on the left etc. The rifles shot on command, as one, and being crack shots, all the group would be culled. The only proviso was that if there were more deer than rifles, they would be left alone so that any survivors would not become educated.

Using this method more than 50% of deer culled have been taken at night and the Galloway deer are now as rare as hen's teeth.

I have already touched upon the choice of rifle in the section on firearms, but I would like to voice my opinion on the moves to legalise .22 centre-fires for use on small deer including roe in England. .22 centre-fires have been used in Scotland on roe for years and I have shot over 1,000 using .222 or .22/250. However, I would not recommend them to anyone, especially the inexperienced or someone embarking on a substantial cull within a limited timescale. The three quarter shot through the shoulder of a large roe with either can mean a long hunt before you find your beast: indeed with the .222 you may not find it at all. Little blood will be left (if any) to help you or your dog as there is often no exit wound. In short, it wastes time finding beasts, especially in rough country, so I can only advise the young keeper to use a .243, 25/06, .308 or 30/06.

Many highland keepers will scoff at this, many using .22 centre calibre fires for everything, the smaller the calibre the larger the badge of honour worn by such men. We lesser mortals have to use big calibres and while on this subject, I can remember talking to an old retired head stalker who thought that a .222 was a cannon; he never used anything other than a .22 long rifle to shoot red deer. He was skilled enough to stalk to 50 yards and shoot his quarry through the eye.

Difficult beasts in areas where it would be difficult to extract were shot in the leg, usually in the joint, the stalker following on, often with a dog, until the beast reached an accessible spot where it was despatched. Such skill is beyond mere mortals as myself.

The irony of the current attitude to deer is that they appear to be something of a bête noire to the modern conservationists. These people are prepared to take any action, even introducing lynx and wolves to control them. The death of a large herbivore by a wolf pack is not a kind one and this does not even take into account the unpleasant side-effects from the re-introduction of this cunning predator. Domestic dogs would be in grave danger from wolves, who seem to find them a particularly appealing delicacy. No dog could be allowed to run loose, either in the countryside or in the vicinity of houses and would have to be housed in extremely wolf-proof kennels and runs if they were kept outside. I personally find it a strange concept that an inhumane death inflicted by one animal on another is more acceptable than a humane death carried out by man on an animal. The greatest advocates of the reintroduction of large carnivores are often the most vehement critics of fieldsports, gamekeepers and deer stalkers. If only we could ask the deer what they thought, I am sure they would prefer to be managed and looked after by professional deer managers than to be harassed by wolves all year round. It was once said of a certain King of England that 'he loved the deer as if he was their father'. If this was the case, the deer of modern times are but orphans who are sentenced to death for the slightest transgression against the state.

CONCLUSION

In the writing of this book I have been careful not to be too precise on the legality of certain practices. Where they have been illegal I have said so, but there are certain areas where a keeper may in the future be breaking the law inadvertently, indeed the law has already changed regarding wildlife legislation during the writing of this book. I would therefore advise anyone who has any doubt as to the legality of his actions to check with BASC, NGO or the SGA. The complexities of wildlife legislation mean that a separate book such as *Fair Game* (Pelham Books) would need to be consulted to keep abreast of current laws. Even so the situation is fluid and the law can change several times a year. Add to this the fact that England, Scotland, Wales and Northern Ireland have different laws and different interpretations of laws (even between certain police forces) and this means that the reader should always contact the above bodies for up-to-date advice.

Much of the legislation which has been passed regarding the hunting of mammals and the rights of access to land is almost deliberately vague, and much will depend on interpretation and test cases before anyone can say for certain how successful prosecutions can be achieved. For this reason the keeper should be wary and take steps to protect his game, while at the same time staying within the law. The keeper should never underestimate how much of a target he is, especially if his employer is of high rank and status, and he should think carefully if ever he is tempted to break the law, bearing in mind that seemingly innocent possessions, comments or written records can be construed as incriminating evidence. An example of this was the keeper who was the subject of a police search, during the course of which his diary was seized. This contained the records of the vermin he had killed over a number of years including foxes, which he described as dogs and vixens. This common phraseology sent an over-enthusiastic police officer into overdrive and he spent several man hours checking if any domestic dogs had gone missing at the same time as the keeper recorded the killing of a dog fox. Luckily there was no correlation but one can only wonder what would have happened if there had been a co-incidental disappearance of someone's pet dog.

As anyone who has read this book will have gathered there has been an almost complete reversal in the status of the gamekeeper from the beginning of the twentieth century, when he was second only to his employer in authority on a country estate, to the early part of the twenty first century where he has become regarded almost as a labourer. I find this a sad state of affairs and in the long term I feel that the wildlife and game of our countryside will suffer and almost certainly already has.

The Grey Partridge is the litmus test of the lowland countryside. Only when this species starts to thrive and expand its range can we feel that we are making progress but I am pessimistic on this score and can only predict a gloomy future for this bird, the true lowland keeper's favourite bird. I hope that I am wrong on this score and would love to think that coming generations can once more hear the coveys calling to each other in the gloaming of a summer's evening.

The first World War was meant to end all wars; it did not, but it did change the world forever, especially the keeper's world. Over 30,000 gamekeepers were employed before the War and only 3,000 employed after. The exact number of keepers killed in the Great War is not known but there can be no doubt that the keepering profession was devastated by death, crippling injuries and the economic melt-down post-1918.

The second challenge to gamekeeping is the current global recession, the worst, it is predicted, for half a century. It can only be assumed that it will not be advantageous to gamekeepers and will probably mean that many will lose their jobs. Perhaps some good may come from this situation with guns being content with smaller bags and more emphasis on wild birds. If this is the case I hope that my book will be of assistance to a young keeper who suddenly finds himself without the safety net of large numbers of spare birds after the years of plenty. He must adapt if he is to survive just as his predecessors had to adapt all those years before when they returned from the two World Wars.